*The American College and
the Culture of Aspiration,
1915–1940*

The American College and the Culture of Aspiration, 1915–1940

David O. Levine

Cornell University Press

Ithaca and London

First published 1986 by Cornell University Press.
Second printing 1987.
First published, Cornell Paperbacks, 1987.

International Standard Book Number 0-8014-1884-4 (cloth)
International Standard Book Number 0-8014-9498-2 (paper)
Library of Congress Catalog Card Number 86-4169
Printed in the United States of America
Librarians: Library of Congress cataloging information
appears on the last page of the book.

The paper in this book is acid-free and meets the guidelines for permanence and durability of the Committee on Production Guidelines for Book Longevity of the Council on Library Resources.

Contents

Preface

"In the absence of a system of hereditary ranks and titles, without a tradition of honors conferred by a monarch, and with no well-known status ladder even of high-class regiments to confer various degrees of cachet," Paul Fussell concluded in an essay for *The New Republic* in 1982, "Americans have had to depend for their mechanism of snobbery far more than other peoples on their college and university hierarchy."[1] For the American historian, Fussell's observation raises fascinating questions. In a nation that heralds the self-made man of action and disdains the man of reflection, when and why did colleges and universities become arbiters of economic and social mobility? In a land of individual opportunity, how can one account for a hierarchical cultural institution? Finally, in what distinctive ways has American soil nurtured schools of higher learning?

This book chronicles the emergence of the American postsecondary school as a central economic, social, and cultural institution in this century; it is intended also to increase awareness of the complexity of the functions of education in the modern United States' egalitarian and technocratic society. We look to the universities to produce the desired number of engineers—and professional basketball players. We provide there a home for many of our creative artists. Schools compete for federal and corporate largess in the hope of enhancing their prestige and stimulating local economic growth. In my lifetime society has repeatedly turned to academe for solutions to its technological and other problems, yet public attitudes and governmental policy are rarely based on an informed understanding of the interrelationships of higher education and the economy, the polity, and our culture.

7

While a research assistant for the Sloan Commission on Government and Higher Education in 1979 and 1980, I was struck by a glaring black hole in both the historiography of American education and contemporary educational policy making: everyone seemed to know what had happened since World War II but little had been written about the important developments in the preceding decades. To those of us who are interested in the disjunction between American rhetoric and reality, the years between the world wars are an illuminating period, an era of unprecedented access to opportunity and of class and ethnic discrimination, of educational entrepreneurship and of intellectual and social snobbery.

My perspective on the role of education in modern American society was shaped in large part during my work for the Sloan Commission, as well as at the University of Pennsylvania, where I spent much time on various policy and search committees. Under the aegis of the Committee on Higher Degrees in the History of American Civilization at Harvard University, I explored these issues with the encouragement and support of Daniel Aaron and David Donald.

Above all, Frank Freidel, Nathan Glazer, and David Riesman have nurtured both my work and me. Various members of the Department of History at the University of California, Los Angeles, have been stimulating and understanding colleagues; in particular Robert Dallek and Richard Weiss made insightful suggestions concerning both content and style. David Jaffe also provided helpful comments on an earlier version of this manuscript. The responsibility for my interpretations, of course, remains mine alone.

This book could not have been written without the help of the librarians and archivists at the many colleges and universities I visited while conducting my research. They opened my eyes to the many neglected treasures in their holdings, as well as to the atmosphere of their institutions.

Peter Agree, Barbara Salazar, and their colleagues at Cornell University Press have been most helpful. Robert Westbrook and Paula Fass read the manuscript with great care for the Press and enabled me to improve the quality of the book.

This work is dedicated to my family. Without the unwavering encouragement and support of my wife, Sherrie Zacharius, and the loving care of my parents, Jacques and Florence Levine, I would not have had the opportunity to pursue this project or my career. My gratitude for their understanding and patience cannot be adequately expressed. And, finally, a special note to my son, Aaron, who has edited some of this book at the age of one by reaching up to press the keys of a word processor. As I have been encouraged by family and friends, so too do I hope he has the opportunity to pursue his dreams. That is what the culture of aspiration is all about.

DAVID O. LEVINE

Los Angeles, California

*The American College and
the Culture of Aspiration,
1915–1940*

1 / Introduction

Today most Americans take it for granted that a college education is an essential ingredient in the formula for success. Not only must lawyers and doctors attend college before beginning professional training, but would-be entrepreneurs and social workers also must acquire several years of postsecondary schooling before Americans deem them qualified to practice their chosen vocations. Even artists and sports and entertainment stars are trained in colleges and universities. Despite our cultural skepticism about the value of formal knowledge and intellect, most Americans are not at all ambivalent about the value of formal education. Education is now firmly linked to growth and national survival, as well as to personal advancement.

Yet amid the fraternity rushes, plasma physics laboratories, student loans, and affirmative action programs of today's universities, it is important to recall that higher education has not always been a critical criterion of economic and social mobility in American society. As late as the first decade of this century, only about two of every hundred young people between the ages of eighteen and twenty-four went to college. At that time, only a handful of universities enrolled as many as two thousand undergraduate and graduate students combined; only five medical schools required any college preparation for admission.[1] Even at the very best universities, few faculty members had earned the degree of Doctor of Philosophy, and even fewer conducted original research—despite William James's warning in 1907 about the "Ph.D. octopus." In the early years of the twentieth century, public attention was rarely focused on the colleges.

Higher education began to play a prominent role in the development of American society during World War I. Between 1915 and

1940 it experienced unprecedented change and growth. For the first time young people looked primarily to education as the avenue to economic and social mobility, businessmen and professionals looked to the college for its talent and its stamp of legitimacy, and society looked to the university for the benefits of its research. This was a time of skyrocketing enrollments and admissions quotas, of new practical courses of study and selective honors programs, of federal financial assistance and social snobbery, of trend-setting fraternity life and sophisticated scientific research. The developments that education has undergone since World War II could not have taken place in the absence of the emotional debates on mission, curriculum, and admissions which stirred the campuses in the 1920s and 1930s.

Scholars and critics have long debated the nature of American society and questioned its distinctiveness. Are Americans idealistic or pragmatic? Have social relations been as egalitarian as our democratic pronouncements suggest? Are we a melting pot or a salad bowl? Generations have tried to reconcile seemingly opposite traits in order to characterize our national personality, and generally have failed to satisfy one another's yearnings for definitive reasons for their self-confidence or disillusionment. Throughout our history, however, one characteristic has united us all, the Pilgrim and the Polish-American, the robber baron and the new freedman: American culture is a culture of aspiration.

Though the United States has not fulfilled its promise of "life, liberty, and the pursuit of happiness" for all of its people, the American dream has always been an essential, if often elusive, variable in our national life. In the twentieth century this dream has manifested itself in the individual pursuit of education and in the expansion of the functions of educational institutions. Since World War I more and more Horatio Algers have sought desperately to go to college, to join the right fraternity or to attain a professional degree, more often than not surpassing their parents' and their own expectations. As a result, an examination of the history of higher education between the world wars becomes a chronicle of American society's ongoing process of self-definition: in a society based on hope, would access to higher education, and therefore opportunity, be apportioned by socioeconomic status or by merit, by intellect or personality, by gender, race, or whim, or perhaps by some combination of all of the above?

Between the world wars, American colleges and universities found themselves in the public limelight. Individually and collectively, consciously and unconsciously, they responded to a cacophony of interests, some petitioning for unlimited expansion of the curriculum and the student body and others calling—sometimes whispering—for restriction of their mission to the preservation of the status quo. The rapid rise of collegiate business education and professional-oriented urban universities suggested that institutions of higher learning would now provide training to an increasing number of students in an ever-increasing array of white-collar professions. Debates about the curriculum focused on the balance between cultural and practical subjects in the undergraduate course of study. Debates about admissions—and later about exclusionary quotas in particular—focused on the relative importance of intelligence and of background in the selection of a self-conscious elite. Debates about the structure of American higher education itself focused on the efficient allocation of occupational training and therefore of access to economic and social privilege. In the 1920s and 1930s the American college welcomed the professions and prestige enthusiastically, but despite its remarkable growth and stunning successes, it did not always welcome democracy. It thus demonstrated how far American society had come and how far it had to go.

In his classic study *The Emergence of the American University,* Laurence Veysey describes what he calls the "symptoms of crystallization." After charting the development of such elite universities as Harvard, Yale, Princeton, and Chicago after the Civil War, Veysey concludes that by 1910 the structure of the American university had assumed its stable twentieth-century form and that few new ideas about the role of higher education have been advanced since that time. He adds in a cryptic note that while many educators consider the junior college movement an exception, he believes two-year institutions to be a part of secondary, not higher, education. According to Veysey, the critical period of innovation in American higher education ended about 1910, with the retirement of such educational giants as Harvard's Charles W. Eliot and Johns Hopkins' Daniel C. Gilman. Indeed, he concludes, "an architect [was] no longer required, only a contractor."[2] Most historians have shared Veysey's view that the major innovations in higher education ended with the professionalization of the elite university around the turn of the century.[3]

In the early years of the new century, the United States continued to change and grow at a startling pace, and the elite universities did show signs of incipient expansion. The desire to harness and rationalize the structure of the United States' vast economic and social resources dominated American thought. Grappling with the conflict between the rhetoric and institutions of individualism and the growing complexity of modern life, leading Americans embarked on a "search for order" to improve the quality of life for most Americans by making society's economic, social, and political institutions more efficient.[4] Nowhere was this quest more evident than in the nation's efforts to foster education.

During the first decade of the twentieth century, the British commentator James Bryce observed, colleges and universities took their first tentative steps "out of an era of relative obscurity into a period of great demand"—a development that contributed to his optimistic view of America's future.[5] The availability of philanthropic support for the elite universities—in particular for research conducted there—was a good omen, and the nascent and successful partnerships between these institutions and the professions provided a model for the future. Debates about the relative value of classical and utilitarian curricula suggested possibilities for a new and more practical conception of higher learning. In these respects, Veysey's perspective is correct. The structure of university influence was in place, if only in about a dozen schools. Still, while their potential was great, their contemporary influence remained limited.

Elite educators trumpeted efforts to raise the standards and therefore the effectiveness of colleges and universities. The Carnegie Foundation for the Advancement of Teaching played a central role by commissioning the influential 1907 study *Academic and Industrial Efficiency* and the 1912 Flexner report on medical education. In addition, when the Carnegie Foundation created a retirement system for faculty, it established rigid standards to determine whether an institution's faculty would qualify to receive its benefits. At the outset, little more than half of the public universities that submitted data (only three in the South) could meet the foundation's criteria in regard to student–faculty ratio, number of books in the library, and the like.[6] The vast majority of colleges and universities looked at the stature, functions, and values of the elite institutions from quite a distance.

Even more important, most young people still chose not to go to any college. As late as 1913, fewer than one in twenty young persons attended college, and even the most prestigious universities were scrambling to fill their classes, drawing students almost exclusively from their own regions and admitting many with academic credentials below their stated admissions requirements. Tuition figures similarly imply that the best institutions had but limited appeal. Owing in part to lack of demand, Yale had not raised its tuition for nearly thirty years; Harvard could not "afford" to charge more tuition than Stevens Institute of Technology until after World War I. While the small coterie of distinguished university presidents enunciated an enlarged conception of the American institution of higher education, it remained largely unrealized during their tenure.

Writing in a popular magazine of the day, Clayton Sedgwick Cooper observed that student life suggested "the subtle charm of youth lost in a sense of its own significance, moving about in a mysterious paradise all its own." He added that the American college was generally regarded as a "place where an extra clever boy may go and still amount to something."[7] Faint praise, indeed. As the United States abounded in opportunities in railroads and oil, department stores and publishing, most American colleges offered essentially the opportunity for four years of pleasant idleness.

The traditional perspective on the history of higher education in the United States is therefore misleading. There can be no doubt that a handful of self-conscious and forceful university presidents did establish the elite university as an integral part of the professional world in the late nineteenth century. Despite the leadership of these influential visionaries, however, the so-called elite universities had less impact than historians, educators, and the public have assumed. Economic and social pressures soon stimulated the growth of American higher education beyond the hopes, expectations, and indeed the fears of progressive, and yet conservative, elite educators.[8]

Our contemporary image of college life between the first and second world wars is limited to visions of raccoon coats and bootleg liquor on a fall football afternoon and the earnest student radical marching for peace at an urban institution. These stereotypes mask the unprecedented growth and intellectual ferment in American colleges and universities in the interwar years. This period was not simply one of drift, as the traditional view suggests;[9] indeed, it was during the 1920s and 1930s that American schools of higher education moved into the mainstream of American economic, social, and cultural life.

As more and more attention was focused on the functions of education in a modern society, it became clear that American attitudes toward education varied widely. Was democratic higher learning a contradiction in terms? Could the demand for specialized training be reconciled with traditional conceptions of knowledge and intellect? Would American colleges and universities facilitate individual mobility by enhancing educational opportunity or limit it by restrictive curriculum, admissions, and pricing policies? Myriad philosophical, social, and practical considerations suggested, in Jay Hudson's term, a confusing "plenitude of educational purposes" and alternatives to educators and the public.[10]

While in the nineteenth century American colleges may have enjoyed relative seclusion from the kinetic society around them, after World War I they could afford no such luxury. In the following decades, each college and university was forced by social and institutional pressures to reevaluate the curriculum it offered, the type of student it wished to attract, and its role in the local or national community it wished to serve. Educational debates raged not just in professional publishing organs but at individual schools. No two institutions reacted alike: each took into account its own unique combination of institutional prerogatives. Why did one college seek to become selective while another sought to accumulate professional-oriented programs and students? Why did one college discriminate in its admissions process and another did not? All institutions confronted new demands for both training and research, and nearly all chose to meet them.

An institution's tradition, its sources of financial support and control, its geographical setting, its applicant pool, its presidential leadership and faculty perspectives, and the specific economic and social currents in which it existed constituted the complex matrix of factors that determined its reaction to the possibilities for growth open to the twentieth-century college and university. During the next few decades, for example, the so-called elite institutions struggled to establish their identity as such by holding to traditional values and constituencies that other colleges did not or could not afford to cultivate. The public sector rose to prominence in the 1920s and 1930s because of its willingness to respond to any and all interests in society, particularly by the creation of new types of postsecondary institutions. For each college that chose to limit its size, many more chose to enlarge and recast themselves: normal schools became teachers' colleges and teachers' colleges became state colleges and universities.

The growth of American higher education was stimulated by a

remarkable confluence of economic, social, and intellectual developments that appeared first in the Progressive Era and gathered momentum after World War I. Expansion served the needs of the rapidly growing professional and service-oriented sectors for training and legitimacy. It permitted educators to seek and to establish a larger place for their institutions in a practical and heretofore generally disdainful world. It also catered to the desire for status of an emerging white-collar, consumption-oriented middle class. Increased public, business, and governmental concern for higher education demonstrated its newly won acceptance as an integral part of the nation's present and future.

After World War I, institutions of higher learning were no longer content to educate; they now set out to train, accredit, and impart social status to their students. The curriculum became inextricably tied to the nation's economic structure, particularly its burgeoning white-collar, middle-class sector. New types of students were taught new subjects at an increasingly diverse array of postsecondary institutions. Hundreds of new institutions were founded; the colleges enjoyed an unprecedented enrollment boom. In conception and curriculum, higher education became more accessible to more Americans than ever before. New avenues of economic and social mobility became available.

This transformation was radical in many respects, yet it manifested itself in conservative ways. The college student was no longer on the fringe of his generation; now he would take his place as a future leader of society, but only after careful selection, generally based on family background, and socialization. Faculty members no longer toiled in obscurity; they assumed responsibility for the creation of new knowledge as well as the transmission of the old, but only with the support of America's public and private establishments. Colleges and universities pursued greater visibility in society, often by devoting themselves to such nonintellectual and noncontroversial activities as intercollegiate athletics. The functions of institutions of higher learning and of their students, faculty, and administrators were no longer antithetical to the broad economic and social values of society; indeed, the colleges became the primary champions of those values. The campus became a center for the ethos of an emergent white-collar, consumption-oriented middle class.

Despite the universal appeal of education's democratic promise, however, enrollment data show that the higher the prestige of an institution, the greater the numerical predominance of the children of the upper middle class. During this era of change and opportunity, they seized the nascent possibilities of college attendance first. The presence—real or sometimes threatened—of an increasing number of ethnic and poor students on such campuses showed how vital higher education had become to the aspirations of American young people in general. They all believed that college training prepared one for a good job and that the collegiate experience assured one of important social connections and the good life thereafter. Yet, while the ambitious of all backgrounds flocked to the colleges, most of the ambitious poor could not afford to attend. Furthermore, once there, though they all shared the same hopes, collegiate culture only occasionally brought young people from diverse socioeconomic backgrounds together in the same classes, activities, and fraternities.

More typically, differentiated tracks of achievement and social life were established, among institutions and even on the same campus, to distinguish between those young people who came to school with better socioeconomic backgrounds and those who came to school in the hope of moving up the socioeconomic ladder. Examples of this often ambiguous situation abound: after they were admitted to the best institutions, if they were admitted, ethnic students were relegated to "B" rather than "A" fraternities and non–liberal arts divisions were sometimes located on a different and less attractive campus than the more prestigious liberal arts departments. Still, despite the obvious and more subtle forms of discrimination, most ethnic and poor students continued to share the dreams of their middle-class peers and saw college as the key to a better life. And for all but a few, even during the depths of the Depression, it was.

Consequently, the evolution of modern American higher education between the world wars is a story not only of steady progress but of ambivalence. In the 1920s and 1930s, reality failed to match American democratic rhetoric. Many institutions resisted the trend toward a more liberal curriculum. Suddenly young people were not only eager to attend college in a general sense but concerned about the social implications of the school they went to and the fraternity they joined. For the most part, institutions at the apex of American higher education were not open to all young people of ability or potential without regard to their socioeconomic status, gender, race, or religion. While hundreds of thousands of less privileged young people joined their more privileged peers in college, by the late 1930s the continued disparity in educational attainment among young people of different socioeconomic classes and the segregation of most students of ethnic or poor backgrounds became a source of concern and social tension.

Between 1915 and 1940 American educational institutions reinforced the barriers that enabled young people from the "best" homes to strengthen their numerical predominance at the best schools and in the most prestigious professions. The culture of aspiration stimulated an unprecedented demand for higher education of any kind as a symbol of economic and social mobility; it also created the demand for status that enabled some colleges to select their students for the first time. Ethnic and poor students often surpassed their more affluent peers in academic ability and drive, but more often than not they were channeled into less acclaimed schools and less prestigious occupations. Urban and public institutions offered new courses and new hope to those who clamored for an opportunity to move up the economic and social ladder, while at the same time the now-selective liberal arts college provided a check against undesired democratization to those who wished to preserve the hegemony of the white Anglo-Saxon Protestant upper middle class.

The collective impact of thousands of individual and institutional decisions during the 1920s and 1930s suggests the self-conscious development of a differentiated system of higher education in the United States. Each society must select its leaders and train its citizens for occupations that call for different skills and offer differential status. In the United States, higher education has come to play the most prominent role in this process. Expansion of existing and new institutions met much of the increased demand for the broad dissemination of education and training, but time and again the prerogatives and prestige of well-established groups in society were ensured before significant numbers of equally, if not more, talented ethnic and poor students were given their chance. The prospect of mass and democratic education in the aftermath of World War I therefore fostered both the selective liberal arts college and the public junior college, and each in many respects owes its existence to the other.

Change and expansion encouraged diverse institutions to respond to new and divergent interests. At stake was not simply the nature of higher learning in the United States; here, too, in large measure, would be determined the American economic and social structure.

Still, before World War II prompted passage of the G.I. Bill and the establishment of President Harry Truman's Commission on Higher Education, access to American higher education remained a privilege, not a right of all young people. Because it did so, it embodied both the promise of America's culture of aspiration and the limitations of its economic and social institutions' ability to realize that promise.

2 / The Colleges Go to War

Although enrollment had been growing at an unprecedented rate since the final decade of the nineteenth century, World War I proved to be the watershed in the history of American higher education. On the eve of the war, most college students and faculty still remained apart from the mainstream of American life. Few young people believed that college provided the best opportunities for economic and social mobility; few professors were called upon to lend their knowledge to the solution of society's problems. With some notable exceptions, while the administrative structure and educational ideology necessary for expansion were in place, the colleges had failed to capture wide support from business, government, and the public. World War I changed all that: no institution could avoid—or could afford to avoid—its influence. The war experience generally and the establishment of the Student Army Training Corps in particular consolidated the formation of a social consensus about the value of higher education.

Preparations for the war effort fostered recognition of new opportunities for service and cooperation between institutions of higher education and other sectors of the society. As Jay Hudson has pointed out, the war created a widespread need for "skilled intelligence of a special sort,"[1] as in the fields of engineering and administration, and the colleges were given the opportunity to demonstrate their usefulness to society. Parke R. Kolbe proudly reported that "even the staid old colleges which had formerly put up rigid bars between themselves and the modern ideas of community obligation . . . awoke to the call of patriotism and introduced unheard of innovations."[2] Institutions modified their curricula and admissions procedures; faculty offered their advice and expertise. Impressed by the effectiveness of wartime curricular innovations, educators left them in place. As a result, American higher education established its reputation as an essential partner in, rather than a hindrance to, the pursuit of a more efficient and prosperous society in an increasingly technocratic world.

In the public eye World War I transformed the college student from a frivolous young fellow into a prospective leader of society. Young people were encouraged to attend college to gain access to the war-related technical and management occupations that promised economic and social mobility in the postwar world. *The Case Tech*, the student newspaper of the Case School of Applied Science in Cleveland, advised its readers to "THINK TWICE before you leave. Is that job you've got lined up now worth the sacrifice of the job that awaits you at the end of four years when you step forth a TRAINED MAN, A COLLEGE GRADUATE?"[3] As a result of such advice, many young men who flocked to the colleges during the war stayed on after it ended. Business reformers and government officials became eager to acquire the expertise, ambition, and social conservatism of the college-educated. By 1922 a professor was writing in *The New Republic*, "The old jibe of futility no longer holds against our colleges; their training pays in cash and power, and their influence is compounding at usurous rates."[4] By showing higher education's potential for service to young people and diverse sectors of society and by creating economic and social incentives for college attendance, the war effort accelerated the expansion of the structure, size, and functions of American higher education.

Students Go to War

At first, however, it was feared that the war would contribute to the demise of most American colleges. In large measure because of the war, enrollment declined substantially between 1915 and 1918. Well over half of the nation's colleges suffered a drop in attendance, some losing as many as two-thirds of their students. As a majority of American colleges had enrolled fewer than 300 students, the widespread siphoning of students into the war effort threatened college after college with extinction. The situation at DePauw University, a Methodist school in central Indiana, was typical: nearly a quarter of the male student body enlisted in the army or in an ambulance corps before the spring of 1917; a third of the remaining male students followed suit the following fall. By the spring of 1918, 1,185 of the University of North Carolina's students and alumni had enlisted; indeed, only a telegram from President Woodrow Wilson dissuaded the university's young president, Edward K. Graham, from signing up as a private himself. "In a moment of hysteria," a historian has since reported, Indiana University's president, William L. Bryan, even wired President Wilson to offer to close his institution for the duration of the war. The trustees of one small school, Olivet College in Wisconsin, did vote to close their institution, but later gave the faculty permission to keep it open on a curtailed basis. "With no end of the war in sight, with constant recruiting campaigns taking steady toll of students, and with the prospect of a lowered draft age imminent," Kolbe recalled, "there seemed to be little prospect of continuing work without seriously mortgaging the future."[5]

Claiming that the public interest demanded an uninterrupted flow of trained leaders for the war effort, educators took unprecedented steps to promote their institutions. "There ought to be a conviction aroused which should amount to a propaganda," President Ernest M. Hopkins of Dartmouth College suggested in 1917, "that every man who is qualified to enter an institution of higher education should do so, and that the young men and women of the country should understand that a stronger argument exists for such a course this year than ever before."[6] New brochures issued by colleges and universities stressed that tuition was an investment in new opportunities that would open up after the war. The administration of President Wilson's former university, Princeton, argued that "the true soldierly course for next year's Princeton student will be to give himself wholeheartedly to the daily task of education, remembering that 'peace, too, hath her heroes like fame and fortune.'" Still, advice that sitting tight required as much courage as joining the war effort apparently failed to convince F. Scott Fitzgerald and his peers who joined the ambulance corps or the army. Similarly, Emory College in Georgia urged high school seniors to "ENLIST IN COLLEGE IN ORDER TO RENDER YOUR COUNTRY A LARGER SERVICE," but only the addition of military training to its curriculum in the fall of 1917 halted the decline in attendance there.[7]

Not all institutions suffered from a drastic reduction in attendance. A 1918 Bureau of Education survey noted that while colleges of agriculture lost more than a third of their enrollment and engineering schools lost slightly less than a fifth of their students, liberal arts colleges lost little more than a tenth of their prewar attendance, and the decline in male enrollment was softened by a modest increase in the number of women attending liberal arts colleges during the war. The socioeconomic backgrounds of students—generally higher at the more prestigious liberal arts institutions—probably account for the differences in these figures.[8] Young men at the nation's technical schools seem to have been the first college students drafted. As young women were not encouraged to replace those young men in technical fields who had left for the front, public attention was soon focused on an imminent shortage of trained engineers, researchers, and administrators.

After war was declared in April 1917, educators turned to the federal government for help. Pressing the president and Congress for assistance, they emphasized the importance to society of "not only unbroken columns for the Army and Navy, but also unbroken columns of engineers and architects, unbroken columns of physicians and surgeons, unbroken columns of chaplains and nurses, and a thousand other unbroken columns of skilled civilians."[9] They stressed the long-term benefits of federal support for higher education. The president was soon asked to issue an "absolutely imperative" order to "stop the wholesale running off of college students to the front," one college head reported, "[because] the greatest construction period in the world will follow this war." "The demand for trained men in all lines—financial, economical, social, and industrial—will be ten times greater than it ever has been before," he predicted. "Where will the trained men come from if the colleges are depleted?"[10] A generation before, this argument would have been excessive and premature; now it was persuasive.

The Student Army Training Corps

Higher education had friends in high places in the federal government. In July 1917 President Wilson—who as president of Princeton had written an article titled "Princeton in the Nation's Service"—wrote a widely circulated letter urging young men to stay in school. But it was Newton D. Baker, the secretary of war and a trustee of Western Reserve University, who took the lead in encouraging the colleges to guide public opinion and "to keep the lamp of learning burning among the young." Responding to educators' lobbying, Baker authorized the creation of a committee of college presidents to advise the Advisory Commission of the Council of National Defense in the summer of 1917. The year before, Congress had authorized the creation of the Reserve Officers Training Corps (ROTC), but fewer than a hundred units had been established at the nation's colleges before the United States entered the war. Still faced with critical manpower shortages, an impatient President Wilson issued General Order 15 on February 2, 1918, which formalized the army's links to the higher education community; in early May he supported the formation of National Army Training Detachments at more than a hundred schools. The War Department also asked local draft boards to defer technical experts and students and formed an advisory board to assist the newly created Committee on Education and Special Training, which provided leading educators with an even more direct line to wartime policy makers.[11] Then the sympathetic president and his cabinet convinced a reluctant Congress that college attendance should be encouraged even more directly by the establishment of the Student Army Training Corps (SATC).

Until the summer of 1918, most members of Congress pressed for a universal draft. The effort to keep the army "democratic" had decimated the colleges in the fall of 1917; the Bureau of Education estimated that male enrollment declined 40 percent. Congress was still considering a bill to lower the draft age; if it had passed intact, the effect on the colleges would probably have been catastrophic. But finally, pointing to the success of the training detachments, the War Department and educators turned a skeptical Congress around. Congressional approval for the formation of the SATC in August 1918 signaled to the dean of the University of Kentucky that "our educational system [is] . . . virile enough to make of itself a tool for a special purpose."[12] Now all but forgotten, the SATC was viewed by contemporaries as an unprecedented and important development, a rite of passage for American higher education from carefree adolescence to manhood.

Under the SATC, participating colleges were run as full-time army training facilities. The federal government took over the colleges in all but name: it used existing plants, equipment, and personnel and funded expansion to enable the nation's colleges to select and train officer candidates and technical and administrative experts. Most colleges set up two separate but related programs, Section A (collegiate-oriented) and Section B (vocation-oriented). This cooperative venture promised to alleviate army manpower shortages and to keep the colleges open.

The federal government established minimum standards for participation in the program. Each college was required to have offered at least two years of collegiate-grade education to at least 100 men the previous academic year. In addition, the War Department insisted that each school guarantee a place in its SATC unit to any high school graduate who requested one. Even such a staunch elitist as President A. Lawrence Lowell of Harvard announced that his college would matriculate any applicant over eighteen years of age with a diploma from an approved high school. In return, institutions received about $900 to cover tuition, room, and board for each student-soldier. In their zeal, few college presidents voiced concern about federal interference in their affairs. Indeed, Western Reserve University's Charles F. Thwing lauded "this most generous provision . . . without precedent in the history of liberal education or of the conduct of war." "It's Patriotic to Go to College!" proclaimed the Emergency Council on Education, the newly created voice of the higher education establishment, and thousands of young men got the message.[13]

On October 1, 1918, more than 140,000 male students were sworn into the United States Army at simultaneous ceremonies at 525 colleges. At most schools the newly commissioned student-soldiers marched in awkward formation on the athletic field before fellow students, faculty, administrators, and army officials, and listened to inspiring speeches. "In America you have come to college this autumn at your country's call," President Edgar O. Lovett of Rice Institute in Houston, Texas, told his assembled student-soldiers. "Go to college! Return to college! are not the mere seasonable exhortations of college presidents: they are governmental slogans." "It was an impressive occasion and one of deep moment for the higher educational system of the United States," Kolbe recalled, "for it represented the culmination of collegiate effort for official recognition and the final coming of the opportunity for service to the fullest extent."[14]

Enrollment increased significantly at many institutions. Attendance at Emory College reached 296, up 100 from the previous spring. Enrollment at Alabama Polytechnic Institute (now Auburn University), with the largest SATC unit in the South, climbed from 803 in 1917–18 to 1,280 in 1918–19. The number of freshman and sophomore students at the University of Chicago increased by one-third.

Harvard had lost about a fifth of its enrollment during the early years of the war, but when school opened in the fall of 1918, Samuel E. Morison later recalled, attendance went up as "everyone but the near-sighted, the flat-footed, and the very young" joined the SATC.[15] During previous wars, American college enrollment had declined; now, in contrast, the formation of the SATC stimulated attendance.

Campus life changed dramatically after the establishment of the SATC. Dartmouth College's historian believed that the upheaval was far more serious than any previous one in the college's long past. Military training became an obsession with most students; learning lagged far behind. "Every day Princeton becomes less an academic college and more a school of war," reported its alumni magazine. At the University of Illinois, some 3,000 men moved into fraternity houses converted into barracks for the duration of the war. Their daily schedule included two hours of drill and eight hours of supervised study and recitations. The typical male student's day, the *Daily Illini* reported, consisted of "a melange of calisthenics, close order drill, bayonet practice, studies, more calisthenics, more close order drill, and topped off with a little additional study after supper." This schedule was followed even at Fordham College, an urban Catholic institution. Students ate their meals in new dining halls built with federal money, then marched in formation through campus to class. Student activities and fraternities, the mainstays of peacetime college life, were all but ignored. In short, as the president of the University of Arizona observed, "curriculum and traditions have been literally pulled to pieces."[16]

Most faculty encouraged and took great pride in the SATC experiment and the changes it fostered on their campuses. They perceived a greater public appreciation of the colleges' usefulness to society, and they welcomed the program's substantial financial benefits. Though relatively few faculty were asked to join the Intercollegiate Intelligence Bureau, a voluntary project that provided government agencies with the names and specialties of academic experts, or The Inquiry, the small group of social scientists organized to provide President Wilson with background information on diplomatic issues, these ground-breaking efforts to incorporate faculty into the public policy process boosted faculty morale. Committees on War Information were formed on many campuses to coordinate the local dissemination of technical information and propaganda. Emphasizing work related to the war effort, faculty encouraged innovation in the curriculum, not only in the physical sciences but in the social sciences as well. Most applauded the creation of new divisions, such as programs in naval engineering, aeronautical science, and statistics, which brought an infusion of cash, students, excitement, and status to their schools.[17] A postwar memorandum suggesting that the army saw great potential in continued cooperation with the academic community on research and personnel matters was generally warmly received.[18] Most faculty members recognized and supported the aggressive expansion of the size and functions of the American university catalyzed by the war effort.

Not all faculty appreciated the tenor of campus life during the war. These dissidents were disturbed by their colleagues' willingness to accommodate the transformation of the colleges into facilities for the training of technical personnel. Furthermore, they were angered by their colleagues' readiness to promulgate the government's propaganda. Some campuses were torn apart by the xenophobic ostracism of German subjects and pro-German professors. One of Columbia University's best-known professors, the historian Charles Beard, resigned because of the alleged violations of the principle of academic freedom condoned, if not perpetrated, by the university's president Nicholas Murray Butler. Aware that failure to participate in the SATC program would hurt attendance, the trustees, administration, and faculty of Juniata College in Pennsylvania still refused to establish a unit because of the pacifist beliefs of its sponsor, the Church of the Brethren. The trustees considered the presence of uniformed men on campus unthinkable; several faculty members even visited army camps to counsel resisters kept under detention. Others were opposed to the SATC for nonideological reasons. The change in daily routine irked some: when faculty meetings dealt with such questions as how many hours of drill should be required of non-SATC students and whether non-SATC students should wear uniforms, many faculty disputed the relevance of the program to the educational process.[19]

Still, the short-lived SATC was judged a resounding success when the Armistice heralded its termination barely three months after its inauguration. The wartime experience of California's Pomona College demonstrates how most institutions adjusted to and benefited from the program. Four days after war was declared, the Pomona trustees voted to proffer the use of the college's grounds and facilities to the government; when the government did not respond, the college floundered. The faculty abolished the recently established limitation on freshman admissions in an attempt to replace enlisted upper-classmen with additional new students, but enrollment declined from 598 students to 544 in the fall of 1917. With the introduction of the SATC the following fall, attendance jumped to 649. In December 1918, one month after the end of the war, construction was completed on a barracks designed and paid for by the army; it was converted into a new gymnasium at little cost to the college. The student newspaper hailed the program for encouraging the adoption of new curricula. Most important, it added, "one hundred men have gotten a taste of a college education which would have been denied them had it not been for the training corps."[20] At Pomona and elsewhere the SATC provided new buildings, new students, and a new self-confidence.

Students at Illinois viewed membership in the SATC as "merely a means of separating the wheat from the chaff."[21] The war appeared to prove the usefulness of the college student as well as of the college. While most young men were being drafted into the army, the more ambitious—or more well educated and financially comfortable—of them were being paid to attend college and to prepare for leadership positions in the war effort and the postwar world. Fearing a lack of technicians, scientists, officers, and administrators, the federal government chose to excuse from combat service those young men it felt could fill those manpower shortages, and to send them to college instead. As a result, although an estimated 6,500 college students or graduates died in the war, many of the nation's most promising youth avoided the conflict. Admittedly, even proudly, World War I was "a college man's war," a war planned and directed—but not fought—by college men trained to mobilize and lead the nation.[22] Whereas any young northerner with the necessary means could pay his way out of the Union Army during the Civil War, in World War I the federal government paid young men to stay in college.

The events of World War I, most notably the establishment of the SATC, accelerated the emergence of a new privileged class in American society—the college-educated man. The college diploma became a key sign of economic status and social responsibility. In the confusing postwar world, The DePauw Daily noted, "if there ever was a time for leadership it is now. . . . And where will men look for leadership if not to the nation's universities?" The college graduate is "the captain of today," the student newspaper asserted boldly. "[He] has been an asset to the life of the past. To the life of the future he is a necessity." "Multitudes of men have seen in the army that opportunities for leadership frequently go to the trained man," a college newspaper editorial declared in 1919. "The people as a whole have observed that education and democracy are inseparable."[23] The creation of the SATC legitimized the claims of educators and the influence of the college graduate.

The Rise of the Academic Expert

World War I proved the preeminence of the expert in modern society. Events at home and abroad in the early twentieth century convinced contemporaries that knowledge and training were essential to the efficient organization of economic, social, and political institutions and to the solution of human problems. Educated individuals studied the nation's problems, suggested appropriate responses, and were called upon in ever-increasing numbers to administer the newly created programs and to staff the strengthened and new commissions. The diverse individuals and coalitions that sponsored the varied reforms we now gather under the umbrella of the Progressive movement did not agree on most issues, but they did concur in their reliance on the expert and his ability to apply theory and scientific principles to resolve the issues of the day. Society looked to the engineer and the economist, the chemist and the political scientist, and it found them increasingly in the nation's institutions of higher learning.

The establishment of the National Bureau of Standards in 1901 was the model for the interaction of business, government, and experts from institutions of higher education. With the increasing technical complexity of industry came the need for uniform standards of weights and measures; the lack of national standards was considered both costly and humiliating. Urged on by a coalition of scientists and businessmen, Congress created a national laboratory to establish and monitor such standards in order to make American business more efficient. With an initial capitalization of $250,000, which made it perhaps the most elaborate research facility in the country, the National Bureau of Standards was authorized to engage in whatever research it deemed necessary and to hire and protect its employees under civil service rules. The first director was Samuel W. Stratton, a University of Chicago physicist and future president of the Massachusetts Institute of Technology, who had led the effort to form the bureau as a professional and scientific agency, free of economic and political influence. The public gained more confidence in the academic expert, a new and supposedly disinterested and objective participant in a public policy process otherwise endangered by corrupt special interests.

American educators welcomed the opportunity to provide new knowledge and new experts. Charles Thwing, like most college presidents, insisted that his institution no longer wished to be worshiped; now it sought to be "in touch with life." The appointment and acceptance of academicians to government positions was "evidence of the common sense of the American people that the prejudice against the College Professors, like that of the men of letters, is rapidly dying down, and that there is beginning to be public recognition and public appreciation of the service they are rendering to the Commonwealth," Brander Matthews observed in 1909. "It is partly due to a growing understanding of the real value of the expert and the theorist."[24] With the extraordinary proliferation of knowledge in field after field in the late nineteenth and early twentieth centuries, it was no longer possible for dedicated amateurs to keep up with the explosion of important and increasingly complex discoveries. In nearly every discipline, a handful of institutions of higher education were soon at the forefront of American research and training.

Individuals interested in the physical and social sciences congregated in the changing American universities, relatively free from the pressures of the profit motive and partisan political passions found in other sectors of society. They cooperated in the formation of professional societies and competed for peer prestige, the best graduate students, and research funds, thereby stimulating the pace of research. These professors believed they had a responsibility not only to transmit the culture and knowledge of the past to their students but to create new knowledge as well. This newer type of academic felt much the same way about his traditional role as Theodore Roosevelt had felt about his father's generation of Mugwump political reformers: ideas and intellect were useless unless they were fused with a sense of moral responsibility and a willingness to act on those ideas and ideals. In a modern society dependent on technology for its economic and social progress, knowledge is power. Knowledge and the power it brought now resided on the college campus.

The recruitment of properly trained professional personnel at all levels of government was a high priority on the Progressive agenda.

The increasing interdependence of sections of the country and its diverse peoples, the traumatic rise of the cities with its attendant problems, and America's new role as a leading actor on the international scene enlarged substantially the number and range of services of local, state, and national governments. The nation responded to these new demands not by increasing the size of government alone but by altering the nature of American government itself. Government was viewed increasingly as the most effective and efficient agent of social change. Young intellectuals stood at the vanguard of political reform; they argued that only men of "finish, efficacy, and permanence"—as E. L. Godkin, the editor of *The Nation,* put it—could provide the "enlightened statesmanship" necessary to maintain the smooth functioning of democracy. Seventy years before, Alexis de Tocqueville had observed that government in America appeared to be run by the "invisible machine" of popular sovereignty. Now government would be staffed by a college-educated bureaucracy.[25]

In the twentieth-century United States, government service would no longer be a matter of privilege or patronage alone; it would become a profession. In his classic *Anti-Intellectualism in American Life,* Richard Hofstadter describes how Americans' distrust of expertise, their dislike of centralization, their desire to uproot entrenched powerful classes, and their belief in the simplicity of government "amounted to a repudiation . . . of the special value of the educated classes in civic life." During the Progressive Era, however, experts worked their way into the good graces of the American public. Hofstadter shows that the dynamic Roosevelt removed the "stigma of effeminacy and ineffectuality" from intellectuals and invited many of them into government service.[26] By the force of his intellect, personality, and popularity he drew the public's attention to the liberal ideas of such thinkers as Herbert Croly, the author of *The Promise of American Life,* and the young Walter Lippmann, whose *Drift and Mastery* captured the spirited self-confidence of his generation of concerned expert reformers.

Yet distrust of experts remained widespread. Ironically, Woodrow Wilson, the former political scientist and college president, was not disposed to consult and appoint academicians to public office. "What I fear is a government of experts," he said during his victorious 1912 presidential campaign. "God forbid that in a democratic country we should resign the task and give the government over to experts. What are we for if we are to be scientifically taken care of by a small number of gentlemen who are the only men who understand the job? Because if we don't understand the job, then we are not a free people."[27] Wilson insisted he had rarely heard more penetrating debate on the issues than in workingmen's clubs. His early appointments and policies confirm his opposition to the ideas enunciated by Roosevelt's young supporters. Wilson's rhetoric strikes a chord that still echoes in American politics today. But the events of World War I forced the president to change his mind.

The war effort demonstrated the indispensability of college-trained scientists, administrators, and social scientists. After meeting with several of the nation's top scientists, Wilson approved the formation of the National Research Council and the Naval Research Laboratory in 1916; indeed, a White House press release announcing the creation of the former advisory body asserted that "preparedness, to be sound and complete, must be solidly based on science." Most of the dollar-a-year men brought to Washington to run such wartime agencies as the War Industries Board were college graduates. Professional associations placed the resources of academic personnel at the disposal of the federal government; the American Historical Association, for example, formed the National Board for Historical Services in April 1917 to "render useful public service during the war." The Wilson administration soon tapped so many academicians for wartime government service that lunch at the capital's Cosmos Club was reported to resemble an intercollegiate faculty meeting.[28]

The best example of academicians' involvement in public policy during World War I could be found not in Washington but in the dusty back rooms of New York City's Public Library and the American Geographical Society. There about 150 scholars were gathered into small study groups collectively called The Inquiry to prepare working papers for the president in preparation for the eventual peace conference. Sponsored by Colonel Edward M. House, perhaps Wilson's closest associate, The Inquiry was organized in September 1917 under the direction of Sidney E. Mezes, president of the College of the City of New York and House's brother-in-law. The Columbia University historian James T. Shotwell, head of the National Board for Historical Services, and Walter Lippmann, now a Wilson supporter, also accepted key positions with the fledgling group, perhaps the nation's first government-sponsored public policy think tank.

Despite academicians' enthusiasm and the project's success, the history of The Inquiry demonstrates that the expert was not yet a fully accepted part of the American political scene. A few social scientists had been consulted during the peace conferences at the Hague in 1899 and 1907, but no experts had been asked to advise the Department of State since then. Nor were professors encouraged to study or to teach contemporary history or international affairs. The State Department itself was unable to provide expert strategic planning. As a result, Lippmann admitted that "there is a real famine in men and we have been compelled practically to train and create our own experts."[29] Even though the war effort dramatized the need for experts on Eastern Europe, the Middle East, and Asia, few could be found anywhere in the United States. Groups of scholars at the leading universities cooperated with The Inquiry's staff; still, historians from such remote fields as ancient and classical history were assigned such critical tasks as redrawing the boundary lines of modern Europe.

The complicated peace process dramatized the usefulness of the expert. In all, The Inquiry produced and collected nearly 2,000 reports and 1,200 maps; thirty-five scholars accompanied President Wilson to the Paris Peace Conference. As a result, Europeans deferred to the American delegation as the best source for documented information there. Many of the recommendations of its scholars were incorporated into the president's Fourteen Points, his blueprint for world peace, and into the final treaty itself. Just five institutions—Harvard, Yale, Princeton, Columbia, and the American Geographical Society—contributed half of the organization's young and inexperienced staff. The quality of their reports belied the authors' limited qualifications and the unavailability in this country of current source materials on other countries. Despite its effectiveness, then, its weaknesses pointed out that the United States could not afford to be caught so unaware and unprepared again.[30]

The postwar world accepted the college-trained expert as an indispensable spoke in the wheel of government. "We can no longer adhere to the outworn Jacksonian notion that 'the duties of public officers are, or at least admit of being made, so plain and simple that men of intelligence may readily qualify themselves for their performance,'" warned Lloyd Short, a University of Missouri political scientist. "The duties of public officers of our day are, for the most part, technical or professional, highly specialized, and immensely important, and they can be adequately performed only by permanent officials who have the requisite training and experience. Our universities, in an ever-increasing degree, should be a recruiting ground for the public service."[31] In the 1920s Herbert Hoover was instrumental in bringing increased numbers of college professors and graduates to Washington. He provided a haven for them in the Commerce Department and at the Conferences he sponsored on a wide-ranging array of issues. Political rhetoric aside, college-educated bureaucrats were given more responsibility following the war. Business also looked to the colleges and universities for its middle-level managers and industrial scientists and engineers.

During the Depression academicians gained an even more secure foothold in the federal government. Franklin D. Roosevelt's administration was faced with unprecedented challenges in its efforts to revitalize the American economy. Now that the Republican businessmen appointed by Hoover had failed to bring the nation out of its depression, a Roosevelt confidant asked, "Why not go to the universities of the country?" The so-called Brains Trust constituted only the tip of the iceberg of academicians' participation in the New Deal. "Government in this age is no theatre for amateur actors," Princeton's president, Harold W. Dodds, told the 1936 graduating class at Rice Institute. The hard times demanded a new civil service, one that "will combine the politician's responsibility to the public, the executive's knowledge of administration, and the student's grasp of underlying theory"; and he predicted that such college graduates would not be found wanting. He was right: while only about 10 percent of the relevant age cohort had attended college, 90 percent of the most important New Deal officials had gone to college and nearly 60 percent of them had earned advanced or professional degrees. Social scientists and lawyers populated nearly every level of the many New Deal agencies. Though the public perception of their power was exaggerated then, as now, academicians nonetheless exercised pervasive and unprecedented influence on public policy during the New Deal.[32]

The burgeoning size and responsibilities of government in the early decades of the twentieth century opened up new possibilities for service and status for college graduates and professors. The first generation of progressives emphasized civil service reform; the next, the city manager system, designed to wrest the direction of government away from the people, but only when administratively necessary; and the last, a government of college-trained and -socialized bureaucrats to fine-tune the organization of American society. In the complex modern world, educational credentials rather than experience became of necessity the critical measure of competence in the professions, in government, and in business. Supported by other sectors of society, particularly after World War I, academicians entered the "real world" of modern America. Yet at the same time they entered an imaginary world in which only technical expertise gained through a college education could solve the world's problems. Ironically, as American higher education has moved into the mainstream of American life, its faculty, its research and training, its graduates, and its potential personal and social benefits have been put on a pedestal.

Postwar Expansion

World War I was the take-off point in the history of American higher education. Attendance had been increasing steadily since about 1890, but the rate of growth had slowed slightly in the decade before the war. A study by the Association of American Colleges revealed that the average liberal arts college had but 14 instructors and 165 students on the eve of the war. As late as 1918, more than half of American institutions of higher learning enrolled fewer than 300 students; only 37 of 672 universities, colleges, and technical schools had more than 2,000 students, and just 8 enrolled more than 5,000 students in all of their departments combined. The unprecedented postwar boom alone boosted enrollment an estimated 25 percent nationwide between 1917 and 1920.[33]

When the war ended and the SATC units disbanded, educators encouraged students to look to the future, to view the completion of their college education as what economists would now call an opportunity cost investment. A member of the Board of Curators of the University of Missouri urged young people to apply the "standardized American test" of practicality to college; he was confident that the modern college was "an investment in citizenship . . . usefulness . . . [and] careers." The federal commissioner of education assured students that "the new era upon which we are entering will require the services of a much larger number of college men and women than the old era which passed away with the war." Economists estimated that more than 600,000 new technical and management positions would be created each year of the following decade, leaving more than enough room for any young man who expected to go from college to a promising position.[34] The unprecedented demand for college graduates, particularly in the expanding sectors of the economy, augured well for the young men who could afford higher education.

With such possibilities dangled before them in the hard postwar times, young people flocked confidently to American colleges and universities. The enrollment crush in the fall of 1918 started an enrollment boom that lasted for a decade. A survey of thirty colleges and universities showed that while they had lost nearly one-fifth of their 1914 enrollment by 1917, in 1919 these same schools were faced with an enrollment nearly 50 percent higher than their 1914 total. The class that entered the Case School of Applied Science in 1919, for example, was 75 percent larger than any previous freshman class. Wisconsin's passage of a soldier's bonus law that provided educational benefits from the state treasury stimulated an increase in attendance at the University of Wisconsin far beyond the predicted level. Widespread shortages of professors, housing, and equipment resulted when four times as many freshmen as expected began classes that fall at the University of Illinois. Illinois soon doubled its enrollment: it enrolled 5,009 students in 1916–17, only 4,030 in 1917–18, an SATC-propelled high of 5,721 in 1918–19, and a total of 10,103 students by 1926. The University of North Carolina enjoyed a growth rate in attendance of nearly 8 percent a year between 1918 and 1928; the University of Chicago's enrollment grew at 9.8 percent a year from 1918 to 1926, significantly higher than the 5.8 percent annual rate of increase between 1903 and 1918. Typical of the nation's liberal arts colleges, DePauw University drew 753 students in 1916 and 1,765 a decade later; indeed, its 1925 freshman class of 706 was twice as large as the entire student body of twenty years before.[35]

The biennial surveys sponsored by the Bureau of Education shed further light on the unprecedented magnitude of enrollment growth: in 1919–20 there were 597,857 undergraduates; in 1921–22, 681,076, an increase of 14.9 percent; in 1923–24, 823,063, an increase of 20.8 percent; in 1925–26, 917,462, an increase of 11.5 percent; in 1927–28, 1,053,955, an increase of 14.9 percent; and in 1929–30, 1,100,737, an increase of 4.4 percent. Though this rate of increase pales in comparison with the rate of growth in the twenty-five years after the end of World War II, it is clear that the 1920s witnessed the United States' first era of mass higher education.[36]

The rush to the colleges surprised even the most optimistic of educators. Enrollment projections made as late as the early 1920s fell far short. A commission predicted attendance for the next twenty-five years at the University of Minnesota in 1920; the 1929–30 estimate was surpassed in 1925–26, and attendance in 1926–27 nearly equaled the 1934–35 prediction. One professor at tiny Juniata College remarked in 1916 that by 1956 the college would enroll 300 students; by the end of the 1920s, more than 500 attended the Pennsylvania school. Looking at the national picture, New York University's chancellor Elmer E. Brown forecast in 1921 that as much as 10 percent of the college-age cohort and 1 percent of the country's total population would attend college; "it seems unlikely," he added, however, "that this proportion may be realized within the next twenty to thirty years." In 1924, just three years later, over 10 percent of the nation's young people attended college and slightly more than 1 percent of the American people were enrolled in college in 1937–38— years ahead of Brown's seemingly farsighted projections. No one could have predicted in 1910 that the proportion of college-age youth in college would more than triple to 15.4 percent in just thirty years.[37]

The wartime rhetoric legitimized students' interest in a college education with a definite vocational bent. Studies showed that nearly two-thirds of American undergraduates came to college to prepare for a specific occupation or profession. A 1923 poll at Indiana University indicated that 1,380 of the 1,511 respondents intended to enter nonteaching careers, a substantial shift from the early days of the century, when nearly half of Indiana's graduates went into education. Speaking for its peers, the Cornell Daily Sun noted that the success-oriented young man was in college to prepare for a business career: "Businessmen are demanding something more than a personality and they are paying for their demands. . . . A real university education has a concrete value." College presidents echoed the progressive themes of efficiency and elite moral leadership; the students were there for training and social cachet.[38]

World War I triggered the proliferation of subjects offered by American colleges. Government and business now willingly provided support for courses in technical fields of study. As a result, the relative strength of the traditional liberal arts declined in favor of the vocation-oriented course of study at most institutions of higher learning. The Bureau of Education reported at the end of the war that colleges and universities were "forced by public demand to add numerous professional curricula, such as commerce, journalism, and the several varieties of engineering." Between 1918 and 1925, 143 new collegiate departments of commerce were opened; only 40 such programs had existed before the war. Enrollment in engineering climbed from 29,784 to 49,139 between 1918 and 1920, an increase of 65 percent.[39]

Contemporaries could not help being struck by the rapid expansion of their institutions. "It is not merely that the student body has increased, or that the faculty has increased," wrote Harry W. Chase, president of the University of North Carolina (which had formed schools or departments of education, engineering, public welfare, psychology, music, and sociology in the previous five years) in 1923, "but that department after department has been added, school after school has been organized, until today 60 percent of the student body is enrolled in other than liberal arts courses; and that the conception of what a University is for has altered and broadened to an immense degree."[40] Eager to be responsive to economic and social changes, educators modified their institutions to cater to the demand for practical higher education. The postwar American institution of higher learning was wholly different from its ancestor in size, kind, and clientele, though separated in time by only a decade.

By responding so quickly and so confidently to the public demand for practical higher education, American universities contrasted sharply with their European forebears. Visitors crossed the Atlantic Ocean to examine the kind of university that American energy, democracy, prosperity, and pragmatism had wrought. All were amazed by the magnitude and quality of America's collegiate facilities. During and after World War I, research laboratories and libraries were being built in the United States on a scale envied in contemporary England and on the Continent. The vice-chancellor of the University of London was shocked that Catholic University of America had as fully equipped and nearly as large a chemistry laboratory as any in Great Britain, that Swarthmore College had as beautiful and lavish facilities as any at home, and that Yale's pathology department was more advanced than any in its field in Europe. He and his traveling colleagues found at Northwestern University "the same freshness of view, and belief in the future, the same numerous staff and adequate equipment that we had found elsewhere." "For awhile," he reluctantly admitted, "the world will wend west-ward."[41] The qualitative and quantitative expansion of American colleges and universities was well beyond the scope of what visiting Europeans deemed appropriate or even imaginable in their own homelands.

Still, foreign visitors believed that the quality of American higher education suffered because its human and physical resources were spread too thin. American institutions of higher learning were criticized for catering to ever-increasing numbers of students with a broadened range of courses of study. Matthew Arnold had long before assailed the land-grant colleges for being "calculated to produce miners, or engineers, or architects, not sweetness and light." Furthermore, despite its diversity and size, higher education was widely held to exert little moral leadership in American culture. Europeans attacked the impact of business and businessmen on American higher education. They also asserted—rightly—that European scientists still overshadowed the American upstarts in their contributions to knowledge, even if many of the experts saw their advantage slipping away.[42]

European educators were most ambivalent about the strong desire for a university degree among American young people. Some admired the fact that—in their view—a college education had come to be taken for granted among middle-class Americans and even attainable by working-class citizens after World War I; indeed, the great diffusion of education was adduced by these visitors to be a critical reason for the absence of class feeling in this country. Even Ramsay Muir, a skeptical European, could not help admiring "the crowning efforts of a whole community determined to secure the fullest benefits of the highest education for the greatest number" when he visited the great public universities of the Middle West, such as Wisconsin and Minnesota.[43] These visitors were faced with the paradox of a more broadly based conception of higher education—too many students and too many subjects might result from increased interest in and support for higher education—and chose to back away from its democratic implications.

This point was dramatically confirmed by enrollment data of the 1920s. In 1925, when about 800,000 persons out of a total population of 117 million in the United States were enrolled in college, only about 46,000 of Great Britain's 43 million people and 68,000 of Germany's population of 63 million attended a university. One educator in 1930 claimed that there were more persons above the age of fourteen in school in the United States than in all other countries in the world combined.[44] Although the bulk of this enrollment growth came in practical fields that Europeans did not yet recognize as legitimate concerns for institutions of higher learning, they conceded that such expansion was an innovation they might soon be forced to emulate. World War I had proved that the future of modern society was inextricably tied to the widespread diffusion of education and research, and the pragmatic Americans had a head start.

Education for Conservative Leadership

Between the two world wars, for the first time in American history, a college education became an essential part of the success strategy of those who sought fortune or prestige in the United States. And the strategy worked: when Pitirim Sorokin studied the backgrounds of more than 600 millionaires and self-made men in the 1920s, less than 12 percent had attended college; in the mid-1940s, when C. Wright Mills conducted a similar survey, over 20 percent of the most successful men in the United States had gone to college.[45] The day of the self-made man was passing; the era of the college-trained expert had arrived. No longer just a home for dilletantes, the college attracted the ambitious as well, and in rapidly increasing numbers.

Educators wanted to be "in touch with American life," and they succeeded. While some protested and defended the traditional collegiate curriculum and student life, most chose to respond to the public demand that institutions of higher learning devote their resources to the training of future business and social leaders. They welcomed the increased clout brought about by the many changes and innovations, as well as the rapid growth stimulated by postwar educational priorities. College after college modified its curriculum, admissions standards, and student life to accommodate the practical and status-minded perspectives of its new students and benefactors. By reaching out for new functions and to new constituencies, the American college revolutionized its culture.

The rising prestige of a college education in the 1920s reflected some progressives' fears for the future of democracy in the United States. By stressing the need for formal education as a prerequisite for entrance to a growing number of positions of economic and social influence, progressives limited opportunity to those who could afford to attend college and to those few others whose expenses were borne, in one way or another, by the economic and social establishment. There was no doubt that the college graduate, taught progressive values and twentieth-century techniques, was intended to provide constructive but also conservative leadership in a society undergoing rapid change. As the American population grew and became increasingly heterogeneous, success on the college campus became a yardstick by which to measure an individual's suitability to practice law or manage a corporation. By virtue of the training made available largely if not exclusively to young people of means, college graduates enjoyed greater opportunity than their uneducated peers to share and lead in the nation's prosperity and newfound power. This obvious fact might have focused attention on the need to ensure equality of educational opportunity for talented poor and ethnic Americans, but it did not. As a result, few cultural artifacts of this age are so telling as the postwar college student: typically a child of the modern world, with his specialized course of study and his automobile, he was also a child of an American Protestant middle-class world, with its safe values and aspirations.

Surely the demand for practical higher education and equality of educational opportunity would have arisen one day if World War I had not occurred. Progressives had already begun to turn to experts for advice; the American economy had already begun its shift toward managerial and professional administrative structures. Many immigrant groups already viewed education as their key to economic and social mobility. But it is now clear that the war effort, with its attendant economic and social changes, altered dramatically Americans' conception of higher learning. The war was a turning point, and American higher education was led by a generation insistent upon growth but anxious about change.

3 / Business Goes to the Colleges

Practical incentives stimulated the dramatic and diffuse expansion of collegiate business education in the United States in the decade following World War I. Before the war, American universities had benefited from the professionalization of law, medicine, engineering, and several academic disciplines, but these changes had little effect on undergraduate life and on the public perception of the value of a college education. It was not until World War I had demonstrated the benefits that business and education would derive from collaboration that the foundation was laid for the rapid expansion of both the curriculum and enrollment. As a result, occupations formerly regarded as entirely outside the learned professions were now considered worthy of collegiate and university study; whereas fifty years before, perhaps five professions were deemed suitable for university attention, in the 1920s American colleges were providing training in fifty or more white-collar fields.[1]

Proponents and critics alike agreed that the needs of American business—and the intense desire of educators and students to fulfill those needs—dominated American higher education in the 1920s, just as they did most aspects of American life during the decade of "normalcy." Unlike their predecessors, businessmen of the 1920s did not look askance at learning. During this decade, businessmen, educators, and potential students agreed with the *Harvard Crimson* that "business success no longer involves a mere doing of the right thing by intuition or experience, but is only obtained by those whose minds are trained to recognize the entire implication of the affairs with which they deal."[2] In supporting the colleges, businessmen expected them to become both training facilities and socializing agents for the burgeoning white-collar middle class; in reaching out to new business and technical constituencies, educators responded to the perceived need for more and better-educated experts. Particularly in light of traditional intellectual values, there is no better example of American higher education's entrance into the mainstream of American life than its responsiveness to the interests of the business sector and business-oriented, ambitious young men.

Specialization and Individual Ambition

The alliance between business and higher education encouraged the rapid shifts in the occupational structure of the American economy which had begun in the latter third of the nineteenth century. In its landmark 1933 study, President Herbert Hoover's Research Committee on Recent Social Trends emphasized "a remarkable expansion of the technical professions and an increasing demand for specialized training [as] the proportion of the population in white collar work has shot upward."[3] These occupational shifts accelerated during the first three decades of the twentieth century, exhibiting the characteristics of a maturing industrial and commercial civilization. Table 1 indicates that those sectors of the economy that were growing most rapidly were also most likely to require a more educated work force. Just as the need for more clerical personnel spurred the growth of secondary education, so the need for technical and management personnel encouraged the growth of the college. The years just before the war witnessed a brief slackening of the growth of white-collar occupations, but the expansion of economic activity after the war sparked a further explosion in the number and range of professional occupations. The increased availability of training for these occupations at American colleges and universities led in turn to a decade of unprecedented popularity for higher education.

The increased demand for sophisticated industrial processes and administrative techniques led to technical and business training on a larger scale. The shift toward standardization and the use of mass-production methods diminished the need for skilled workers in many jobs, but it also brought a striking rise in the proportion of occupations that did require special training. Not only were more educated men essential in an expanding economy, but more specialized men were needed as well. "The banker today needs his trained statistician,

Table 1. Number of workers and percentage change in selected occupational fields, 1870–1930

Occupational field	1870*	1900 Number	1900 Percent change	1910 Number	1910 Percent change	1920 Number	1920 Percent change	1930 Number	1930 Percent change
Agriculture	6,428	9,802	+53%	10,872	+11%	10,524	−3%	10,242	−3%
Trade and transportation	†		†	3,447	*	4,215	+22	6,094	+45
Clerical occupations	206	781	+279	1,635	+109	2,952	+81	3,935	+33
Public service	73	260	+256	382	+47	642	+68	692	+8
Professional services	338	1,196	+254	1,727	+44	2,203	+28	3,110	+42
Law	39	106	+172	115	+9	123	+7	161	+30
Education	127	446	+251	615	+38	795	+29	1,125	+42
Engineering	7	93	+1,229	209	+125	349	+67	507	+45
Chemistry	1	9	+800	16	+78	33	+106	47	+42
Medicine	62	130	+110	151	+16	150	—	160	−7
Other	102	412	+304	621	+51	753	+21	1,110	+47
Manufacturing	2,674	7,537	+182	10,253	+36	12,425	+21	13,790	+11
Other	2,445	7,747	+217	7,529	−3	7,832	+4	10,296	+31
All fields	12,164	27,323	+125	35,845	+31	40,793	+14	48,163	+18

*Percentages not computed.
†Data not collected.
Source: President's Research Committee on Social Trends, *Recent Social Trends in the United States* (New York, 1933), pp. 281–82.

his trained investment counsel, his advertising manager, and his men trained in engineering and production methods," Wallace B. Donham, dean of the Harvard Business School, insisted. "He cannot wait for the long, hourglass method of training these men by apprenticeship."[4] What was true of banking was also true of numerous other industries, and once the colleges met the demand for more specialized expertise, their growth was assured.

The decline of apprenticeship marked the emergence of the college as a training facility for American industry. In a complex industrial order and an increasingly heterogeneous society, college students constituted a select group trained for the specialized tasks and social atmosphere awaiting them in the growing number of large corporate and research structures. The economist André Siegfried noted that education was coming to be indispensable at both the middle and the top of the corporate ladder; "the time is past when a youth is initiated into business by sweeping out the office." On-the-job training no longer seemed practicable. *The New York Times* conceded that the old rules did not produce modern business leaders: "In the past we have cited it as a triumph of free institutions and a prime cause of our industrial efficiency that so many of our corporation presidents have risen from the ranks, but that past is closing behind us," it concluded in 1920.[5] Businessmen now preferred to hire trained chemists and skilled accountants.

No previous generation of businessmen or ambitious young people had relied on the colleges for training. But now economic progress appeared to be dependent on new skills more clearly linked to learning, and if a young man wanted to become a chemist or a businessman in the 1920s, rather than going directly to work he went to college for the professional training and socialization that would ensure him ready access to the modern American upper middle class. The growth and transformation of American higher education after World War I was due to this symbiotic interrelationship of modern economic and social life, the recognition of advances in vast fields of new knowledge, the influx of new students interested in those new subjects, and the unique inclination, if not zeal, among American educators to seek and foster connections between change in the economic structure and the development of academic institutions. As a result, while the industrial giants of earlier eras, the Henry Fords and Thomas Alva Edisons, tinkered in their barns and attics, twentieth-century Horatio Algers toiled first in the classrooms, athletic fields, and fraternities of the nation's colleges. Educators pointed out that the presidents of General Motors, General Electric, Du Pont, and Goodyear in the 1920s had been classmates at the Massachusetts Institute of Technology.[6] There could be no greater incentive for the pursuit of higher learning than individual ambition.

Engineering and Scientific Research

Engineering was the first field in which links were established between industry and institutions of higher education. Before the Civil War there were only 6 engineering schools in the country; 85 were founded by 1880; by 1917 the number of engineering programs had reached 126. The proportion of engineers in the general population multiplied fifteen-fold between 1880 and World War I. The most important innovation in engineering education during this period was the Cooperative Plan, first established at the University of Cincinnati in 1906. Each participating student divided his undergraduate years between classroom work and experience in an industrial setting; in the words of its founder, the plan was "based upon the philosophy that practice and theory should be taught concurrently and should be coordinated." By the 1920s, it was estimated that at least 137 institutions offered a variation of the Cooperative Plan, often to business as well as to engineering students.[7] A twentieth-century version of apprenticeship, the plan showed industry and education just how much each could benefit by cooperating with the other. Engineering demonstrated that it made sense for business to encourage enrollment in institutions of higher learning, which would in turn provide it with qualified personnel.

This pattern of mutually advantageous cooperation was soon repeated in the area of university research. World War I accelerated the pace of industrial research in the business sector, which in turn encouraged the growth of engineering education and research at American universities. Before the war, in large part owing to the legacy of the "inspired gadgeteer," industrial research was still at an embryonic stage. Few private companies had extensive research laboratories: in 1901 William McMurtie, president of the American Chemical Society, observed, "We cannot yet boast with the Germans that single works employ more than 100 thoroughly educated chemists." In the next decade, American Telephone and Telegraph, Du Pont, Westinghouse, General Electric, and Standard Oil of Indiana opened ground-breaking research facilities. These laboratories were the exceptions rather than the rule, but between 1918 and 1940 the number of industrial laboratories skyrocketed from 300 to 2,300 and the number of research workers on the payrolls of America's largest corporations climbed from 1,200 to 27,000. During the Depression, although the funds devoted to industrial research and development declined by nearly 25 percent, the number of laboratories still climbed by 12 percent.[8] When companies boosted their research and development efforts during and after the war, the impact was felt not only in the economy but in the nation's colleges as well.

The federal government began to take an interest in research in the years before World War I. In the late nineteenth century, the charismatic John Wesley Powell, renowned for his exploits in the West, was able to secure funding for a handful of geologists and physicists in the U.S. Geological Survey. During the Progressive Era, the establishment of the National Bureau of Standards and the enactment of the Pure Food and Drug Act created additional research positions for scientists inside and outside of the federal government. With the passage of the Adams Act in 1906, Congress authorized the funding of a modest amount of original research at each state agricultural experimental station. Research contributed to the efficient production and regulation of goods and services, which enhanced the quality of American life and also added to Americans' confidence in their corporations and in the efficacy of their educational institutions.

Educators had begun to solicit private and public support for university research before the war, but with only limited success. Until the war, the largest source of funding for university research was the universities themselves, and they had little money to spare. When Andrew Carnegie established the Carnegie Institution of Washington in 1902, his initial gift of $10 million equaled Harvard's entire endowment and amounted to far more than the total endowment funds spent on research at all of the nation's colleges and universities combined. The physics departments at Harvard and Princeton spent only $2,500 and $1,600 a year, respectively, of their institutions' own money on research on the eve of the war. The creation of the Rockefeller Institute for Medical Research and the Carnegie Institution as independent research facilities during the first decade of the twentieth century suggests further that business and philanthropic organizations were not yet convinced of the value of university research. In a speech at the opening of Rice Institute in 1912, the provost of Columbia University argued that industry should recognize that "out of the laboratories of the universities are coming to an increasing extent the influences that make for economic and industrial improvement and contribute to the betterment of human living and to the good of mankind." Still, the universities did not receive any substantial corporate funds for research until the 1920s.[9]

The military stepped up its own research efforts once American involvement in the war became imminent. According to the chemist James B. Conant, later president of Harvard University, when the American Chemical Society offered its services to the federal government at the beginning of the war, the War Department declined the offer on the grounds that it already had a chemist in its employ. But the armed services soon changed their minds. Of the twenty-two members of the Naval Consulting Board at its founding in 1915, only four had no engineering or science degree; one was the aging Thomas Alva Edison. Edison and his colleagues were instrumental in the formation of the Naval Research Laboratory, which was started with a grant of $1.5 million from Congress in 1916. While reluctant at first, the military soon asked local draft boards to defer technical experts from the combat draft and later supported the creation of the Student Army Training Corps. In addition, with President Wilson's blessings, the National Academy of Science set up the National Research Council in 1916. By the end of the war, though little public money had been invested in research, future federal support seemed assured.[10]

These newly forged links between economic development and education increased enrollment and research in a wide range of engineering and technical fields. The land-grant institutions saw their attendance jump 65 percent between 1910 and 1920, primarily because of the accelerated demand for engineers. At the Massachusetts Institute of Technology, enrollment in the fall of 1919 reached 3,033 students, 1,183—or 64 percent—more than in the previous peak year of 1916–17. Attendance at the Municipal University of Akron doubled between 1921 and 1923 after the introduction of an industrial engineering program that catered to local industry needs.[11] The organization of the California Institute of Technology in 1921 pointed up the recognition of the role of science and engineering in American higher education. The Society for the Promotion of Engineering Education even conducted a four-year study in the 1920s which analyzed manpower conditions in the various engineering specialties and urged institutions to steer students into certain fields.[12]

Engineering educators accepted without apology the premise that their destiny was to serve the business community and the general public. Particularly at the land-grant institutions, they set the standard for drawing from and contributing to the resources of the local community. Typical of the more ambitious engineering schools in the United States was the College of Engineering at the University of Illinois, the fourth largest school of its kind, which in the early 1920s offered undergraduate degrees in architecture, architectural engineering, ceramic engineering, civil engineering, electrical engineering, mechanical engineering, mining engineering, municipal and sanitary engineering, general engineering, physics, railway civil engineering, railway electrical engineering, and railway mechanical engineering. Nearly every industry and government agency in Illinois had its own department at the state university in Urbana-Champaign.[13]

Agriculture

The same pattern can be seen in agriculture. After the turn of the century, much public attention was focused on the need to improve the quality of life for rural Americans, and the nation's land-grant institutions were at the forefront of these efforts. Several members of President Roosevelt's Country Life Commission were leading figures in the academic community. More important, the federal government also cooperated with educational institutions to raise the rural standard of living. Mechanized farm machinery had ushered in a period of relative prosperity for the nation's farmers; now government support for agricultural extension education, launched by the 1906 Adams Act and the Smith-Lever Act of 1914, enhanced the possibilities for future gains in productivity. Research and extension work expanded after the war: funding for research in agriculture jumped from $1.6 million in 1914 to $19.2 million in 1924. The number of full-time university research personnel in the field increased from 221 to 850 in the same decade. Educators asserted that the development of agricultural education and research between 1914 and the end of the 1920s surpassed the progress made during the fifty years following passage of the Morrill Act in 1861. The land-grant colleges earned the congratulations of President Calvin Coolidge for "rescuing agriculture from an almost chronic status as the Cinderella in the industrial family, and placing it on a higher plane of scientific accuracy and permanent prosperity."[14]

As mechanization began to free more people from farm routine before World War I, farm youngsters started to take advantage of the many opportunities available at the land-grant schools. Later Mill-burn Wilson, a New Deal farm official, recalled that while it had been unusual for him to attend an agricultural college in 1902, such an education was far more commonplace for those who could afford it a decade or fifteen years later. In 1912 Eugene Davenport, the dean of one college of agriculture, reported that many of the better agri-cultural schools were overflowing with students and seeking ways to limit attendance; in retrospect, these colleges were perhaps the first selective institutions of higher education in the country. They were popular because they offered a way off the farm and into other lu-crative fields. After all, students were not preparing to return to the small family farm they had left; rather, they were studying a wide range of subjects—including, it was said, "several new agricultural sciences [that were] christened every time a new catalogue [went] to press"—and looking to enter a variety of agricultural- or science-related occupations. The University of Illinois trained its students for teaching and research, the marketing and processing of agricultural products, landscape architecture, and other middle-class business positions; only one-quarter of its graduates became farmers or farm managers.[15]

In the early twentieth century the possibilities of mass production were already transforming farming into agribusiness. Like jour-neyman mechanics, yeoman farmers had been replaced by trained experts. As the family farm gave way to commercial and scientific agricultural enterprises, colleges of agriculture expanded their influ-ence by increasing research and steering their students to areas of study leading to related middle-class professions. A broad social con-sensus evolved that institutions of higher education properly played a leading role in the structure of an occupation and the training of its future practitioners. Now that the pattern had been established in engineering and agriculture, the same process of professionalization took place in the largest and most important of all American occupa-tions—business administration.

Business Administration

No field underwent a more complete metamorphosis into a profes-sion than business administration. A popular 1928 guidebook to

American colleges suggested—with some exaggeration—a remarkable shift in public perception: "Business, which used to be a mere matter of buying and selling, with some sort of simple bookkeeping, and for which one prepared by a brief apprenticeship, has now become a complex profession, in which courses are given in colleges and universities all over the country."[16] Managerial capitalism had created new industries as well as new levels of management. Knowledge replaced instinct as the practitioners' chief asset, if only because most business decisions were made by middle-level managers far removed from "the big picture" and from ownership. The growing sectors of the economy—finance capitalism and mass marketing—appeared to require a different kind of businessman from the traditional industrial entrepreneur. These trends continued unabated in the decade following World War I, and one of its ripple effects was the rapid growth of the American college. The businessman of the 1920s believed that higher education provided a perspective that was not only helpful but necessary.

During most of the last half of the nineteenth century, as the managerial ethos began to revolutionize the structure of American capitalism, businessmen tended to reject the suggestion that an undergraduate education of any kind could enhance an individual's ability to succeed in the business world. Though a study of Amherst College graduates of this era showed that half had entered business careers,[17] most businessmen echoed Andrew Carnegie's casual dismissal of the college education of the late nineteenth century:

> While the college student has been learning a little about the barbarous and petty squabbles of a far-distant past, or trying to master languages which are dead, such knowledge as seems adapted for life upon another planet than this as far as business affairs are concerned, the future captain of industry is hotly engaged in the school of experience, obtaining the very knowledge required for his triumphs.[18]

By the turn of the century, however, the attitudes of many businessmen began to change, in part because fewer captains and more lieutenants were running corporations.

Curiously enough, those robber barons who castigated education the most were among American higher education's most generous benefactors, as Carnegie's own extraordinary munificence toward institutions of higher education amply demonstrated. While the "school of experience" still kept its nostalgic appeal, these legendary self-made individualists soon admitted that the future of American business should be in the hands of knowledgeable college-educated experts and administrators. Cornelius Vanderbilt once remarked that "if I had learned education I would not have had time to learn anything else"; indeed, he claimed the only book he had ever read in his life was *Pilgrim's Progress,* at the age of seventy. Yet the older he got, the more he resented his lack of education, and he gave $1 million to the university that bears his name. Leland Stanford similarly had no faith in education; he complained that the most helpless job applicants he interviewed were college men. But he hoped that his university would offer "a practical, not a theoretical education," so that its graduates would possess a clear aim in life.[19]

Businessmen did not engage in a sinister plot to absorb higher education into their orbit; rather, most educators were eager to tap the wealth and influence of American business. Such men as Carnegie, Vanderbilt, and Stanford were not transformed overnight into supporters of the classical curriculum. They remained skeptics in the face of ideas and intellectuals. There were exceptions, of course: John D. Rockefeller encouraged the development of a school of theology as a cornerstone of the new University of Chicago and Johns Hopkins started the nation's first center of graduate studies in the humanities and social sciences. Once businessmen began to send their own sons and daughters to college, to build monuments to their new wealth and even look for future employees there, the colleges were no longer dismissed out of hand. It took some time for long-held prejudices to fade, but both businessmen and educators recognized that their mutual desire for efficiency and enhanced status converged in educational policies that encouraged the diversification and specialization of the curriculum and increased enrollment.

In the early years of the twentieth century, progressive businessmen began to assert more fervently that the times demanded more college-trained personnel. Frank Vanderlip, president of the National City Bank of New York, told a 1905 audience at the convocation of the University of the State of New York that the mutual distrust felt by businessmen and educators had to dissipate for the sake of the future of society. Striking familiar progressive themes, he insisted that better-educated businessmen were needed to develop new principles of business conduct. The growth of American business could no longer rely on the exploitation of natural resources; now progress was predicated on the ability of businessmen to organize and allocate such resources more effectively. "The great man in commerce today," Vanderlip declared, "is the cooperative man, the man who sees clearly the right thing to be accomplished and is willing to sink his individuality to accomplish it."[20] This new businessman required the intellectual and social training of the college experience.

The events of World War I played an important role in business acceptance of the value of a college education. In 1913 a survey of the Illinois Manufacturers Association revealed that fewer than half of its members required any university education for *any* of their technical or management positions; a 1921 report of a survey conducted by the National Association of Corporation Training—an organization founded during the war by businessmen and educators—pointed out that there was now a "progressive dependence upon higher education institutions as sources of employee supply [as] the prejudice of many businessmen . . . is being rapidly overcome."[21] The war effort showed that the colleges were the best source of supply for enlightened, trained, and socially acceptable middle-level managers.

Upper-middle-class parents generally shared businessmen's attitudes toward higher education. They sent their children to college because it was the thing to do, even if they were dubious about its value.[22] Once these children, the young people considered most suitable for business positions, went to college, it followed that businessmen would recruit their future employees there. Typical of this ambivalent combination of skepticism and social ambition was the response of Sinclair Lewis's George F. Babbitt to his son's reluctance to go to college: while he discounted the value of education, he insisted that the only way to gain admittance to "the class that [is] just as red-blooded as the Common People but still [has] power and personality" was to attend the state university, join a fraternity, and participate in college activities.[23]

This unprecedented interest in education had little to do with any appreciation of learning. Rather, it depended on businessmen's and the public's perception of both the technical and the social legitimacy of the college experience. In the 1920s more and more businessmen and parents became convinced that the colleges promoted the efficiency of American business and the happiness of individual students in their careers and social lives.[24] Still a radical notion in the early decades of the twentieth century, this conception of the functions of higher education quickly became the foundation for the popularity of American higher education. As late as 1931, however, a leading study of collegiate business programs was only cautiously optimistic: "The ancient prejudice against the college man in business has gradually disappeared," it concluded. "This does not mean that the bachelor's degree has at last become an open-sesame to fame and fortune . . . but at least it is no longer regarded as a liability."[25]

Businessmen still found fault with education. The college student was no longer lazy; he was arrogant. In a 1924 article, "Why I Never Hire Brilliant Men," an anonymous businessman explained that he promoted "raw material" rather than college graduates because "business and life are built upon successful mediocrity, and victory comes to companies not through the employment of brilliant men, but through knowing how to get the most out of ordinary folks." Yet in 1925 *The New York Times* reported that "only a few of the oldest 'captains of industry' repeat the old charges about the bad effects of higher education . . . so there is nothing surprising [in the fact] that the representatives of big business are 'scouting,' as the managers say, around the campus and keeping a longing eye on the seniors."[26] Despite some complaints, businessmen of the mid-1920s could see that the curricula of the colleges had been modified to accommodate both business suitors and potential students. Business administration became a profession, and in turn American higher education assumed many of the structural characteristics of a competitive and dynamic industry.

Schools of Business

Efforts to establish collegiate schools of business followed logically the change in business perceptions of the worth of a college education. With few exceptions, these efforts were unsuccessful until World War I, when for the first time the widespread creation of such programs within universities was viewed as a natural expression of both American educational ideals and American economic development. "In view of our general acceptance of the idea that the higher levels of practical education are quite properly a function of the university," an educator stressed, "it is only to be expected that business—overwhelmingly our largest practical activity—should have its training schools at the university level."[27] As in other spheres of American life, growth had assumed a logic of its own. Philosophical arguments and intellectual content notwithstanding, business education affected the characteristics of the learned professions, to the alleged benefit of all concerned parties.

The first collegiate school of business was founded at the University of Pennsylvania in 1881 when an industrialist, Joseph Wharton, gave $100,000 to establish a program in business and commerce. The object of the Wharton School, in the words of one of its early guiding lights, Edmund J. James, later president of the University of Illinois, was

> to provide for young men special means of training and of correct instruction in the knowledge and arts of modern Finance and Economy, both public and private, in order that, being well-informed and free from delusions upon these important subjects, they may either serve the community skillfully as well as faithfully in offices of trust, or remaining in private life, may prudently manage their own affairs and aid in maintaining sound financial morality; in short, to establish the means for imparting a Liberal Education in all matters concerning Finance and Economy.[28]

But the Wharton School's message fell mainly on deaf ears: only thirteen students showed up its first year, and it was seventeen years before the second school of business was founded, at the University of Chicago.

Business education gained support, both inside and outside academia, as the managerial revolution took hold. Then, as one Harvard Business School professor recalled, "in reality the business world summoned the school into being."[29] Individuals were no longer the sole financial and philosophical supports for these programs; now the driving force became a self-conscious and progressive business community. The efforts of New Orleans businessmen to establish a business program at Tulane University were typical: 104 businessmen guaranteed the financial stability of the new program and the local Association of Commerce provided the classroom space for the school when it opened in the fall of 1914.[30]

Educators responded to the opportunity to foster collegiate business education with unprecedented entrepreneurial zeal. Despite the active opposition of liberal arts faculty at many institutions—it was not until 1913 that a professor could claim that "for the first time the Wharton School stands on the same independent footing as the other schools in the University of Pennsylvania"[31]—more schools of business were created each year. Between 1900 and 1910, ten more departments were added to the seven in existence at the turn of the century; between 1910 and 1915, twenty-three additional programs were founded.[32] Elite universities with the longest history of performance and status in the traditional learned professions were generally among the first to seek curricular reform in the new and prestigious profession of business management.

After World War I, other schools followed suit as business education became something of a craze. Between 1919 and 1924, 117 new programs were introduced at colleges and universities across the nation. In 1919, for example, business programs were started at the College of the City of New York, an urban public institution; Villanova University, an urban denominational school; the University of North Carolina, a southern public university; Kalamazoo College, a midwestern liberal arts college; the University of Minnesota, one of the nation's largest universities; the western University of Montana; and nineteen other institutions from coast to coast. Contrary to the tepid reception the Wharton School received during its early years, 150 students enrolled the first year of the University of North Carolina's experiment in business education; by its third year, 358 attended. Most telling are the data on the number of degrees granted in business: in 1915–16, 789; in 1920, 1,397; in 1922, 3,205; and in 1928, 5,474. By the late 1920s there were more undergraduate male business students in each of seven geographical sections of the United States than there had been graduates of business programs nationwide a little more than a decade before.[33]

These programs were created rapidly—perhaps too rapidly, some contemporaries felt—in response to public demand and competition between institutional rivals. In 1915, for example, the Iowa legislature rejected a petition calling for the establishment of a school of commerce at the state university, citing a lack of funds; a year later, a survey commissioned by the state supported the legislature, claiming that rural Iowa should not invest in urban-oriented educational programs, particularly since business management had not yet attained professional status everywhere. But within the next decade Iowa succumbed to the prevailing trend. In 1916 the American Association of Collegiate Schools of Business was formed to raise the standards of the fledgling programs; throughout the 1920s it established minimum accreditation standards—such as the presence of at least three faculty members who had earned the Ph.D. degree and sufficient library facilities—for these new schools.[34] The formation of collegiate business schools demonstrates the entrepreneurial spirit of American educators. Universities met the market on the latter's terms; the creation and quality of new educational products depended on each institution's desired segment of the market, local, regional, or national, middle-class or high-status.

Liberal Arts Schools

Liberal arts colleges also fashioned a more utilitarian image. Driven by the same keen desire for students that animated universities, colleges tried to portray themselves as forward-looking schools, training the next generation's leaders with a mixture of liberal culture and practical education. Claiming that the American college had always prided itself on preparing its students for leadership roles in society, educators acted as if it were only natural for the liberal arts college to bend its curriculum to the prevailing interest in business subjects. A businessman-educator, President Ernest M. Hopkins of Dartmouth College, a former telephone company executive, was hailed this way when he was awarded an honorary degree by Colby College: "His remarkable achievements in the field of applied economics are abundant prophecy of the better correlation between college training and practical life which President Hopkins will help all of us to understand and to achieve."[35] This was no small task, but one worth undertaking in view of the financial and popular support it promised the colleges.

Liberal arts colleges struggled to find a balance between the traditional classical curriculum and the new practical courses added to keep them competitive. At DePauw University, for example, the English department added a course in business writing, with elementary psychology as a prerequisite, in 1915. A college pamphlet published after World War I noted that events had "placed on the universities the duty of giving students systematic preparation for a business career," and listed DePauw's new electives in insurance and accounting. Though the school lacked a department of business administration, DePauw's economics department offered twelve courses that it considered "pre-business." The president of Grinnell College rationalized the introduction of business courses there by insisting that students should be familiar with the material aspects of American life, as well as with its culture: "Our aim is not only to impart knowledge," he said, "but also to urge upon students the business spirit and the businessman's point of view."[36] Few students needed such encouragement; most liberal arts colleges added business-oriented courses to meet the demands of potential students and benefactors for practical higher education.

More than any other college in the nation, Antioch transformed itself when it embraced practical training in the early 1920s, but it did so with a reformer's zeal that first appeared to buck the materialistic trend of the age. In 1919 the Ohio school was an unaccredited college that had fallen on hard times since the days when it boasted of having the famous educator Horace Mann as its president. The appointment of Arthur E. Morgan, a self-made millionaire engineer and reformer from nearby Dayton, to its board of trustees that year shook the institution out of its doldrums. Morgan and his wife, a former Wellesley College instructor, had dreamed of establishing their own college, and now he had his chance.

Morgan proposed that Antioch form a work-study curriculum, which "would in no sense lower the standard of education here required but would add to the efficiency of our undergraduates in all lines of future endeavor." Within one year the trustees voted to implement a six-year cooperative plan and, at his request, named Morgan as president to direct the "new Antioch." Thereafter, students alternated between studies on the campus—mainly general education and self-directed courses—and employment in a variety of businesses around the country. In the next two years Morgan embarked on a national effort to advertise Antioch: he brought to the board of trustees such national figures as Charles Kettering, an old friend and wealthy Dayton industrialist and philanthropist, and Jerome Greene, former right-hand man to Harvard's president, Charles Eliot, and former dean of the business school there. Work, he asserted in the numerous magazine articles he wrote to popularize his progressive yet conservative philosophy, ought to be integrated into the curriculum of the liberal arts college to build the character and broaden the experience of the nation's future leaders.

Few institutions achieved so much popular acclaim as Antioch in the 1920s. It was the first liberal arts college to adopt the cooperative plan, and Morgan's tireless efforts to gain publicity were amply rewarded. Wealthy students from the East began to apply in large numbers to this innovative college, and it quickly became one of the nation's most selective schools. During the first few years, Morgan interviewed the applicants and made the admissions decisions himself, and he took great pride in turning down ill-suited young men who ended up at Harvard or Yale. In 1920 Antioch enrolled just 75 students, nearly all from the Midwest; in 1926 it enrolled more than 700 students from all but five states and turned away twice as many interested students at a time when rejection of potential students was still a rare luxury. By the mid-1920s Antioch students were working in more than thirty occupations, from accounting to animal husbandry, from nursing to journalism, in at least fifteen states. When on campus they took a large number of required courses, generally in the sciences and social sciences, before they could choose electives at the end of their fourth year. Physical education was stressed as part of the design to instill healthy personal habits as well as to inspire intellectual growth. Antioch "trains primarily for proprietorship and management, not for subordinate employment," Morgan proclaimed, and the school's extraordinary growth demonstrated the popularity of its progressive philosophy, personified in its resident guru, role model, and president.[37]

The close ties between the business world and the nation's colleges were made quite explicit in the 1920s. Most colleges quickly altered the content of professional undergraduate courses when employers suggested they do so. A General Electric executive advised the Association of American Collegiate Schools of Business on the desired proportion of general education and other courses in the curriculum. The Western Reserve University student newspaper hailed the formation of an "Adjustment to Life" discussion series to bring local businessmen and undergraduates together "in order to meet [the students'] lack of definitiveness and at the same time grasp the advantage presented by various industries, businesses, and professions which feel an actual need for college-trained men." Many schools set up research bureaus to focus on local civic and business issues. Colleges aggressively sought corporate philanthropy for these efforts: Colorado's Regis College even promoted a $1 million endowment campaign in the early 1920s with the slogan of "reciprocal business" and the argument that a healthy college was a bulwark against socialism.[38]

College Placement Services and Corporate Recruitment

The formation of college placement bureaus was a symbol of the strengthened ties between business and educational institutions during the postwar years. Beginning in the second decade of the twentieth century, companies began to visit colleges to recruit their graduates in significant numbers; in 1915–16, seventy-two companies visited the School of Commerce and Administration at the University of Chicago. These visits were still rare at the vast majority of schools, but the trend gathered momentum after World War I. The number of companies that sought to be included on the mailing list of Stanford's vocational guidance committee, for example, increased from 57 to 184 during 1918–19 and reached 391 in 1921–22.

Placement services were turned over from faculty committees or the school's Christian Association to a separate administrator. Dartmouth College named an associate dean for employment matters in 1919; he prepared for the new post by reading all he could about a variety of occupations, establishing a student records system, interviewing students about their vocational interests, administering the latest psychological tests to seniors, traveling for three months to visit corporations, and working with selected other elite colleges and universities to set up an Intercollegiate Employment Bureau in New York City. Similarly, several Atlanta companies established the Georgia College Placement Office in the early 1920s because "the greatest good that Emory, or any other university, is doing for Atlanta and the state of Georgia is in the giving each year of the hundreds of young men who with their trained minds step out to take up business reins in our cities and towns." By 1925, 44 percent of all large universities, 12 percent of medium-sized universities, and 11 percent of the nation's small colleges had organized placement bureaus. College presidents hailed these bureaus as proof of the colleges' enhanced role in society; in his stump speech to local groups and high school seniors, DePauw's president, for example, boasted, " 'Big Business' is learning the value of the trained energy of youth. It sends representatives to DePauw."[39]

Corporate representatives and advertising stressed the variety of opportunities available to the college-trained student. As part of one of the most extensive recruitment programs in the country, one General Electric official personally visited 75 colleges and universities and interviewed 1,200 students a year in the late 1920s. Western Electric advertised extensively in college newspapers across the nation, seeking to attract liberal arts graduates as well as business and engineering students with such captions as "But the Whole Team Doesn't Play First Base" and "Isn't It Better to Be a First-Rate A.B. than a Second-

Rate E.E.?" Public utilities and construction firms, which benefited from economic development in the 1920s, promised college graduates that "the nationwide Good Roads program spells OPPORTUNITY for hundreds of engineers."[40]

The formation of placement offices and campus recruiting efforts encouraged young people to focus on the links between college attendance and their own future success. In an issue of *The Case Tech* carrying advertisements placed by five corporations, a student editorial commented on the enhanced reputation of a college education in the postwar United States: "A score of years back the college man was recognized with awe and only a select few recognized the value of an education. . . . At present, a college education is no longer considered a luxury, it is a requisite. . . . Employers have been fast to see that in the college of today lie the leaders of tomorrow and have hired accordingly."[41]

American higher education in the 1920s contrasted sharply with its past because an unprecedented number of businessmen and young people shared this utilitarian view of the value of a college education. The American college was useful for more than just polishing the elite of the learned professions; now it was touched by and helped shape a wide range of professional and business occupations. For the first time, the pursuit of a college education appeared to be indispensable to those who aspired to a prosperous and modern America's economic and social privileges.

Opposition to Vocational Education

Not everyone welcomed the alliance of business and higher education. The growing prestige of business and technical subjects in American colleges and universities, as well as the stronger voice of businessmen in university affairs, had its vociferous critics. While the president of the University of Illinois was confident that the victory of specialized curricula "is as sure in the domain of iron and wood work as in that of law and medicine . . . and that victory is sure and speedy in proportion as the demand for efficiency becomes more imperative," he stressed that "it would be a grave mistake to suppose that this development has gone on spontaneously, or quietly, or uniformly." Every progressive step, in his view, had been met with active and often bitter opposition.[42] The president of Beloit College bewailed the encroachment of vocational studies into the liberal arts curriculum and tried to minimize their influence after being approached by a trustee who wanted to know why a course in the English department could not include a session on how to write a business letter.[43]

Institutional tradition and faculty opposition affected a school's response to the social and financial pressures to include business subjects in the curriculum. Most institutions, seeking a broader base of support, found it desirable or necessary to expand their offerings. Only a few bastions of cultural conservatism, such as Yale and Princeton, excluded business from the classroom. Many liberal academics doubted that any college could continue to permit its faculty members free play in their own fields of interest if control over academic policy shifted from the campus to the corporate boardroom. Efforts by some educators and outsiders to persuade schools to refuse foundation and corporation philanthropy went unheeded. But ultimately, as "fighting Bob" La Follette of Wisconsin observed, for most schools no money was "too vile or debased in its source to devote to the cause of higher education."[44]

The most strident protest against business influence in American higher education came in Upton Sinclair's book *The Goose-Step,* published in 1922. "It is the Jabbergrabs of America who have created a good part of our 'higher' education and placed upon it the stamp of their crude and simple faith in material success," this gadfly of the left declared. The famous socialist muckraker railed against the presence of businessmen on boards of trustees; he called Columbia University, for example, "the palatial University of the House of Morgan." He feared that the influence of business courses would destroy the intellectual tone of the American college: "The commercial men and women who specialize in such subjects come into the universities, and they bid against the professors of liberal arts for power and prestige and pay—and how much chance do you think a scholar or lover of belles-lettres stands against such people?" Pointing to the ouster of the radical economist Scott Nearing from the University of Pennsylvania faculty, Sinclair sarcastically predicted that academic freedom would be preserved by the appointments of a professor of stock watering and an instructor in political manipulation. Despite its "grotesque exaggerations," the well-known educator and author Percy Marks admitted there was "indubitable truth" in Sinclair's analysis.[45]

The Professionalization of Business

The acceptance of business education into the curricula of American colleges and universities was the culmination of efforts to raise business to a professional ethos. Such efforts began in the late nineteenth century, when, in the course of his lectures on professional ethics and civic morals, the French sociologist Emile Durkheim asked, "There are professional ethics for the priest, the lawyer, the magistrate. . . . Why should there not be one for trade and industry?" American progressives echoed this view: it was believed that the professionalization of business would improve its efficiency and contribute to the smooth functioning of society. Louis Brandeis, among others, thought that it would heighten businessmen's awareness of their responsibility to help alleviate social problems. The application of Frederick Taylor's principles of scientific management in some 240 volumes of studies published before World War I was weighty evidence of the good intentions of this commitment.[46]

The professionalization of business not only was new in this country, it also marked the unique nature of American higher education. The learned professions had found a home in universities everywhere by this time, but only American institutions of higher learning were generally willing to reach out to new constituencies. Business provided the means for expansion; in return, the university gave the business profession legitimacy. In seeking to affiliate with institutions of higher education, businessmen hoped to legitimate their claims to specialized expertise and shared principles in the conduct of their occupation, and by doing so to enhance their status in the society. The absence of business programs in Europe at the turn of the century—and their relative absence there even today—suggests that this process of professionalization was at first a distinctly American phenomenon. Where business programs were formed overseas, they were set up in urban institutes of technology, rarely in prestigious universities: in Great Britain, of the three most important institutions, only the London School of Economics of the University of London sponsored a business program, and it enrolled only 818 full-time students in 1919. Collegiate business education on a broad scale was an American innovation, blamed by the Europeans on our "cult of the 'concrete.' "[47]

The spread of business education in American colleges and universities demonstrated that higher education reinforced the worst as well as the best of conservative values. Concerned for the stability of a highly mobile and increasingly heterogeneous society and anxious about their own economic and social hegemony, many conservative progressives linked occupational mobility to higher education: the requirement of a degree would restrict the new professional business opportunities available to those young people whose backgrounds suggested they shared the same social values—and prejudices. A reliance on expertise and efficiency alone need not have preserved existing privilege. But the admissions policies of leading institutions and the differentiation of higher education in the 1920s show that the efforts to raise the standards of professional conduct were also intended to ensure that the custodianship of American society remained in safe hands.

Since the 1920s this mixture of technical rationale and social motivation for the development of business and other collegiate professional programs has been particularly suited to American modern corporate and professional structures, traditional rhetoric about American individualism notwithstanding. The decline in the proportion of self-employed college graduates from 51.9 percent in the first decade of the twentieth century to 32.0 percent in the 1920s and even further to 24.9 percent in the 1930s signaled the good health of modern American higher education.[48] During these decades, as the total number of college graduates increased dramatically, the university secured its function as the purveyor of technical and social training for the burgeoning white-collar and peer-oriented middle class. Not only did the proportion of college-educated businessmen increase substantially after World War I, but other occupations that required a college education also enjoyed a disproportionate share of the economic growth during the prosperous 1920s and suffered less than old-style occupations during the Depression of the 1930s.[49] The value of a college degree rose as institutions of higher learning widened their orbit of influence to white-collar occupations beyond the pale of the learned professions. The day of the self-made man had passed; the decades between the two world wars witnessed the ascendancy of the college-educated man.

4 / Expansion and the Urban University

During the first three decades of the twentieth century, while the nation's population increased by 75 percent, attendance at American colleges and universities skyrocketed an astounding 400 percent. Despite the prominence of collegiate business programs, they did not account for most of this growth. Economic, social, and political changes transformed the size, functions, and characteristics of a wide array of white-collar occupations. Most of these new professions found a home in the country's rapidly expanding metropolitan areas and in plastic urban universities eager to strengthen their ties to local constituencies. By 1927 the colleges and universities of New York City enrolled more students than all American colleges and universities in 1890. The University of Pittsburgh's "Cathedral of Learning," a skyscraper of classrooms and offices built in the 1920s, was a towering reminder of the new status of urban institutions of higher learning.

The 1920 census revealed that the United States had become an urban nation. In the late nineteenth century, the American industrial revolution took place largely in the city, with its concentration of large labor pools and potential consumer markets. Following decades of rapid growth, the cities became the focus of the nation's economic, social, and intellectual life. Urbanization had produced an array of economic and social problems. Hundreds of thousands of immigrants, from rural areas as well as from foreign lands, settled in ghettos that stood in crowded and filthy contrast to the traditional American small town. By the first years of the twentieth century, while Democrats and Republicans, conservatives and liberals, progressives and bosses might disagree about the means to be used, all agreed that the quality of urban life needed improvement. Reformers, stressing the desirability of cooperation between voluntary organizations and governmental agencies, founded settlement houses and promoted the development of the public schools, symbols of their concern and hope for America's future. These efforts were often inspired as much by fear as by optimistic faith, but by the 1920s even those who deplored the rise of the city recognized that it was here to stay.

The Rise of the Urban Professional

Between the two world wars a growing number of urban-based middle-class professions enhanced the prestige of a college education. Census data demonstrate that of twenty-eight professional and semi-professional occupations examined, twenty grew during the 1920s and 1930s, despite the Depression. The number of college teachers jumped 20 percent, chemists 25 percent, librarians 32 percent, and welfare workers 70 percent. It was widely observed that the Depression had less impact on white-collar occupational groups than on lower occupational classes.[1] By 1940, at a time when only 5 percent of the work force were professionals of one kind or another, the college graduate had moved into the highest economic and social ranks in the nation.

A 1941 study showed that an increasing proportion of college graduates entered these new professions between the two world wars. The traditional emphasis on the learned professions gave way to the modern imperative to prepare young people to assume intermediate positions in business and other sectors of society. As a result, the numbers and proportions of male college graduates in such fields as teaching, science, and business increased dramatically during this era, as Table 2 indicates. These professions were likely targets for educational entrepreneurs, who received the enthusiastic support of professionals, reformers, and potential students. As formal education became a prerequisite for individual mobility, the sphere of influence of American higher education was widened.

In the years following World War I the urban university assumed a strategic place in its community. The establishment of collegiate business programs suggested the willingness of American society and its educators to bend educational institutions to economic and social

Table 2. Percentages of male college graduates employed in professional fields and in business, 1940, by age group

Field	All ages	Under 30	30–39	40 and over
Professions				
Education	16.8%	18.2%	17.2%	15.6%
Medicine and dentistry	15.2	7.1	15.4	20.5
Sciences	10.5	12.6	9.9	9.7
Law	9.5	6.1	9.3	11.9
Government	5.4	6.3	5.3	4.7
Ministry	3.0	1.6	2.9	4.0
Arts	2.4	3.2	2.3	2.0
All professions	62.8%	55.1%	62.3%	68.4%
Business	37.2	44.9	37.7	31.6
Total	100.0%	100.0%	100.0%	100.0%

Source: F. Lawrence Babcock, *The U.S. College Graduate* (New York: Macmillan, 1941), p. 22.

trends, and no type of institution proved more receptive to change than the urban college. As the number of urban youngsters swelled, so did university-trained teachers. As the number of city services increased, so did university-trained economists and social workers. Further expansion into varied white-collar fields signaled the triumph of this pragmatic philosophy. During the Depression, schools were forced to maintain their diverse curricula in order to attract as many students as they could from their surrounding region. Professionalization of the work force fueled the growth and secularization of urban institutions; by linking their destinies to the professions, small—and often denominational—schools became large, secularized, multi-faceted organizations practically overnight.

The legacy of the urban institution of higher learning is not merely its dedication to the professional ethos but its commitment to the culture of aspiration. Hundreds of thousands of ethnic young people entered the mainstream of American society through its classrooms. And with but a few exceptions, the doors were wide open to students from any of the city's diverse socioeconomic and religious communities. Conservatives often shuddered, but market forces in the economy and in education impelled the dramatic expansion of these colleges. That the tremendous growth of the urban university did not depend on public or private, nonsectarian or denominational control confirms the widespread social consensus that fostered the acceptance of higher education and its connections to individual mobility and social progress.

The Private Urban University and Its Community

Like its urban setting, as Parke R. Kolbe observed, the urban university was "condemned for its materialism and undue specialization, and praised for its true vision of life and its efficiency." It typified the modern American university's commitment to meeting the practical needs of its community and students. Urban population increased by over 50 percent between 1900 and 1930, and middle-class white-collar opportunities opened up at perhaps an even greater rate. Kolbe, president of the Polytechnic Institute of New York in Brooklyn, attributed the amazing increase in urban college attendance to the growing complexity and importance of urban life and the need for experts to solve its complicated problems and to provide its necessary services, the growing number of college graduates who worked in urban areas and provided role models for city youth, and increased funding from the public and government for an enlarged and modern version of the university. By virtue of the urban university's location, let alone the competitive and philosophical pressures it experienced, the urban university administrator felt a special responsibility to the surrounding community, if only after a strong nudge or two from economically or politically powerful interest groups in the city. In 1924, although only 145 of the 913 colleges and universities in the United States were in cities of 100,000 people or more, those urban schools enrolled nearly 270,000, or over one-third, of the 664,000 full-time undergraduates, and an even greater share of part-time and extension students.[2]

An urban-oriented higher education constituted a departure from American tradition. Early in the twentieth century, Columbia's Nicholas Murray Butler defended the urban college by refuting the conventional view that rural schools offered a more pristine environment. "There is no ground whatever for the apparently widespread belief that to send a young man to a college in a great city is to subject him to a kind, an amount, and a variety of temptation that would be spared him if he were elsewhere," he insisted.[3] Urban educators claimed that while rural institutions offered their students fewer distractions, the rural college student took advantage of their comparative isolation to behave in an inappropriate manner. This argument was largely unconvincing. Urban educators could not successfully debunk the traditional belief in the virtues of rural life, but in time the momentum of urbanization and modernization established the legitimacy of their institutions.

In the 1920s, the older and more prestigious urban institutions did not subscribe fully to the urban values they proclaimed. Such schools as Columbia, the University of Pennsylvania, New York University, and Western Reserve University tried to walk the fine line between trumpeting the advantages of an urban locale and insisting that they offered a campus life not unlike that of a rural liberal arts college. These institutions were seeking to attract urban and suburban upper-middle-class and upper-class Protestants, many of whom were uncomfortable with the thought of sending their children to college in the corrupt and immigrant-populated city. Caught between their efforts to maintain the interest and participation of their traditional clientele and their desire to appeal to new interests and new social groups, many universities forged a compromise by distinguishing between their liberal arts college in lovely neighborhoods and their professional schools in "downtown branches."

At the most elite level, then, the ethnic students who tended to gravitate to urban schools could damage an institution's reputation in influential circles. Pennsylvania's "democracy of the street car" had been hailed in some quarters since the turn of the twentieth century, but such tolerance in admissions and undergraduate life was largely responsible for the institution's lack of prestige between the two world wars. Although Pennsylvania leaned toward its old families when the moment seemed propitious, as a Jewish commuter student argued in an *American Mercury* contest in the 1920s, the school still failed to abate the drain of Philadelphia's "best" children to less urban and less ethnic institutions, such as Princeton and the New England colleges. In the late 1920s a group of alumni explored the possibility of separating the college of liberal arts from the undergraduate professional schools at the present West Philadelphia location (to which the university had moved from downtown in the early 1870s) by building a new rural campus at Valley Forge, some twenty-five miles outside of the city. This plan to attract Philadelphia's old families and their social allies proved too expensive and was abandoned.[4] New York University did move its liberal arts programs uptown and Western Reserve University did found a branch down-town, but both still lost substantial local upper-class support. In other respects, though, these institutions shared in the prosperous expan-sion of urban higher education: more often than not, urban univer-sities cast their lot with the future, with new courses of study and new types of students.

Like their state university counterparts, urban universities strove to become identified as a model of service to the diverse economic and social interests of their communities. The experience of Cleveland's Western Reserve University in the 1920s typifies the efforts to estab-lish closer ties between the urban school and its many local constitu-encies. Western Reserve's Charles Thwing repeatedly emphasized that a university was founded by a community and was accountable to it: "It does not exist for itself. . . . It is a method and means." A great university in a great city had the opportunity and the duty "to serve the community in every grade and form" and should therefore "increase its power of service by cooperation and union" with the city's business interests and public schools. To Thwing, and to those powerful men he cultivated, higher education was "essentially a mis-sionary undertaking," a source of training and social stability in a rapidly changing urban environment.[5]

The Cleveland Foundation spoke for the city's progressive civic and business leadership when it called for the expansion of higher educa-tion in the mid-1920s. After sponsoring a survey on the state of higher education in Cleveland, the foundation stressed that the city's reputation and progress depended on its support of a great university. "Such an outstanding university in Cleveland would engage in an eternal search for truth in a thousand avenues touching the life of the people in the community. It would shine as a great light on a hill, drawing all men and women under its beneficent influence," the study dramatically predicted. "Indeed, such a university in Cleveland might well serve as a climax of the numerous evidences of civic spirit and community welfare organizations in which the citizens of the city justly take so much pride." More than pride was at stake: education was the key to progress. Local support for higher education would convince young people of the importance of investing a few years in some form of college training "in order not only that they may secure the benefit of a larger income which normally accompanies spe-cialized education, but that they may help to increase more effectively the material resources of the city and nation."[6]

In field after field, the foundation supported the expansion of higher education to meet the needs of a dynamic economy. Perhaps the most important item on its agenda was the merger of Western Reserve and its neighbor, the Case School of Applied Science. Its effort to bring together the two well-known schools—separated only by shrubbery—failed in the 1920s, but it did succeed in making Western Reserve a model urban school in many respects. Noting that the natural development of scientific industrial life since 1890 had created the need for more formally trained businessmen, the foundation found the absence of business education at Western Reserve "astonishing" and suggested that undergraduate and graduate curricula in business and a Bureau of Business Research be established. The creation of a "Downtown Center" to meet the needs of part-time, professional-oriented, and so-called disadvantaged ethnic students was also suggested; once started, it became the fastest growing division of Western Reserve. Only about 10 percent of the city's high school teachers were trained locally, so it was proposed that teacher training be enlarged and improved. As local industry could accommodate 400 new engineers each year and the Case School was supplying little more than 100 eligible graduates a year, engineering education could be expanded as well. Although both Western Reserve and Case had increased their enrollments in the postwar period, the foundation estimated that the potential attendance growth could be measured in the thousands rather than the hundreds, if only the institutions and their supporters would resolve to raise enrollments to the levels of such similar cities as Philadelphia and Pittsburgh.

Expansion seemed to be a natural imperative for the urban university, overwhelming any philosophical or parochial reluctance to meet the perceived needs of its community. "This great institution you are launching here is not a private institution," Chancellor James H. Kirkland of Vanderbilt University said at the opening of Houston's Rice Institute in 1912. "There are no private institutions, gentlemen. All institutions for the education of a people are public institutions, devoted to public acts and public enterprise, and always part of the great public interest."[7] Whatever the source of their income or the form of trustee control, all American colleges and universities, but particularly those in urban areas, were expected to be governed by public opinion and, of course, to benefit from their sensitivity to changes in public sentiment in regard to the value of education. In progressive eyes, as in the eyes of most educators and ambitious students, the public interest was not the sole province of any specific government or denomination.

In fact, the private sector of higher education maintained its predominance in most urban areas. These schools' willingness to bend the educational and denominational principles on which many of them had been founded was critical to their remarkable growth. Most denominational schools demonstrated their ability to meet the needs of their coreligionists and of other supporters who simply preferred private rather than public control of any social institution. Furthermore, powerful voices of support for private urban schools repeatedly fought attempts to expand or raise the quality of public urban higher education. As long as private urban institutions continued to be responsive to their cities' diverse economic and social constituencies, their competitive edge remained.

The urban university's success was also assured by its willingness to attract the huge local pool of potential students from less privileged socioeconomic backgrounds. Urban college students cited the nearness of an institution as the chief criterion for attendance. Indeed, the proportion of commuters at urban universities was generally higher than 50 percent and occasionally as high as 80 percent or more.[8] Particularly during the Depression, the typical urban student came from a working-class home and attended college primarily for vocational reasons. These facts—and not a school's source of control—dominated institutional decision making. Urban institutions were dedicated to bringing the mountain to Mohammed, contrary to the traditional conviction that college students should be detached from the distractions of urban life.[9] Access, not isolation, ruled the modern day.

The Secularization of Urban Institutions

The secularization of the nation's urban denominational institutions testifies to the transformation of American higher education in the early decades of the twentieth century. No college could avoid—nor did many want to avoid—the pervasive influences of urbanization and professionalization. Most educators and nearly all students sought to identify their institutions more closely with the urban environment and the economic and social opportunities it presented. Foundations enhanced this process: the Carnegie Foundation for the

Advancement of Teaching, for example, stipulated that institutions must be free from any and all denominational control in the selection of trustees, administrators, faculty, and students in order to receive faculty retirement allowances. More important, however, were the larger forces of professionalization, which prompted the extension of the curriculum to more and more practical fields and thus increased competition between institutions, and individual ambition, which manifested itself in the priority students placed on practical training and social assimilation.

Sectarian institutions were pulled between their desire to retain some denominational distinctiveness and their desire to adapt to new sources of financial support and students. One study showed that the number of college catalogues that included religious aims among the functions of higher education declined by more than 50 percent among those surveyed between 1910 and 1920. Even though the vast majority of students still went to church, the large number of faculty that did not—one survey estimated that as many as 90 percent of the social and biological scientists at American colleges doubted the existence of God—set a more secular tone for campus life. While two dozen state-supported institutions still subsidized campus branches of the Young Men's Christian Association, the YMCA no longer served as the de facto student affairs office at most universities by the 1920s. Most colleges' chapel services lost whatever religious overtone they had once had; now focused on talks on "right living," these daily or weekly services were attacked by students who wished to end mandatory attendance at them in the 1920s.[10] Most sectarian institutions surrendered to these social pressures and modified their emphasis on religion in the curriculum and other aspects of campus life. Many officials had done little to encourage religious influence as early as the late nineteenth century, but secularization's biggest triumphs came after 1910, and particularly following World War I.

Change came to the top of the educational hierarchy in the 1920s when most denominational universities appointed their first non-clergy presidents and altered the composition of their boards of trustees. Large urban Methodist institutions, in particular, seemed to undergo this transition to a greater extent than other denominational schools. At the University of Southern California, for example, the appointment of Rufus von Kleinsmid, a former DePauw University professor and University of Arizona president, as president in 1920 led to the termination of the university's governance by the Southern

California Methodist Conference in 1928. The first non-Methodist to head the University of Denver was Frederick A. Hunter, appointed in 1928, two years after the pastor of a local church resigned from the board of trustees because of the loss of sectarian control over curriculum policy.[11]

It was not until the 1920s that Catholic colleges and universities fully accepted American ideals of higher education. The separation of the colleges from affiliated preparatory schools was a critical step in the development of independent universities; another was the establishment of professional and graduate schools and the introduction of electives into the curriculum in the early 1920s. As a result, attendance surged: in 1916 some 32,000 students were enrolled in Catholic colleges; in 1930 there were approximately 102,000 students; by 1940 the number had climbed to 162,000. The establishment of business administration and education programs at New York City's Fordham University doubled enrollment there in the mid-1920s. As Edward Power, a historian of Catholic higher education, has written, "it was not [the desire] to form good Catholics which led founders to establish colleges after 1850, although this purpose has not left and should not leave the Catholic college, but it was to educate Catholics in the best traditions of higher education." After decades of static enrollments and sporadic closures, Catholic institutions thrived when greater emphasis was given to meeting general educational rather than religious needs.[12]

Led by the Jesuit-controlled urban universities, Catholic colleges reached out to potential students by increasing the number of professional opportunities available there. Unlike other denominations, the Catholic church had no policy of "strategic withdrawal," the federal Bureau of Education reported in 1926. The federal government's one specialist in higher education praised the Catholic church for "meet[ing] the challenge of extraordinary demands by immediate and general expansion of facilities to accommodate all who are prepared to seek admission." Yet Catholic universities did not differ from most other urban universities, both private and public, in their determination to broaden their curricula to entice ambitious students. Serving the self-conscious minority they did, however, Catholic universities exemplified the effort of many urban and sectarian institutions to act as a bridge between the Old World and the New for thousands of students not yet prepared psychologically to attend nonsectarian institutions. As David Riesman has remarked, these schools constituted "decompression chambers for those edging their way out of the ghetto."[13]

The acceptance—indeed, recruitment—of practical-minded ethnic students by urban universities testified to the vitality of the culture of aspiration and its importance to the transformation of American institutions of higher education. The tension between religious traditions and contemporary social pressures should not be minimized, but most sectarian schools proved flexible enough to provide the training essential to the needs of potential employers and the dreams of their ambitious students. When prestigious liberal arts colleges established quota systems to restrict the numbers of Jews and Catholics they admitted, such students entered the professions after graduation from expanded and secularized urban universities. Indeed, they soon dominated such professions as teaching and accounting in most American cities. The universities' desire to be typically American institutions and ethnic students' ambitions for upward mobility were both served.[14]

A Prototype of the Urban School: Emory University

The development of Emory University in Atlanta between the two world wars is prototypical of the urbanization and secularization of American higher education. By the second decade of the twentieth century, the image of the South as an economically backward section was etched in the minds of most Americans, including many southerners. Despite the tireless efforts of its conscientious boosters, the New South movement had failed to produce much substantive improvement in the quality of life for most of the population. Rural poverty was widespread; rural electrification, for example, was not common until the end of the New Deal. The South also lagged far behind in the emergence of a white-collar and professional-oriented middle class. Census figures in 1920 showed that bankers, lawyers, teachers, and chemical engineers, among other trained professionals, were underrepresented in Georgia's population; whereas there were forty-nine inhabitants for each professional in the entire United States, there were eighty-one persons for each professional in the state of Georgia.[15]

The South trailed behind in education much as it did in other measures of contemporary economic and social development. Speaking at a northern college in 1915, William P. Few, president of Trinity College (not yet transformed into Duke University), admitted that educational conditions in the South were "altogether chaotic," but he believed that "the long, tedious years of convalescence" after the Civil War and Reconstruction were ended at last, now that efforts was under way to standardize and raise the quality of all types of schools and colleges.[16] Support for secondary education was still abysmal: a 1922 study showed that Georgia ranked forty-third among the forty-eight states in public education expenditures per child and that sixty-four of the state's counties lacked a high school of standard grade.[17]

Southern colleges and universities had a long way to go to catch up with other American schools. In the first years of the twentieth century, the total annual income of all higher educational institutions in eight southern states *combined* was less than that of Harvard University alone; even as late as World War I, Columbia University had a larger endowment than all of the southern colleges and universities put together.[18] No southern institution was included on any list of the nation's best schools. Of urban institutions in the South, only Vanderbilt University—and perhaps Tulane—received any attention at all. The Southeast's most important commercial center, Atlanta, lacked a university as late as 1915. The small thirty-year-old Georgia Institute of Technology, tiny denominational and women's colleges, and a few proprietary schools of dubious legitimacy dotted the landscape there, as elsewhere in the South, but for all practical purposes Atlanta was an educational desert.

A soft drink came to the rescue. Asa G. Candler, founder of the Coca-Cola Company, provided the financial backing necessary to move a small Methodist college from Oxford, about forty miles away, to Atlanta and to buy a proprietary medical school and a proprietary law school in order to establish a university. With the support of the Southern Methodist church (of which Asa's brother, Bishop Warren A. Candler, was an influential leader) and the Atlanta Chamber of Commerce, little Emory College became one of the South's most important institutions practically overnight. Founded during the latter days of the Jacksonian period, as so many other denominational colleges had been, Emory had carved out a niche for itself as one of the better colleges in the South in the late nineteenth century, but in size and reputation it was dwarfed by colleges in the North and Midwest. Until the Candlers' efforts, southern philanthropy was unable and unwilling to nurture the development of a modern university.

The founding of Emory University demonstrates its deep sectarian roots and its modern entrepreneurial spirit. Although the establishment of Emory in Atlanta had been contemplated before, it was not until the Educational Commission of the Methodist Episcopal Church, South, voiced its support for the move that it became a reality in 1914. The commission became determined to found a university after the church lost control of Vanderbilt's board of trustees. Two cities vied for the new institution: Birmingham, Alabama, and Atlanta. In a dramatic move, Bishop Candler, a former president of Emory College, produced a letter from his brother pledging to donate $1 million if the university were established in Atlanta. The deal was struck. A school of theology was founded, the proprietary Atlanta Medical College became a department of the institution, and the Lamar School of Law was opened as part of the new university in 1915 and 1916. The liberal arts college remained in Oxford until a new campus was built in fashionable suburban Druid Hills, on land also donated by Asa G. Candler.[19]

The Candler family presents an interesting picture of the cultural ambivalence of the New South movement. For much of his adult life, Warren Candler, called a "genteel conservative" by his biographer, had opposed any signs of modernization in college life.[20] When he became president of Emory College in 1888, he cut business and technical courses out of the curriculum. He steadfastly opposed such "student distractions" as intercollegiate athletics—and the "materialistic psychology" it bred—and the "immeasurable folly" of the elective system. Even after he assumed the chancellorship of the new Emory University, he fought against the acceptance of substantial contributions from such "secular" foundations as the General Education Board and the Rockefeller Foundation. Warren lost most of these battles to his brother Asa, the energetic businessman-reformer. Asa hoped to bring Atlanta up to date as quickly as he had transformed a little-known elixir into the nation's most popular soft drink. In 1917, while funding the new Emory, he served as both mayor of Atlanta and president of its chamber of commerce. Not unlike Houston's William Marsh Rice, who also made a substantial fortune, served as his city's mayor, and donated the funds to create Rice Institute, Asa saw the creation of a university as spearheading urban and regional economic and social development.

Both themes were addressed at Emory's opening ceremony. Bishop Warren Candler, now chancellor, spoke of the religious and southern origins of the new institution. An official of the local chamber of commerce emphasized the importance of the connection between the university and the business community. Indeed, the college faculty were the guests of the Atlanta Rotary Club the following week. The bishop notwithstanding, the move to Atlanta was engineered by civic leaders who were fully conscious and supportive of the revolutionary changes it would bring to the functions of Emory College: as the university historian has written, "No longer could it be mainly concerned with the education of a gentleman, as in the preceding century; now it must be occupied with fitting a large proportion of its students with the prerequisites for professional training in the professional schools of which it was the center." Since other sections of the country had many adequately equipped and generously endowed universities, Bishop Candler conceded, "surely the South should have at least one, and if we will Emory will be that one."[21]

From the outset, then, the institution's destiny was tied to the professions. Howard Odum, a 1904 graduate of Emory College, not yet the nationally renowned social scientist he would become in the 1920s, played a critical role as dean of the college its first year in Atlanta; he wrote the trustees, "I find a universal opinion that Emory should begin at the beginning to stress her professional education, and it will manifestly be unwise to wait a year." As a result, although the classroom buildings and faculty housing were still unfinished, and while the roads and sidewalks on and near the campus remained unpaved, young men crowded into the new college in unprecedented numbers in 1919. Owing largely to the formation of a school of business administration, more than 400 students enrolled, half of them as freshmen, though the trustees had expected only 300 students. In the 1920s, programs in engineering, journalism, public affairs, and library science were added to the curriculum. After a decade, enrollment had nearly doubled, to about 750 students. Though Emory still lagged far behind the leading universities in research facilities and size, it improved sufficiently to join their ranks. In 1924 Emory was admitted to the Association of American Universities; four years later, a chapter of Phi Beta Kappa was installed. By 1932, the president of the Julius Rosenwald Foundation considered it one of the most important institutions in the region.[22]

From its inception, Emory University wanted to play a strategic role in the South's industrial development. Its publicity campaigns stressed that progress depended on the emergence of an educated business- and professional-oriented middle class. In 1925, for example, one Emory advertisement warned that the South would never move forward economically and socially unless adequate facilities for promoting research and for training scientific workers were developed at the region's universities. Emory officials hoped to educate and train young men who shared in the progressive belief that social progress and individual mobility went hand in hand, a vision accepted more widely outside the South. In a region burdened by its history, Emory looked to the future: the model southerner of the twentieth century would be a college-educated lawyer, doctor, educator, or businessman.[23]

The formation and expansion of Emory University was coincident with the spirit of progress and professionalism which emerged during the Progressive Era and grew during World War I. After moving from a rural to an urban setting, it attracted rural youth to its professional training. Though firmly rooted in its provincial and conservative past (no women or minorities were admitted), Emory did aspire to offer an education suitable for those young southerners expected to be the future leaders of a modern and prosperous South.

Emory's transformation is now complete; in fact, it is one of the very few universities founded in this century that has achieved national renown. Aside from a handful of others—most notably, perhaps, Duke University, the University of California at Los Angeles, the California Institute of Technology, and Brandeis University—today's most highly regarded institutions had already established themselves as such before World War I. The emphasis on professional and technical education and research has enjoyed such support that nearly every leading institution has exploited the possibilities for expansion and growth. Private universities, particularly those in urban areas, have taken great advantage of these opportunities, but they shared the spotlight between the two world wars with public institutions even more committed to opening the doors of higher education to new subjects and new students.

Municipal Universities

"The development of the municipal university may be regarded simply as a further step in the great democratic movement for the extension of educational privileges among the people," proclaimed a historian of municipal universities in 1932. The public urban institution was dedicated to providing access for new students to new courses of study unavailable at other nearby schools at a low cost. In 1923 a survey indicated that 54 percent of the students at the University of Louisville and 61 percent of those at the University of Cincinnati would not have gone to college at all if those municipal institutions had not existed. Most of these students were lower-middle-class young people who saw a college degree—any college degree—as a ticket out of their neighborhood and into the mainstream of American life.[24]

University of Akron

The public urban university sought aggressively to meet any and all of the diverse manpower needs of industry and education in its community. No better example can be found than the University of Akron in Ohio. Buchtel University was bought by the city of Akron and transformed into a free municipal university in 1913. Between 1914 and 1921, a college of engineering, a school of home economics, and programs in commerce and teaching were instituted. In the early 1920s, George Zook, later head of the American Council on Education, assumed the presidency; at his inauguration he stressed the business-education partnership that constituted the heart of the municipal university's mission:

> I conceive the future University of Akron to be an enlarged institution with buildings, equipment, and faculty which are adequate to offer courses of study demanded by young men and women in this city and which can supply the industries, the schools, and other interests, public and private, with a much larger proportion of the trained engineers, chemists, teachers, and others who are needed in technical and professional work.[25]

The availability of professional-oriented courses of study at other municipal universities was also dependent on the local need for such training and its accessibility at nearby private institutions. In the early 1920s the citizens of several cities even passed bond issues to fund the expansion of public urban universities and to guarantee free tuition.[26] The future of the modern city was linked not only to the growth of its public institutions of higher education but to the social investment in the aspirations of young people eager to enroll there.

Wayne State University

The federal commissioner of education considered the municipal university the soul of the city. In 1930 he envisioned a day when a free, high-quality university would be the capstone of the educational system in each major city in the United States. He pointed to Detroit as the best contemporary example of this ideal.[27] Only a decade earlier it would have been impossible to do so. After all, Detroit had had no public college until 1917, when a public junior college was started with 300 students and a faculty borrowed from its landlord, Central High School. Detroit Junior College was begun by the high school's principal, David Mackenzie, to meet the needs of students who did not intend to enter the learned professions and who could not afford to go away to college. Within five years, seven vocational and preprofessional fields were added to its curriculum. Still, as late as 1923 Detroit, the nation's fourth largest city, more populous than eighteen states that operated public universities, had no four-year public college of its own. By that year the junior college—still located in Central High School—had become the third largest postsecondary school of any kind in Michigan. The state legislature finally passed a bill that enabled the city board of education to merge it with the city's teachers' college, which had been a normal school until 1920, and form the College of the City of Detroit. The new school enrolled 1,400 students its first year.[28]

The history of Detroit public higher education between the world wars reveals the role played by the local economy in educational expansion. Between 1923 and 1930, as Detroit expanded rapidly as a result of the extraordinary growth of the automobile and related industries, day enrollment at the City College leaped 47 percent and the number of part-time evening students increased by five times. Programs in engineering and nursing were added. During the depths of the Depression, however, the city council was forced to pass (but soon rescinded) a desperate proposal to keep the college open by charging tuition and paying the faculty in scrip. The institution survived one bitter budget fight after another and was renamed Wayne State University in 1934. The rapid growth of the city, with its concomitant demand for large numbers of technical- and professional-oriented young people, sparked the expansion of public higher education there. While shaken, Detroit's belief in public higher education was reaffirmed time and time again during the 1930s.

College of the City of New York

The most famous public urban institution of the day was the so-called Harvard of the proletariat, the College of the City of New York (CCNY). Its growth between the wars was nothing less than astronomical. In 1920 City College enrolled little more than 3,000 students; by 1930, attendance had increased by 353 percent, to well over 10,000; and in 1940, enrollment had climbed by an additional 228 percent, to over 24,000. Yet its historian, S. Willis Rudy, has properly called this growth "an educational evolution [rather] than an educational revolution," since its expansion was a logical response to New York City's own development. Curriculum reform in the first few years after World War I paved the way for the dramatic increases in enrollment: City College granted the nation's first Bachelor of Science degree in the social sciences in 1916; in 1917 it reorganized itself and added separate divisions of engineering and civic administration; in 1920 a school of business was founded; and in 1921 a school of education was created. As a result, attendance doubled in less than half a decade.[29]

In the 1920s, increased demand for public higher education in New York led to the establishment of the Brooklyn College of CCNY. When a Brooklyn college was first publicly proposed in 1906, Columbia's president wrote his City College counterpart that the idea was preposterous; it was only after several false starts that it finally gained some headway during World War I. In 1917 a small branch of City College was set up in Brooklyn's Boys High School for would-be college freshmen who hoped to transfer to four-year institutions. This approach worked in Brooklyn as it did in many other cities: by 1925, 2,000 students were attending these classes. At the same time, Brooklyn residents constituted over one-third of the student body at City College's main campus.

Intensive lobbying efforts drew attention to the vast potential for public higher education in the outer boroughs of New York City. The Brooklyn Chamber of Commerce petitioned the New York State legislature and the City College board of trustees to urge that Brooklyn be given its own public college. The proper facilities, it argued, would encourage more young people to attend college. In 1930, when Brooklyn College was founded, its four-year program drew 2,800 day and more than 5,000 evening students. Similarly, Queens College was formally established in 1937 after a decade as a thriving branch of the main campus. Enrollment at City College itself still increased as thousands of new Americans crowded the Gothic buildings.[30]

The rapid growth of public higher education in New York City shows just how important new Americans considered the attainment of a college degree in the 1920s and 1930s. City College students in this era, Rudy points out, "came largely from lower income groups, and had grown up in homes where there had been a continuous and severe struggle for existence." Only about one-fifth of the students in the late 1930s had fathers born in the United States.[31] As early as World War I, nearly four of every five City College students were Jewish. The preponderance of Jewish students at the free City College both reflected and nourished the widespread belief among American Jews that education offered the opportunity for a miraculous rise in economic and social status.

The history of City College suggests not only the possibilities of public urban higher education but its limitations as well. Indeed, it deserved its reputation as "the Harvard of the proletariat" because it was the most selective college in the country throughout most of the interwar period. Its dedication to democratic access was remarkable: the family income of City College students was significantly lower than that of New York City public high school graduates who went to private institutions of higher education, and 85.6 percent of its students in the late 1930s reported that without free tuition they would not have been able to go to college. On the other hand, free tuition did not guarantee open admissions: the entrance requirement increased nearly every year between 1928, when an average high school grade of 60 was sufficient, to 1941, when an average of 88 was required for admission. Leaders of the state's and city's social establishment did as little as possible to build on the tremendous achievements of City College.[32]

Access to higher education in New York City was restricted not necessarily by ability but by the inadequacy of public higher education to meet the demand for it. The socioeconomic and ethnic composition of the City College student body and the predominance of private (often denominational) institutions in the New York area limited support for continued expansion of public higher education there. For thousands of talented children of immigrants, and Jews in particular, City College offered a way out of the lower middle class into teaching and other white-collar professions; yet for many, its promise remained elusive, for its doors were not open to all who qualified, and many of those who did have the opportunity to enter City College found later on that the doors to most medical and other professional schools were closed to them. Still, thousands did gain access to City College or its private counterparts, and went on to take advantage of the opportunities that awaited them in the growing array of urban white-collar occupations.

Education as a Secular Religion

An emphasis on growth and quantity had long been evident in American higher education, even at the most elite institutions: in 1897, President Charles W. Eliot of Harvard wrote his Johns Hopkins colleague Daniel C. Gilman, "I find that I am not content unless Harvard grows each year, in spite of the size which it has attained."[33] Size was seen as a measure of success. Besides, in the 1920s—and since—most educators believed that if their college or university did not respond to the demands for new courses and for the matriculation of new types of students, other colleges would. After World War I institutions of higher learning enthusiastically extended their influence and services into more and more spheres of American life. Progressive rhetoric and the entrepreneurial spirit were embodied by the United States' urban colleges and universities.

Education became the secular religion of twentieth-century American society. To progressives and their successors, institutions of higher education could train and socialize the expert leaders needed to guide society in such disparate fields as business, teaching, and government. To parents and their children, college attendance seemed to offer the safest and most promising route to occupational training and social status in a changing world. In 1936, employing a common metaphor, Roscoe Pound, the law educator and social observer, commented that "in its hold upon popular faith and popular imagination, organized higher learning has the place in American society of today which organized religion had in the society of the Middle Ages."[34] Education was viewed increasingly as the salvation of progress and democracy. The urban university was our largest cathedral: there

Americans paid homage to the culture of aspiration and prepared themselves to seize its opportunities. When such a school is posed against the liberal arts college on one side and the junior college on the other, its limitations as a democratic social institution were clear, but more important were its hundreds of thousands of successes.

5 / *Curriculum Reform between the World Wars*

The nineteenth-century ideal of the liberal arts college was not strong enough to prevent the intrusion of utilitarian studies and job-oriented students into university life. Technological and social pressures compelled ambitious educators, parents, and their allies in other spheres to alter a form of higher learning they considered essentially undemocratic and increasingly unsuited to the needs of an industrial society. Still, the battle between those who supported expansion of the curriculum and those who remained steadfast against it was fierce. The very definition of higher learning hung in the balance of the argument: "Dr. A. fears that any man who uses the term 'vocational' has surrendered to utilitarianism," William H. Crawford, president of Allegheny College, observed in 1915, "while Dr. B. fears that any man who uses the term 'culture' apart from purpose may be working in a vacuum."[1] With the rise of business and other professional programs and with the influx of vocational-oriented students, educational institutions were pushed and pulled between the values of expansion and consolidation, utility and liberal culture, democracy and elitism.

No issue divided educators more than whether practical subjects ought to be included in the curriculum; no question seemed more basic as educators struggled to develop a role for higher education in a modern society. President Robert M. Hutchins of the University of Chicago, one of the most outspoken critics of the "department-store" American university, asserted, "Vocationalism leads to triviality and isolation; it debases the course of study and the staff." He added, "It deprives the university of its only excuse for existence, which is to provide a haven where the search for truth may go on unhampered by utility or pressure 'for results.' "[2] More often than not, however, this traditional view found expression not in the elimination of professional programs from universities but in a revitalization of intellectual values in undergraduate programs designed for the more serious student. Dismayed by what Julian Park termed "the implication that modern life was scaled up to such a rapid tempo as to leave little or no time for subjects without immediate vocational or professional outlets,"[3] educators proposed college-house and honors plans to create distinctions between intellectually oriented students and their more numerous and presumably more practical peers.

Alternatives were not only available, they were pursued. But the forces of expansion and democracy prevailed. If Hutchins and other like-minded educators had had their way, institutions of higher education would have ignored many of the changes in American economic and social life and scorned the new types of students attracted to the modern university. These educators hoped that intellectual values would dictate curriculum and admissions decisions. Most American colleges, however, whether public or private, chose to expand their conception of higher education and to reconcile the traditional liberal arts with the wishes and needs of their new publics. With only a few exceptions, practical and pecuniary considerations emerged triumphant in higher education, as elsewhere in American life. Faced with choices, then, most institutions chose to be responsive and sympathetic to modern economic and social pressures rather than to an academic ideal.

The Roots of Change

No one described the roots of change in American higher education in starker terms than Thorstein Veblen. In 1918, nearly a decade after he had completed much of the manuscript, Veblen published *The Higher Learning in America,* a scholarly broadside warning of the centrality of business values to the American academic enterprise. Having won acceptance in other social institutions, Veblen wrote, business principles and standards of organization, control, and achievement had now asserted themselves as indispensible to the conduct of affairs in education as well. The pursuit of knowledge for its own sake—he called it "idle curiosity"—was no longer legitimate because it was considered unproductive. After all, the iconoclastic social scientist observed, "pecuniary canons are definitive" in a technological society. Once a college education was linked to the materialistic and individualistic values of American society, the acquisition of higher learning ascribed social status in much the same way as did religions, political prestige, wealth, and even conspicuous comsumption.[4]

Veblen believed that the vocational aims of students did not impinge upon American colleges until the late nineteenth century. But as professional interests entrusted training to the universities, college became an intermediate step, rather than an end in itself, for its forward-looking students. Though still affected by the idealistic drift of "a long-term bias . . . such as will not enduringly tolerate the sordid effects of pursuing an educational policy that looks mainly to the main chance," rhetoric about the high moral purpose of higher learning in America was essentially window dressing, Veblen felt. Now that "by force of conventional propriety a 'college course' . . . has become a requisite of gentility," Veblen observed from his cabin in the woods near the campus of Stanford University, the college catered to young people who had no interest in learning itself: "It aims to afford a rounded discipline to those whose goal is the life of fashion or of affairs." Once status was associated with a college degree, Veblen concluded, the expansion and diffusion of educational opportunities in American society was inevitable, as indeed it proved to be in the next decade.[5]

Recognizing that higher education was at a turning point in its development, Veblen urged that professional and technical schools be separated from the emerging university. Otherwise, American colleges, torn as they were between the values of the past and those of the present, between the pursuit of learning and preparation for the modern professions, would remain "confused with the bootless illusion that they are, in some recondite way, parallel variants of a single line of work." The object of the university had always been to cultivate its community's highest aspirations and ideals; in the twentieth century it would have to reassert the distinction between its true function and its newfound pragmatic concerns by removing research and scholarship from its purview. With the expansion of the university into vocational training—the school of commerce was the "broadest and baldest example [of] the supercession of learning by worldly wisdom"—intellectual values had given way to business values. When the pursuit of knowledge was no longer differentiated from training for professional work, the traditional functions of the university would sink under the weight of new courses of study created to cater to ambitious students, anxious parents, self-aggrandizing businessmen, and entrepreneurial educators (he called them "captains of erudition").[6]

Max McConn, dean of Lehigh University, offered a similar analysis in his 1928 book, *College or Kindergarten?* He suggested the creation of separate colleges for serious students on the one hand and frivolous young people seeking professional training or a good time on the other. Most professors, he wrote, dreamed "of a student body which should consist of real students, lovers of learning, fired with intellectual ardor, who should voluntarily crowd the lecture halls, libraries, and laboratories, rather than the stadium, the dancing floor, and the movies." Scholars', or Real, Colleges would serve the interests of such professors and those few students—he estimated they made up about one-half of 1 percent of the college-age cohort—who were serious about their education. Athletics and "activities" would predominate in the so-called Gentlemen's Colleges, whose curriculum would consist of courses similar to those offered at private secondary schools. Enrollment at the Gentlemen's Colleges would be limited to those willing to pay the high tuition McConn envisioned.[7] Veblen and McConn agreed that the intellectual functions of the American college would survive only if they were sharply distinguished from its social functions, but their proposals were more utopian than realistic.

These often bitter critiques of American higher education exaggerated the transformation of American colleges from pristine to pragmatic institutions. Veblen, in particular, underestimated the strength of the bias in favor of a traditional conception of higher learning, even at the most practical-oriented universities. He failed to foresee just how many faculty and student committees would be appointed throughout the interwar period to establish a curriculum that would satisfy both those who sought to preserve a cultural orientation and those who welcomed a more utilitarian emphasis. One student observed that "the modern college student is attempting to ride two horses—vocation and general culture—at the same time," and that while both were good horses, they were "not temperamentally suited to be mastered simultaneously."[8] Nonetheless, educators tried their best to reorganize the curriculum so that both could be mastered by graduation.

Historians have paid little attention to the efforts of those educators who attempted to guide the adjustment of the college curriculum to the modern world without sacrificing their intellectual integrity. Robert M. Hutchins and Abraham Flexner are more familiar names than Lotus D. Coffmann. Yet it was men such as Coffmann, James R. Angell, and Leonard Koos who articulated and reshaped the democratic American institution of higher education. In the widely read *Universities: American, English, German,* Flexner lamented that the American university provided mass education and offered too many practical courses of study. While conceding that the abuses to which Flexner pointed were intolerable, Coffmann, president of the University of Minnesota, insisted that compromise with the twentieth century was the best and only realistic alternative: "What is included in the program of a university is not altogether a matter of what someone thinks. Resistance may be a fine and noble thing, but carried too far the individual may become a martyr to his exclusive thinking, and the institution he hopes to save may become impotent by its very isolation."[9]

In contrast to those educators who clung to the vestiges of the classical curriculum—a curriculum criticized for having "mystical significance . . . but often little specific meaning"—modern educators asserted that a definite cleavage between liberal and vocational education was not inevitable. Frederick Robinson, the controversial president of CCNY, stressed that "our ideal is the scholar who can be of practical service and the workman who brings the scholarly attitude to his work." The goal of modern American higher education was to produce idealistic materialists—and there was no reason to limit their numbers.[10]

World War I proved to be the catalyst sought by those who protested that the classical curriculum was hopelessly outdated. "The deadening conservation of academic reverence for the traditional curriculum is an obstacle in the path of educational progress and expansion," remarked the dean of the school of education at the University of North Carolina, "but the conditions which have dictated the S.A.T.C. courses and which have fought the war to such a glorious finish have already shaped up and pointed out a new future." The chief quarrel with the classical curriculum was that it left the student well acquainted with the past but unprepared for the future, and the United States had always placed a premium on the future, on the recognition of the possibilities of change and progress. Such educators as Luther Gulick, director of Columbia University's Institute of Public Administration, argued that higher education must link itself with "those motive forces of the human mind, which, outside of our schools and colleges, play the controlling role in high achievement."[11]

The conflict between those who respectively supported and condemned the modern curriculum was focused on the issue of the elimination of ancient languages as entrance and graduation requirements. In 1928, Lehigh's McConn wrote that "the great battle between Science and the Classics, the echoes of which may still be heard in many a faculty meeting," had only intensified in the twentieth century; "the slogan of the scientists was, of course, utility and the needs of modern life [while] the classicists fell back upon Mental Discipline." Heated debates on this issue were common at Emory University in the 1920s; in his diary, the social scientist Ross McClean attributed these disputes to the conflict between younger science- and university-oriented faculty and older faculty nostalgic for the small, sectarian liberal arts college of the nineteenth century. Educators such as Wisconsin's Charles Van Hise argued that since Greek was generally taught in a far more narrow manner than the vocational courses, there was no reason to preserve its traditional privileged place in the university curriculum.[12]

The social as well as educational significance of the decline of the classics at liberal arts colleges was not lost on this generation. By the time of World War I, only a small group of colleges could attract enough prepared students if the strict Latin or Greek admissions requirements were enforced; in 1923, only Amherst and Williams colleges still kept the faith. Other schools, such as Harvard, Princeton, and Dartmouth, offered the B.S. degree in large measure to circumvent the question. Columbia University's decision in 1916 to discontinue the B.S. degree and to abolish the Latin requirement for admission was blamed by unsympathetic conservative educators and alumni for opening the school's doors to undesirable ethnic students. A similar battle at Yale University lasted the better part of a decade, until 1931, when President James R. Angell and his supporters—among them western alumni and high schools—finally used some devious parliamentary procedures to overcome the opposition of conservative faculty members and the Yale Corporation to abandonment of the Latin admissions requirement.[13] Competition for public high school students without training in the classics soon overshadowed educational and social considerations: after all, if Duke University no longer required its freshmen to take Latin, could the University of North Carolina afford to insist that they must?[14]

In any case, most educators were philosophically opposed to traditional theories of education and knowledge. Few agreed with Chicago's Hutchins, for example, that metaphysics should constitute the foundation of a college education for all students in the twentieth century. No individual discipline could argue persuasively that it should be the core of the curriculum; "in truth," Professor Leon Richardson of Dartmouth wrote of the decline of the classics in 1924, "the old carefully guarded distinctions are gone." Even the most conservative professional humanist, Angell added, had to admit that science now constituted an invaluable part of culture and that the engineer was as worthy a member of the university faculty as the classicist. Specialized faculties in the arts and sciences could offer little resistance to curricular decisions that gave equal value to different disciplines, in part since the lack of such qualitative judgments enhanced the legitimacy of so many fields and heightened their practitioners' self-esteem. Critic Norman Foerster conceded that the equivalence of subjects in the twentieth-century college curriculum reflected "the relativity of culture" in modern society.[15]

While they sought to make higher education more practical—and therefore, they assumed, more accessible—most educators also subscribed to the progressive value of training a well-rounded elite and, to a lesser extent, to the traditional ideal of imparting a sense of the legacy of Western civilization. While many conservative educators saw a stark choice between quantity and quality, others in the 1920s introduced several curricular innovations—such as general education and honors work—which offered the possibility of having one's cake and eating it too. But ultimately, professional-oriented, secularized universities embodied new conceptions of knowledge in their curricula. The establishment of programs or schools in business, education, and the like was not merely a response to economic change and public demand; it was a logical response to modern ideology as well. Could anyone define an educated person? And would everyone else agree to the definition? Still, by establishing programs to allow their best students to explore more fully what interested them most, educators made substantial efforts to maintain a home for traditional intellectual values even as they aggressively sought to expand their institutions' influence in other spheres.

General Education Programs

Beginning in the second decade of the twentieth century, general education courses and programs were developed to deal with the curricular problems posed by the increasingly diverse student body and by the proliferation of knowledge and new fields of inquiry. In 1914, Alexander Meiklejohn, president of Amherst College, established one of the first survey courses, a freshman course called Social and Economic Institutions. The goal of such survey courses was to provide a common intellectual experience to aid those freshmen who came to college from the less rigorous public high schools and to help students develop a sense of class solidarity before they went their separate ways to specialized courses and the various fraternities and activities. The creation of the War Issues course for the Student Army Training Corps in 1918 gave this idea its most important boost.

Aimed at building students' morale by giving them an appreciation of the history and culture of the various warring nations, the War Issues course—also known as War Aims, a title that more accurately reflected an important part of its agenda—laid the groundwork for the survey courses now known as Western Civilization. Developed by teams of professors across the country, it was based on the "Greats" course at Oxford University. Frank Aydelotte, an English professor at MIT and head of the project, had been impressed by the course as one of the first American Rhodes scholars earlier in the century. Now he suggested that the American course consist of one hour of lecture and two hours of discussion in small groups each week. Thus, with the federal government's financial support and encouragement, Aydelotte essentially standardized one part of the educational experience for the thousands of students of varying ability at the 540 colleges that participated in the experiment and established a pattern for lecture-and-discussion courses still common today. Some three hundred schools continued to teach the course even after World War I ended.[16]

Patriotism provided the rationale for the adoption of these courses, but it was sound educational principles and traditional standards that ensured their survival. Calling the War Issues course "the most valuable single course ever given in the College," Ernest M. Hopkins of Dartmouth supported the creation of required freshman orientation courses in the social sciences—titled Citizenship—and in the natural sciences. At Columbia University, the War Issues course fathered a postwar course called Contemporary Civilization, designed to make the student a "citizen who shall be safe for democracy." As late as 1940, more than a hundred colleges still required general education courses based on the War Issues model. While not radically altering the curriculum at any school, they did succeed in providing an anchor for the ideal of a liberal arts education at a critical time in its development. Now dedicated to turning out businessmen and teachers, lawyers and chemists, colleges devised general education courses to reflect their idea of what each of its educated professionals should be familiar with before leaving school. Despite the increasing emphasis on utility and specialization, the concept of a well-rounded intellect gained ground for once.[17]

Redefining the Liberal Arts

Most educators' definition of the liberal arts was considerably broadened in the 1920s and 1930s. To the despair of the traditionalists, courses in journalism and the fine arts took their places alongside Latin in the curriculum. Such courses served as part of the process of professionalization. After prewar opposition, the Illinois Press Association changed its attitude and supported journalism education at the University of Illinois in the early 1920s. In the arts, as elsewhere, a college education now seemed to be more appropriate preparation than practical training; by 1932 there were 200 art departments in American colleges. Compromise was unavoidable: ironically, while a curriculum committee at Western Reserve University called in 1936 for strengthening the school's nonprofessional offerings to combat students' preferences for so-called bread-and-butter courses, it supported the addition of more journalism and art courses to meet the growing demand for their study. "The glare of the applied arts and sciences . . . may yet threaten to atrophy the higher vision" of the college as the seat of humanism, claimed Western Reserve's dean William Leutner, but without the addition of such courses to the curriculum, the development of the twentieth-century college would have been arrested.[18]

The growth of the social sciences is a lasting contribution of the interwar period. The ready acceptance of John Dewey's philosophical concept of pragmatism, the application of scientific methods to the study of society, and the continued professionalization of the social-scientific disciplines all played important roles in the emergence of the social sciences as an integral part of the undergraduate curriculum. No longer isolated from a changing world, the American college of the 1920s was forced to support the social scientists' attempts to make sense of it. The New School for Social Research was founded in 1918; the Social Science Research Council was organized by several groups that seceded from the American Council of Learned Societies in 1923. Pointing to large enrollment increases in their courses, social scientists claimed that the growth of their disciplines was responsible for the popularity of higher education.[19] Critical to the acceptance, if not predominance, of the social sciences in American higher education after World War I was the widespread consensus among educators and professional-oriented students that the disciplines of history, economics, political science, and sociology could help twentieth-century Americans understand, measure, adapt to, and even control change.

The Depression heightened interest in the social sciences. The influence of Keynesian economic principles on social policy confirmed the broad acceptance of social planning, which in turn led to an emphasis on the social sciences in the curriculum, since educators and students alike believed the colleges should be—and were—training the future leaders of society. Students generally felt that the social sciences gave them an insight into the nature of society which other disciplines—particularly the humanities—failed to do. "The liberal college has been accused by its critics of segregating the students among the cloisters of a classical education unrelated to the problems of the outside world," a Dartmouth senior observed, and he declared that only the introduction of the social sciences had corrected a significant deficiency in the curriculum and prepared his peers and him for their entrance to the modern world.[20]

In *Redirecting Education,* Rexford Tugwell and Leon Keyserling, two university social scientists and key members of President Franklin D. Roosevelt's "Brains Trust," argued that twentieth-century American higher education confronted the challenge of reconciling individual initiative and social planning. It resolved this persistent dualism by dignifying the social sciences and the professions. In the modern industrial state, the structure of society had become in large part a function of education; consequently, in the eyes of Tugwell and Keyserling, as well as of most other social scientists, each institution of higher learning had a responsibility to broaden the range and quality of its training in those fields that would prepare young people to take their places in the boardrooms, courtrooms, classrooms, and government offices of America. The social sciences offered the best opportunity for students to enhance their own opportunities for advancement at the same time that they contributed to the smooth functioning of society.[21] Once again, the expansion of the curriculum was linked not only with the democratization of higher education but with the future progress of American civilization.

Junior and Senior Colleges

The separation of the undergraduate experience in the 1920s into two divisions, so-called junior and senior colleges, constituted an important attempt to distinguish between general and professional undergraduate education, yet it has received little attention since then. The battle line between those who favored undergraduate vocational education and those who condemned it was generally drawn between the sophomore and junior years in college. As a result, many educators, particularly those at large public universities, formally divided the first two and last two years of college. In the junior college, a broad general education was required; in the senior college, the student had the opportunity to pursue an area of special interest. The University of California had begun experimenting with upper- and lower-division work as early as 1902; Elmer E. Slosson supported this approach, based loosely on that of the German gymnasium, in his classic 1910 study, *Great American Universities*. During the 1920s this innovation was widely adopted: by 1930, 55 percent of the independent colleges, 80 percent of the endowed universities, and 90 percent of the state universities surveyed had established junior and senior colleges.[22]

At most institutions, the program was designed simply to provide students from different backgrounds with the opportunity to reach an acceptable level of academic achievement by the end of their second year. Also, since attrition rates were still high, particularly at the large state universities, those students who did leave before graduation were exposed at least to the general education program. It was intended to assist the student in adapting to college life, to widen the student's knowledge and interests, and to help the student choose an appropriate field of concentration. Even if some schools did not form two distinct divisions, they generally arranged their courses so that the first two years of college were devoted primarily to prescribed courses and the last two years to electives.

Many administrators' and faculty members' motives were not always so pure, however. Some educators hoped simply to correct excessive abuses of the elective system. At Emory, the plan sparked "a new purposefulness [and] a gratifying intellectual interest" among undergraduates. But Emory University's dean, for example, also argued that the junior college "furnish[ed] a solution, at least partial, to the problem created by the democratic demand that every boy and girl should have a chance at a college education."[23] By requiring examinations or a minimum scholastic average for admission to the senior college, a school or faculty could ferret out unwanted students whose interests and abilities they considered inadequate. Faculty could then draw the line on mass higher education without risking the social and political consequences of limiting enrollment to the university as a whole. For many conservative educators, the junior/senior college plan was a reasonable compromise between the social imperative that increased attendance and their own philosophical predilection for elite higher education.

The number of institutions that maintained junior and senior divisions declined during the 1930s. Some educators attributed this development to falling rates of attrition. By this time, two years or less of college offered less relative status than it had even a decade before. The students of the 1930s were more serious; the Depression offered them few alternatives to working hard, performing better, and staying in school longer. In addition, the widespread acceptance of major and minor concentrations and required freshman courses alleviated much of the educational rationale for the program. Finally, the improved quality and standardization of the nation's high schools also mitigated the need for the plan. By late in the decade, the experiment was generally confined to less prestigious undergraduate professional programs in engineering and commerce, where there was still concern that students would not otherwise receive a general cultural education.[24]

John Dewey

Though John Dewey wrote little on higher education specifically, these efforts to adjust the college curriculum to the modern world bear his unmistakable imprint. The influence of Dewey's philosophy of pragmatism was pervasive in the early twentieth century, and particularly after the publication of *Democracy and Education* in 1916. Dewey's educational thought was based on the idea that education should be focused on meeting the needs of individual students, not on learning for its own sake. Stressing Dewey's contention that culture could not be confined to a fixed body of knowledge, his supporters argued that educational institutions had to adapt continually to a changing social and economic environment. The introduction of the social sciences, the arts, and other practical courses into the curriculum was therefore justified.

Dewey was concerned, however, that modern education's conceptions of cultural education and of practical education were equally narrow. Cultural education alone was condemned to the fate of the genteel tradition. Yet utilitarian education could not be limited to practical training. Now that so many occupations were affected by applied science or the scientific method, a college education that combined cultural and scientific studies offered the best hope for modern society: "The ultimate point is that instruction of this kind . . . is *socially* necessary, and that until it is properly given in educational institutions, the practical activities carried on in society will not be liberalized and humanized, to say nothing of being most efficiently conducted."[25] Though Dewey did not discuss specific reforms in his public lectures, his spirit was an important element in curriculum reform. Now the colleges would be sensitive to a broader range of individual needs and, as a result, to society's needs as well.

The development of individual potential was the cornerstone of Dewey's progressive philosophy, and so it became of the undergraduate experience. Even a system of mass education could encourage each student to prepare himself for the profession and social position he would assume later in life. "Utility, culture, information, preparation for social efficiency, mental discipline or power" were the values Dewey wanted to instill in American college students. Free to develop, tolerant of others, trained in a specialty but cognizant of social values, the college graduate would then contribute to the smooth efficiency and progress of society. One follower of Dewey, Ernest H. Wilkins, a dean at the University of Chicago and later president of Oberlin College, designed a curriculum with just these principles in mind: in order to familiarize the student with all aspects of adult life, it included hygiene and psychology, English and logic, the concepts of major and minor group selections, and required survey courses.[26] Dewey's philosophy of pragmatism encouraged the incorporation of new subjects for study and new students into American higher education as a means of facilitating individual fulfillment and advancement and ensuring social stability and progress. Practical, mass higher education, properly organized, would constitute the apex of American democracy.

The Revolt against Mass Education

Others, however, were disturbed by modern society and mass higher education. "Philosophically speaking, [higher education] lacks a compelling sense of direction and purpose," one commentator wrote. "Contemporary life is fractional, utilitarian, disillusioned, materialistic, and so is the liberal arts college."[27] Efforts by such men as Hutchins, Flexner, Aydelotte, and A. Lawrence Lowell to reassert intellectual values and a less comprehensive conception of the American institution of higher learning drew their inspiration from a more general intellectual revolt against the hegemony of mass society; as Frederick Lewis Allen commented, "they feared the effect upon themselves and upon American culture of mass production and the machine, and saw themselves as fighting at the last ditch for the right to be themselves in a civilization which was being leveled into monotony by Fordisms and the chain-store mind."[28] These men sought to keep much of the twentieth century at bay by creating new forms that retained the values of traditional higher education, and in some measure they succeeded. Hutchins' "Great Books" plan, Aydelotte's honors plan, and Lowell's house plan were the modern embodiment of seemingly outdated principles. Rejecting contemporary educational trends, these educators led a counterattack that by the mid-1920s established the distinctiveness and prestige of the elite liberal arts college.

Opposition to the utilitarian educational philosophy and curriculum became more strident early in the twentieth century. The effort to emphasize the liberal culture ideal was symbolized by the appointment of Lowell to succeed Charles W. Eliot as president of Harvard in 1909. Eliot had pioneered the elective system and supported research in his forty years at the helm, often at the expense of the traditional views of Harvard's faculty and alumni. One of his most outspoken critics was Irving Babbitt, Harvard's well-known literary critic and philosopher, who bewailed this materialistic view of a college education. Babbitt believed that the "religious-humanistic" philosophy of education should prevail over what he termed the "utilitarian-sentimental" philosophy of education. He insisted that "the college must substitute selection for encyclopedic inclusiveness" in the curriculum. Babbitt warned, "It will be found to be no small matter whether our higher education is to have enshrined at its center the idea of leisure in Aristotle's sense, or the idea of service in the sense given to the word by President Eliot and the humanitarians." College should provide the student with a broad vision of his place in Western culture, not merely with competence to participate in the economic development of contemporary America.[29] Babbitt and others hailed Lowell's appointment as an antidote to Eliot's and society's excessive accent on training, rather than education, in institutions of higher learning.

Against substantial odds, conservatives carried on a guerrilla campaign against the practical-oriented curriculum in American colleges and universities and managed to win a number of significant skirmishes. The idea that higher learning constituted a sufficient end in itself still attracted considerable support. When Lemuel Murlin assumed the presidency of DePauw University in the mid-1920s, he criticized the opportunistic educational policy of his predecessor and promised to define and establish a cultural curriculum free "from changes demanded by the blowing winds and fleeting desires of an unknowing public." Some Dartmouth students applauded efforts to inspire them to enjoy "the simple but profound pleasures of a good book and favorite pipe."[30]

James Truslow Adams, among others, disputed the need for a vast apparatus of more than 1,500 colleges when, he remarked, only a few exceptional young men could truly appreciate a college education. Universities should no longer "feel obliged to offer apologies if, in spite of their devoted endeavors, some of the human material emerges, not as doers, but as thinkers," a foreign-born professor added. Such educators as Babbitt, Hutchins, and Flexner hoped to recreate the nineteenth-century college in the twentieth century despite almost irresistible economic and social forces to the contrary.[31] But the key to the success of those few colleges that led the reassertion of traditional values in the 1920s was the implicit suggestion that a liberal arts education connoted higher social status than a practical one did.

In his 1930 book *Universities: American, English, German* (described by one reviewer as "aggressive, thought provoking, mirth provoking, saddening, and irritating") Flexner denounced the modern American university. While acknowledging that the university inevitably was an expression of its age, he accused the nation's schools of being "service stations" for American society, and described how and where American colleges had made "hurtful concessions" to the forces of expansion and mediocrity. Even the elite institutions, responding to local conditions and pressures, contributed to the "wild, uncontrolled, and uncritical expansion" of undergraduate programs beyond "the limits of credibility." The future first director of the Institute for Advanced Study claimed that modern universities influenced by science and democracy could still uphold values represented by the "accumulated treasures of truth, beauty, and knowledge" of the past; they "cannot be excused [for] . . . reaching out for practical responsibilities that do not belong to universities at all." Instead of doing all they could, Flexner believed, American universities should have been doing as little as they could.[32]

To prove his point, Flexner compiled lists of course titles and dissertation topics he found outrageous. When the University of Chicago advertised its Home Study program with the slogan "DEVELOP POWER AT HOME" and accepted a master's thesis titled "A Time and Motion Comparison of Four Methods of Dishwashing," Flexner felt the modern university had gone too far. Indeed, like Veblen, Flexner opposed the addition of any professional school—and a school of commerce in particular—to the research university. He wanted the university to be more circumspect about its functions; it should stress the humanistic disciplines and creative and critical inquiry, not professional training. "Between the student of political and social problems and the journalist, industrialist, merchant, viceroy, member of Parliament or Congress, there is a gap which the university cannot fill, which society must fill in some other way," he pleaded.[33]

Flexner's aspirations for the American university were anachronistic by 1930. His model was the Johns Hopkins University of the late 1880s, in its nascent stage when he was a student there. By the late 1920s, it was unfair as well as unrealistic to judge American universities, even the very best, by that standard. Surely Flexner hoped the Institute for Advanced Study could recreate the Johns Hopkins of his youth, but few, if any, other institutions could afford such a luxury. Times had changed. Though he supported the advancement of knowledge through specialization, he refused to acknowledge that specialization and professionalization went hand in hand in the twentieth-century research university. His disregard for the public clamor for more education—and society's dependence on it for economic growth—goaded one reviewer to argue that "it would doubtless have been better to [devote] the Bamberger millions [which founded the Institute] to extension education." He, too, failed to propose a reasonable alternative model.[34]

Hutchins and the "Great Books" Curriculum

The precocious president of the University of Chicago, Robert M. Hutchins, did propose an alternative. In articles and his seminal work, *The Higher Learning in America,* published in 1936, Hutchins proposed a program of collegiate instruction that more successfully preserved the best features of the traditional institution in the twentieth-century college, and one that a few schools still use today: the "Great Books" curriculum. As president of one of the most important urban research-oriented universities, Hutchins was more aware than Veblen or Flexner of the pressures confronting an institution that aspired to intellectual goals alone. He noted four new influences on the modern university: an institution's dependence on its sources of financial support and their impact on educational policy; an institution's sensitivity to the demands of a broad public; society's demand that higher education be democratic; and modern society's ideal of progress. Hutchins realized that the American university had to be responsive to the vagaries of public opinion. But modern society's emphasis on science and empiricism, he believed, encouraged an ambivalence about higher education which was inherently anti-intellectual. In contrast, Hutchins offered a university dedicated to the pursuit of truth for its own sake, with a number of research institutes gathered nearby as appendages to the central structure, a traditional liberal arts college.[35]

To Hutchins, the university's "only excuse for existence [was] to provide a haven where the search for truth [might] go on unhampered by utility or pressure 'for results.'" In his view, this search required a thorough knowledge of the classics and philosophy. The ideal university should embody a unity of knowledge and purpose difficult to establish elsewhere in the diffuse modern world. Rejecting the elective system, Hutchins hoped to eliminate the influences of unqualified empiricism and vocationalism from the curriculum. In its place, he suggested a program of general education for the first two years which featured metaphysics and the natural and social sciences. For the duration of his undergraduate education, the student selected a branch of knowledge in which to concentrate his efforts, but professional education was out of the question until after he finished college.[36] Hutchins proposed this plan in large part to clarify what he saw as the popular confusion of the immediate and final ends of higher education. Truth, not personal advancement, ought to be the student's sole preoccupation. This proved to be too much to ask of nearly all colleges and universities, even his own.

Lowell and the College House Plan

Still, in the 1920s, while hundreds of thousands of new students sought to attend college to study practical subjects, the elite college dedicated to the preservation of a distinctive tradition of liberal education enjoyed a renaissance. This new liberal arts college intended to be a selective institution, enrolling only those few students who were most capable of taking advantage of the opportunity to sharpen their mental acumen without concern for immediate employment. It would be a cultural-oriented community inside and outside of the classroom. As a result, Lowell's house plan attacked the emphasis on curricular expansion and broad educational opportunity in American educational and social thought. No wonder, then, that Lowell, conservative Boston Brahmin that he was, titled a collection of his speeches and essays *At War with Academic Traditions in America*.

Lowell wanted to "rebuild" Harvard on an English model, and with the formation of the house system, he was somewhat successful. Guided by the example of Oxford University, Lowell encouraged the intellectual and social growth of a privileged class of student-gentlemen. The object of the college student "should be to acquire habits of intellectual application, of clear and accurate thought, and of lucid expression"; specialization should wait until postgraduate work.[37] Further, Lowell hoped to foster the development of social leadership qualities among his undergraduates by instilling a sense of *noblesse oblige* within small circles of selected young men. At first Lowell concentrated his efforts on building new freshman dormitories and on instituting such important academic reforms as the tutorial system and honors concentrations. But his vision of the undergraduate intellectual community went unrealized until Edward Harkness's gifts launched the college houses at Harvard and at Yale University in the late 1920s.

Lowell wished to construct "college houses" that would restore the traditional conception of the unity of collegiate intellectual and social life. Impatient with intellectual mediocrity and social divisions based solely on wealth, Lowell was confident that the houses would increase faculty–student contact and end superficial social cliques. Despite the fact that a Harvard Student Council report in 1926 had called for the creation of just such small residential colleges to improve the intellectual atmosphere, in part by mixing students from diverse backgrounds, most students were opposed to the "radical experiment" when it was announced in November 1928. Along with some faculty, they preferred, in the words of the student newspaper, "the present system of robust neglect to any alternative plan of gentle guidance." Americanization of the house selection process would inevitably break up natural social groups, the newspaper feared (ironically, given Lowell's disinclination to associate with persons of more exotic background than his own), and each house would become "a temple to a new Pantheon of Balanced Forces." The college houses did bring self-motivated students and interested faculty together, yet they were not an unqualified success. Most socially prominent students chose not to participate and many of the least socially prominent students were barred from the houses by their religion or interests. In addition, Harvard elsewhere made its share of compromises with the twentieth century by sponsoring utilitarian courses and big-time college athletics.[38]

While few institutions could afford to build college houses, most liberal arts colleges realized that their interests were best served by a more intimate intellectual and social atmosphere than their university counterparts could provide. Such college presidents as Amherst's Alexander Meiklejohn and Dartmouth's Ernest M. Hopkins expected their students to become the leading professionals and businessmen of their day. These liberal arts educators of the 1920s differed from their university peers in their emphasis on the value of intellectual development itself during the undergraduate years. A liberal education was intended to inculcate not only knowledge of and respect for culture but also a sense of social obligation. The college house constituted one such living-and-learning environment within the large university; it served as a haven for the best students not only at Harvard but at the University of Wisconsin as well, after Meiklejohn founded the

Experimental College there. In smaller schools, honors work came to symbolize efforts to enliven the intellectual tone of the modern American college.

Honors Programs

In 1924 Leon B. Richardson, a Dartmouth chemistry professor, visited various institutions throughout Europe and the United States in order to prepare a report on the future of the liberal arts college and to suggest a curriculum reform plan for his own institution. Richardson proposed twenty-six innovations designed to make the content of the curriculum "a judicious combination" of cultural and utilitarian values. He suggested the reduction of class size, the creation of a distribution system for general education rather than the prescription of specific courses, and the introduction of comprehensive examinations before graduation. But the centerpiece of his effort both to challenge individual students and to give them the freedom to pursue their own academic interests was the formation of an honors program. At the same time, a committee of Dartmouth seniors came to the same conclusion: reiterating their desire for "an emphasis on active learning" and "intimacy and cooperation between learners and teachers," these students, led by a future college president, stressed the need for an honors program if the college was going to meet the interests of its best students.[39]

"No single movement in higher education has been given more interest or promises more far-reaching results" than the widespread formation of honors programs at American colleges, a federal official commented in the mid-1920s. While precedents had been established at Yale and Harvard before World War I, the honors program idea did not receive wide public attention until after Frank Aydelotte brought it to Swarthmore College in the early 1920s. With the enthusiastic support of the Swarthmore faculty, the experiment was launched in 1922–23 in two divisions, English literature and the social sciences. Restricted to juniors and seniors, the program required that students study two (not four) subjects a semester; they would read materials from extensive bibliographies provided them by the faculty, meet weekly in small groups with their supervisor, and prepare for oral and written examinations to be given at the end of their senior year with the assistance of outside referees. The experiment was extended to three more divisions—French, the physical sciences, and the classics—in the next two years, and every department joined the program by 1930. Between 1925 and 1930, the proportion of Swarthmore seniors in the program leaped from 19 percent to 44 percent of the class, and the college drew more and more students and visitors from around the nation. Funded by the General Education Board at the behest of none other than Abraham Flexner, Swarthmore's honors plan became a model for such reform around the country.[40]

Liberal arts educators established these programs not only to improve the quality of education for the minority of students with exceptional ability and serious intellectual interests, but also to encourage a public perception of the academic excellence of their institution. By 1927, ninety-three colleges had introduced some variation of the Swarthmore plan. The General Education Board aided the formation of the programs at Stanford and other schools. Dartmouth expanded its honors program in 1929 by setting up the Senior Fellowships Program, which gave a handful of top students complete freedom during their senior year. A survey of Methodist colleges and universities indicated that nearly half of them offered opportunities for some form of honors and independent work before the Depression.[41]

Honors programs were also established at many of the nation's state universities. After being dismissed from the presidency of Amherst, Meiklejohn moved in the late 1920s to the University of Wisconsin, where he established an experimental college with a program of general education and independent work that met interested students' needs for an intense intellectual environment. The founders of North Carolina's honors program included faculty members similarly disenchanted with the proliferation of specialized courses and practical students. The philosopher Norman Foerster attacked his school and others for "dispensing education for efficiency" and its willingness to meet the demands of "an acquisitive society keen in the arts and sciences of the production of things" but uninterested in the development of humanistic values. In place of the ever-expanding, materialistic state university of the twentieth century, Foerster offered a Jeffersonian vision of a small public institution with a select student body and a humanistic curriculum based on great books, religion, and ancient languages.[42] And he taught in North Carolina's Honors College, which was open to only fifty students in each class.

The Social Implications of Curriculum Reform

As honors work appealed to only a small number of students, its influence was more symbolic than real. Between the two world wars, and since, the ideal of a cultural education has worked better in theory than in practice at nearly all American colleges and universities. No matter how strongly the cultural conservatives of the 1920s defended the values and curriculum of the traditional liberal arts college, it proved impossible to prevent students from thinking practical thoughts. Midwestern liberal arts colleges, such as Carleton and Grinnell, introduced practical courses even before World War I in order to stimulate the enrollment of male students and to make themselves more competitive with the nearby state universities; at Grinnell, for example, the general aim of a proposed Department of Public Affairs was "to make the College, even though dominated as it ought to be by the spirit of culture, useful for businessmen." In fact, in 1924, business administration courses were the most popular choices for male students there.[43] National surveys demonstrated that students at all types of colleges and universities chose courses increasingly for their relation to their own potential occupations as graduation neared; indeed, fully half of the student body at liberal arts colleges was pursuing professional training in education alone.[44]

Students at even the most prestigious liberal arts colleges were not immune. At Amherst College, where students claimed they appreciated the value of a liberal education and applauded Meiklejohn's reforms, the student newspaper also lobbied for a course in business administration and the appointment of a professor "to be the connecting link between the strictly classical ideas of a liberal education and life under modern business conditions." In the early 1920s, Swarthmore College had a strong engineering program and courses in accounting and "modern business practice"; later in the decade, despite its innovative honors program, a Swarthmore student confessed that the importance of a cultural education had been lost in his peers' contemporary material concerns. A 1937 faculty committee at Dartmouth was hardly alone in its disenchantment with the lack of intellectual curiosity on the part of its practical-minded students.[45]

Still, these honors programs did more than just satisfy the faculty and a small number of students. During this era of the emergence of mass higher education, their very presence promised a distinctive alternative. Honors work suggested that small liberal arts colleges could play a special role in the education of the nation's most talented young men. In a society devoted to broadening educational opportunity, these colleges formed the bulwark of a movement to raise standards and restrict admission to college. In a materialistic age, these schools emphasized intellectual pursuits of a less concrete but more permanent value. The effort to preserve and enhance a college that adhered to the notion of education for education's sake and to cultivate the social habits of *noblesse oblige* among its students was an anomaly in twentieth-century America. Yet such colleges thrived just because they appeared to offer a total educational experience that connoted higher social status than the practical-oriented higher education available at larger institutions. What ambitious young man would not want to attend a liberal arts college if it offered an elite education to a selected group of students? Curriculum reform at the nation's most prestigious liberal arts colleges was a manifestation not only of educational philosophy but also of the social values of its educators and students.

Curriculum reform implicitly recognized the right of non-honors students to acquire some form of college education and the responsibility of educators to meet these students' needs as well. Most educators saw in expansion their—and society's—best hope for the future. "Respectful of the great traditions of the past, we must nevertheless recognize the peculiar exigencies of the present, and the radiant promise of the future," James R. Angell advised his Yale audience in 1921. For the next decade or more, despite his own institution's reluctance to pursue his liberal policies, Angell remained an articulate spokesman for the twentieth-century university, an institution "more generous and more inclusive than has been traditional, but one which does no necessary violence to those ideas of superlative excellence which have been the essence of the university spirit." In his address to the Conference on the Obligation of Universities to the Social Order in the fall of 1932, Angell observed that society had a right to look to the nation's institutions of higher learning for intellectual leadership, particularly in a time of great change. Aware of cultural lag, Angell still held that the university could extend its influence to a wide range of fields of study without jeopardizing its standards or endangering its detached and disinterested pursuit of knowledge.[46] Expansion and innovation offered opportunities for service, and most educators were as vigorous in pursuit of them as liberal arts educators in quest of consolidation and privilege.

At issue in curriculum reform was the very definition of modern democratic higher education. The challenge facing American educators then, as now, was to develop, institutionalize, and popularize a curriculum that was a balanced compromise between the study of relatively fixed cultural artifacts and values and technical training responsive to the needs of the day. After World War I, the quickened interest of hundreds of thousands of new and different types of students in a practical education challenged traditional conceptions and provided the rationale for the growth of the urban and professional-oriented university. Yet the idea of education for education's sake enjoyed a renaissance in the 1920s as some educators seized the opportunity to preserve and strengthen conservative bastions of culture and influence. Much is owed to both groups of educators: the innovations of both Coffmann and Aydelotte, among others, have influenced the parameters of subsequent curriculum reform. Higher education in modern America would come in various shapes and sizes, in honors programs and junior colleges; different curricula reflected different aspirations. In the 1920s and 1930s, curriculum revision was part of an effort to enable each institution to find its place—and that of its graduates—in a changing world.

6 / *The Middle-Class Culture on the Campus*

"In this last decade, higher education has become such a fetich in America that all the youth of the country, rich or poor, from the cities and the farms, fit or unfit, are seeking the roads that lead to the universities," a 1928 guidebook to American colleges proclaimed. "To each one, or to his parents, a college degree is a stamp of social superiority, its lack, a social stigma. Each one believes that it is a magic key to happiness, success, and riches." Like previous generations of young Americans, the young men of the post–World War I era were preoccupied by the desire for future success, but now their future began with a college education and not with flight to the frontier or an apprenticeship in a financial house or lawyer's office. The American college and university of the 1920s emphasized professional training and social status; their growing appeal to young people was based on the new belief that in the *Emory Wheel's* words, "a college degree entitles the holder to a free ticket to the Great American Show."[1] Self-confident, students expected higher education to fulfill the democratic promise of modern America.

But it did not. College attendance did offer great advantages to the young man from a socially desirable white Anglo-Saxon Protestant upper-middle-class background. However, young men from socially undesirable homes, young women, and blacks were far less likely to go to college at all or to enjoy its privileges as students or graduates. Hundreds of thousands of young people from diverse socioeconomic and religious backgrounds were able to use higher education as a ladder to success between the two world wars. They shared this same hope. But Americans of different socioeconomic classes had different rates of college-going and even different expectations about the type of institution they could attend: ability notwithstanding, the higher the socioeconomic background of the student, the more likely he was to attend a prestigious school. The American college of the 1920s and 1930s promised young people a chance to pursue the American dream, but it was a dream reserved first and foremost, though not exclusively, for the male children of those who already enjoyed its economic and social benefits.

No group of Americans sensed and encouraged the shift in the perception of the value of a college education more quickly and fervently than middle-class parents. They were eager to secure positions of equal, if not better, standing for their children in technocratic and heterogeneous twentieth-century America. "[The students] are the sons of middle-class parents who look upon a college education, which, perhaps, they have not had, as a vestibule to one of the genteel professions or to a business career, who see the baccalaureate as a passport to law or journalism or business administration," a desienchanted college professor observed in 1924. "They come expecting to be, and expected to be, pillars of society."[2] The culture of the American college replicated the pragmatic, materialistic, and often biased values of these respectable Americans.

The model student of this period was "an expert technician who is also a 'good mixer,'" Robert Angell wrote in the late 1920s.[3] He was (to use a favorite expression of the former university president in the White House, Woodrow Wilson) "a young man on the make," interested in professional training and obsessed by the pursuit of social status. In the age of Babbitt, college life provided many opportunities to develop a highly self-conscious and peer-oriented personality; the student ignored classroom work and sought social success in activities, athletics, and fraternities instead. Anyone who attended college could prepare for a business career, but those who came to college with the appropriate socioeconomic background and personality had far greater access to the positions of influence on campus than their less fortunate, even if more intelligent, peers. In the midst of the democratic rush to the colleges, WASP upper-middle-class male prerogatives were still preserved.

College as Social Opportunity

After studying the emergence of the elite institutions of the late nineteenth and early twentieth centuries, Laurence Veysey concluded, "Stylized social ambition, more than a quest for academic excellence, captured the new American university." The new university featured professional education and big-time varsity football, while intellectual achievements in the arts and sciences received little public attention. At that time, even though the colleges attracted less than one of every twenty-five young persons, many educators were already concerned. In his 1909 inaugural address, Harvard University's A. Lawrence Lowell remarked that "it requires little familiarity with the students to recognize that they . . . regard the athlete, or the man of social prominence, as a far more promising personality than the high scholar." Lowell felt that respect for undergraduate scholarship was at a low ebb, and he set out to alter that situation by proposing a series of academic reforms such as the tutorial and honors concentration programs. Other university presidents—Nicholas Murray Butler of Columbia, Daniel Coit Gilman of Johns Hopkins, Stanford's David Starr Jordan—similarly warned that academic standards were threatened by an increasing number of socially motivated students.[4]

Yet, despite their jeremiads, and in no small measure because of their efforts to expand their schools, these influential leaders watched higher education's influence increase even as the extracurricular side shows took precedence over the university's intellectual functions. Most educators agreed with Butler's 1929 assessment that "education [had] been made as painless as possible" since the late nineteenth century. Perhaps nostalgically, Butler commented that none of Columbia's present students could have passed the entrance examinations offered fifty years before (the faculty, specialized as they were, he added, probably would have been unable to pass the classics-oriented tests as well) and that the late-nineteenth-century student would have shuddered at the thought that a business program and "school spirit" could set the tone of the American college as they did in the 1920s.[5] Survey courses, honors programs, and the like attempted to bolster academic life, but they were largely unsuccessful.

The social motivation for college-going was more influential than ever before. "The close of the War found newly created wealth that could and did send men to college," the Committee on the Bureau of

Personnel Research at Dartmouth College observed. "Moreover, the general point of view regarding college education had changed and the new men who were coming to college accepted college as a part of the social structure rather than as an opportunity for higher education." In an editorial titled "9,796 Students—Why Are They Here?" the *Daily Illini* explained that most students attended the University of Illinois because " 'going to college' is admittedly the modish, fashionable, acceptable thing to do." Family prosperity and professional training were important factors, but "the opportunity to increase one's social prestige, particularly at home," was the chief reason for attendance. To young people, college-going presented the best opportunity to "master the latest etiquette, buy the latest cut in clothing, learn the latest slang expression." In an essay submitted to *The New Republic* titled "A College for Babbitts," Harvard graduate Scudder Mekeel admitted, "We measure the desirability of advanced education by [the] increase in future income and social prestige. Success is our goal, education serving as only one of the valuable means."[6]

"Apparently many students are motivated strongly by the wishes of parents," commented an American Association of University Professors report. "It has been humorously remarked that all young men and women go to college either because their parents did or did not." Family income skyrocketed during these years and middle-class parents bought not only a car, a telephone, and a life insurance policy for themselves, but a college education for their children as well. In all classes in previous generations, a college degree had been a rarity; now the American middle class believed a young man had to have one, not just to open up the possibilities for economic and social advancement, but even to preserve his present station in an increasingly heterogeneous and technocratic society. Even a cab driver allegedly told a faculty member that parents had no right to bring children into the world without expecting to support them through college. Robert Morss Lovett of the University of Chicago observed that parents made nearly any sacrifice to send their sons and daughters to college "in the same pathetic faith with which they once burned candles to win respite for souls of the dead." They could then feel assured of their own moral rightness and their neighbor's approval.[7]

Not surprisingly, many students felt pressure from their parents. Percy Marks, an English professor and noted critic, remarked that parents who attended his lectures across the country were more eager to hear about fraternity life—despite his disparaging view of its influence—than about academic issues. An editorial in the *Massachusetts Collegian* reminded students of the sacrifices their parents had made to send them to college and of their obligation to spend their four years preparing for an occupation that would put them in a position to command rather than obey others. Sadly, a lonely sophomore confided in the education writer John P. Gavit about the intense pressure for social success he faced at home:

> I felt rotten when I went home from college at the end of my freshman year. I knew what my family expected of me, and I hadn't made good. . . . They were sore because I hadn't got to be anything special, even in the freshman class. Dad said it was all right to study hard . . . but he was hoping I would blossom out into some kind of "leadership" and make "valuable connections" . . . that would be profitable in later life, in business, you know. Mother said she hoped I wasn't going to be a recluse or a poor college professor.[8]

The following fall, this student went back to college and "mixed"; his grades suffered, but he improved his social standing by joining a fraternity. Viewing college as a means rather than an end in itself, most parents preferred that their children develop their social skills and connections rather than their intellectual potential at institutions of higher learning.

Surveys of the vocational intentions of students and their socioeconomic backgrounds in the 1920s and 1930s suggest that students aspired to the types of college training that connoted higher status than their parents enjoyed at the time. In an unpublished article, "Like Father, Unlike Son," the University of Illinois's dean of men observed that most male students did not specialize in their father's occupation. The sons of farmers often enrolled in business and physical education programs; half of the sons of teachers went into engineering and most of the others enrolled in liberal arts programs that led to careers in the learned professions; and while nearly two-thirds of the sons of businessmen attended the commerce school, many others, generally the sons of shopkeepers, sought an engineering career.[9] For many, college attendance offered a chance to move up the economic, and therefore social, ladder, if only one rung at a time.

During the interwar period, more prestigious liberal arts colleges began to attract upper-middle-class students from suburban areas far from the regions of the colleges' traditional clientele. The 1937 annual report of Indiana's DePauw University reflected the self-confidence of this new student body. It reported that more than a hundred students had grown up on farms, but only four planned to return there, similarly, nearly 500 students had fathers who engaged in white-collar trades, but fewer than 200 of them planned to follow in their fathers' footsteps. Instead, while only a third of the student body had fathers in the professions, four of every five students expected to pursue a professional career. DePauw shared in a trend noted among well-known liberal arts colleges of the day: the higher the prestige of the institution, the greater the proportion of upper-middle-class students, and the greater their interest in fields that promised economic and social mobility. In a rapidly changing society, a college degree constituted an insurance policy against downward mobility at the same time that it offered middle-class children their best chance to get ahead.[10]

This desire for social prestige and occupational mobility disturbed the conservative critics. Abraham Flexner described college life as an endless search for social contacts at the expense of intellectual efforts; Robert M. Hutchins likened the college to a resort hotel. In the 1920s and 1930s, these critics harked unrealistically back to a day when the middle class allegedly believed in ideas and reform; they applauded the new institution of higher learning of the late nineteenth century. Now, however, they were as offended by the middle class's materialistic view of the value of a college education as they were by the dominance of its social values in the society as a whole. "Going to college has come to a sort of social necessity," the acerbic H. L. Mencken wryly noted. "It almost ranks with having a bathroom and keeping a car. . . . A learned degree, once a pearl of great price, has come to have no more value or significance than the ruby-studded insignia of the Elks."[11]

College life in the 1920s reflected and nourished a desire for social status, not knowledge, in American culture in general. To its critics, this attitude was contemptible; to its proponents, it was not only respectable, it was pragmatic. Sons were sent to college to prepare for a career, but most Americans still felt that success would be determined by a student's social standing. Much of the era's rhetoric about the need for trained experts, then, seems to have fallen on deaf ears. College provided the credential to prevent a young man's fall from the middle class in an increasingly technological society; more important, it provided opportunities for the development of social skills that would enable the student to get ahead in the "real" middle-class world. This was an age in which the transmission and creation of new knowledge was seen increasingly as critical to cultural development and economic growth. Yet the American middle class stubbornly insisted on viewing college as a social opportunity rather than an intellectual experience.

Campus Activities

Activities, athletics, and fraternities took up most of the average male student's time at the American college of the 1920s. One observer estimated that the average student spent 90 percent of his time on nonacademic activities of one kind of another. He busied himself with four years of scrambling for membership in an extraordinary array of organizations and exclusive societies. At DePauw, for example, there were five honorary scholarship clubs, two student government associations, seven intercollegiate sports, two athletic associations, four journalistic enterprises, four debate clubs, twenty-two departmental clubs, five musical organizations, three other student groups, and twenty-four Greek-letter fraternities for 1,500 students, well over half of whom considered themselves active in two or more activities. The pressure to take part and fit in was intense; a Columbia University dean announced that he would refuse to recommend a student for a business position if he chose not to wear his freshman cap. Participation established a student's social contacts. As a mythical senior remarked in a Pomona College brochure, "College is a great opportunity for a man to round out his personality, and to develop the ability to meet other men and leave a good impression. I hate to think of saying goodbye to the old friends but I have the consolation of feeling that some day I am going to call a lot of congressmen and college presidents names that don't sound like Doctor and Honorable."[12] The typical college student aspired to be a socially acceptable "joiner" among like-minded peers.

Leadership roles in these activities were highly prized by undergraduates. At most schools, graduating seniors considered the presidency of the student council the most desirable and valuable honor; the Yale class of 1922 preferred an athletic letter instead. Conceivably, character and talent—not class—could have determined a student's election to a position of leadership on campus. Yet most such positions went to young men who came to the campus from privileged socioeconomic backgrounds; a 1924 study of Harvard showed that graduates of private preparatory schools controlled extracurricular activities "with hardly a single exception."[13] Many students from less privileged backgrounds gained entrance to higher social circles by virtue of their personality, but despite the talk about how democratic these groups were, such students were the exceptions rather than the rule.

Athletics played a most prominent role on the college campus of the 1920s. A football victory set an optimistic tone at many schools in the interwar period. Furthermore, a successful sports program raised the visibility of an institution: it provided a means of entertainment and identification for the local community—and that community could include an entire state—as well as for a college's alumni and students. In the eyes of most people, students and others alike, the stadium was the most important building on campus, and the achievements of a school's athletes there overshadowed the achievements of faculty and students in the laboratory or in the classroom. "Membership in the varsity football team represents the peak of undergraduate attainment," an editorial in the *New York Herald Tribune* (and reprinted in the *Harvard Crimson*) observed in the fall of 1929, "and from that the scale of values grades down through the lesser sports, through the glee and mandolin clubs, the dramatic society and comic weekly to the bottom of scholastic excellence."

The great emphasis placed on football and school spirit thrust football stars into the spotlight. This trend aided lower-class students who were brought to prestigious schools to play on intercollegiate teams, and who then took advantage of their expertise and fame to gain acceptance in formerly exclusive upper-middle-class environs.[14] Then as today, the popularity of college football on and off the campus enabled some athletes to pursue opportunities for mobility. But its most important function was to provide a symbol for college life. The very magnitude of its presence above all suggested that the modern conception of the all-inclusive college went beyond even marginal intellectual boundaries to meet the demand for mass entertainment by students and other nonacademic constituencies. How American could the college be without an American game as the center of attention?

Fraternities became the focal points of social life at most American institutions of higher learning in the 1920s. The total number of fraternity houses in the nation increased from 774 in 1920 to 1,874 in 1929. Nearly half of the students at most large state universities belonged to a fraternity by the end of the decade. Soon after they arrived on campus, freshmen were thrown into the complex mating ritual called "rushing," whereby they were urged to visit several fraternity houses and the members carefully looked them over. A graduating speaker for the class of 1922 at Massachusetts Agricultural College recalled that a student's choice of a fraternity his first month in college constituted the most significant event of his college years: "Now he is on the way to social prominence. He at last comes to realize the real meaning of a college education."[15] Learning the importance of congeniality, the Horatio Algers of the American college of the 1920s worked their way up the social ladder from pledge to brother.

Fraternities were not just glorified dormitories where like-minded upper-middle-class students caroused during the Roaring Twenties. Critics believed fraternities reinforced invidious class distinctions on college campuses across the country. As early as 1909 the Wisconsin state legislature asked the Regents of the University of Wisconsin to investigate charges that the fraternities there were undemocratic; such attacks on the fraternity system accelerated as they gained in numbers and influence. Fraternities were accused of being hotbeds of snobbery and politics, but little was done to curb their control of campus social life. The fees charged by the so-called better fraternities were out of the reach of poorer students, and Jewish or other ethnic students were not invited to join in any case. Jewish students were forced to petition college administrations for the right to found their own fraternities because they were not accepted by existent organizations. At some schools, gentile fraternities refused to compete against Jewish groups in intramural competition. The 1935 Survey of Social Life at Dartmouth, for example, comfirmed that discrimination in fraternity pledging was the rule rather than the exception. "There's no sense in taking men who wouldn't be happy with us and with whom we wouldn't be happy, is there?" commented a character in a college novel by George Weller.[16]

Amidst the activities and fraternities, one type of student was bound to be unhappy—the serious student. Even during a time of rapid technological change, the hard-working "grind" was a target of derision. "I know of no college where high scholarship in and of itself . . . commands great social prestige," John P. Gavit reported after visiting nearly all of the country's best schools in the mid-1920s. Urging educators and parents to remember the fine quiet student, he noted that most graduates who had been elected to Phi Beta Kappa "look back upon their college life with memories of poverty [and] isolation." Camaraderie, not book learning, was the ideal, even at prestigious institutions; at Princeton, James Wechsler reported, a "lust for learning never seriously affected any more than a minute segment of the community." "It may seem an anomalous thing to say," wrote the Harvard dean of freshmen in the *Atlantic Monthly*, but the true scholar, along with the adventurers, the artisans, and the artists, in his view, were swamped by those who attended college for social and practical reasons. He might have added the political-minded student to his list. Such organizations as the Intercollegiate Liberal League and such publications as *The New Student* fought social and political "normalcy," but to no avail; as one Yale student conceded to Wechsler, "It is alarming to watch the spread of soundness in our universities." Most tragic of all was a wave of twenty-six student suicides during the first six months of 1927, blamed on the alienation of bright and serious young people from their so-called academic environment.[17]

Most students adapted to the rules of the social game. Despite their indulgence in dancing and drinking, as one well-known rabbi observed, the iconoclasm of the young had been overplayed, for there was "no more conservative, stand-pat young man in the world than the raccoon-coated 'homo sapiens' on the American campus." Looking back, two elder professors also felt that students had been far more individualistic before the advent of mass higher education: "Students today are much more alike than they were. . . . They wear the same kind of caps, the same cut of trousers, the same variety of 'slickers' and coonskin overcoats—they talk the same slang and have much the same easy air of knowing the world. You may tell a collegian today whenever you meet him."[18] That collegian was a friendly, fashionable fellow—the idol of America's first consumer age.

Preoccupied as they were by economic security and social status, parents, students, and alumni supported a college culture that prepared students for corporate and suburban life. Even the president of the Swarthmore Alumni Association took Frank Aydelotte and his honors program to task for emphasizing academics at the expense of athletic experiences, which were—and still often are—widely believed to develop the qualities that lead to business success. "The standard of student prominence is not scholarship at all," wrote a philosophy professor, "but heroism on the gridiron, social leadership, or the attractive traits of the good fellow, traits, strange to say, that the world, too, will prize in the student's life beyond the college walls." In American colleges, Upton Sinclair remarked trenchantly, students above all "learn the American religion—what William James calls 'the worship of the bitch-goddess success.' "[19]

The American college student's lifestyle in the 1920s suggests the emergence of the other-directed, peer-oriented personality.[20] Unprecedented opportunities for autonomous behavior presented themselves on postwar college campuses, with their larger and more heterogeneous student bodies and their varied curricula. But to the American college student of the 1920s, success was the end-all and be-all of existence, and success was dependent on conformity to narrowly defined patterns of status-seeking behavior. This might have been a double-edged sword: after all, participation in campus activities could have constituted a means of self-expression as well as a capitulation to peer pressure. But, while the culture of aspiration attracted nearly all students, its symbol came in only one model package: the male WASP student.

Women on Campus

Women have been absent from this book for good reason: they were excluded from the occupational opportunities that stimulated the rise of American higher education after World War I. Conventional American ideas about an appropriate sexual division of labor found ready acceptance in the nation's colleges and universities; indeed, as practical functions were added to the university's agenda and enrollment grew, educators enthusiastically applauded a trend toward what might be called the masculinization of American higher education. Between 1890 and 1910, as the rate of increase in enrollment rose twice as much among women as among men, male administrators feared for the future of the American college. If women continued to constitute too large a proportion of the student body, they argued, neither financial support not public acceptance would be forthcoming. Wishing to exercise influence in modern society, male educators discouraged any behavior that did not suggest the virility of the college or of its graduates.

As a result, nearly all coeducational institutions were paranoid about their public image. Despite—or because of—their exemplary academic performance, women at the University of Chicago fought a losing battle against the segregation of women students; even though women constituted approximately half of the student body there in the first decade of the twentieth century, the university administration asserted that the only alternative was their complete elimination from the school. Confronted by the academic superiority of its women students, Stanford soon imposed a strict quota on female admissions. When so many male undergraduates at the College of the Pacific enlisted in the war effort, for example, its administrators feared the college was in imminent danger of becoming a female seminary; faced with such an "unwelcome distinction," its president worked hard to get a SATC unit formed at the school specifically to keep it open and male.[21] In this male-dominated society, the university expanded, but women's role in it was sharply limited.

The segregation of women quickly became a self-fulfilling prophecy. Although their academic achievements justified an increase in their options, as American higher education moved into the mainstream of economic and professional life, women were pushed farther off the critical fields of endeavor and onto the sidelines. The proportion of women at coeducational institutions increased from 31.7 percent to 35.6 percent between 1890 and 1915, yet female educators conceded (to the satisfaction of male educators) that Americans were less wholeheartedly committed to higher education for young women than for men. Beginning after World War I, but accelerating in the mid-1920s, perceived institutional and professional self-interest led to a sharp decline in female attendance at professional and graduate schools, as well as quotas at most coeducational colleges, reversing decades of coeducational and professional opportunity, limited though it was.[22]

Ambitious young women were steered toward "women's work": the less prestigious branches of the arts and sciences. In *Women Scientists in America: Struggles and Strategies to 1940*, Margaret Rossiter chronicles this self-conscious process in painstaking detail. First there had to be a shortage of men in the field, since women would not be appointed to any job a man would want. Then the discipline had to be defined in light of its so-called feminine qualities. Consequently, for example, women microbiologists found themselves confined to research in newly created departments of home economics or government departments of agriculture, when they were sponsored at all. Promotions and pay equity were rare at best.[23]

Still, despite the obvious discrimination, most women were complacent. Marion Talbot, leading female educator observed in 1910, "While the intellectual life of men has become greatly varied, the intellectual life of women continues to be patterned after the same mold, and their leaders are timorous about making a change." Increasing numbers of women went to college between the world wars—female enrollment more than doubled to about 600,000 by 1940—but the proportion of women in college declined from nearly half of the undergraduate population to 40 percent. And more and more of them studied only the subjects carefully prescribed for them. Prejudice kept them out of the professional schools and the professions; quotas on female admissions were common at most coeducational institutions, implicitly at public schools and merely quietly at private ones. Of course, Jewish and black women faced additional barriers. The Intercollegiate Bureau of Occupations, a placement bureau for women college graduates, went out of business in 1919. Female students were counseled to prepare themselves for marriage and, as a temporary goal, perhaps teaching, social work, or librarianship.[24]

Even if the record showed—as it generally did—that female students were more serious than their male peers, concerned educators were pressed to defend a young woman's right to an education. After all, it was widely held, while men's futures depended on their attainment of a college education, women only went to college because they enjoyed learning. Questions were raised once again about whether higher education could injure its female students. Stanford's David Starr Jordan, in a *defense* of coeducation published shortly before his school imposed a quota on the number of women students, insisted, "There is not the slightest evidence that highly educated women are necessarily rendered sterile or celibate by their education." After the issues of sex and marriage were settled, many supporters of women's higher education still had to contend with claims that education lessened a woman's desirability. A Smith College student complained in the *Harvard Crimson* that "hitherto we have not been accorded the respect the debutante inspires." "I am going to make a rash generalization," asserted William Allen Neilsen, president of Smith. "No girl endagers her social status or her chances to marry by going to college."[25] Whatever interest there might have been in teaching the best students, the desperate tone of Neilsen's remarks pointed up the potency of existent social mores.

In the 1920s, the emphasis on practical higher education sharpened the lines between those who favored and those who were opposed to the idea of separate spheres for men and women. Most educators and parents agreed that professional-oriented undergraduate education for women was inefficient because it prepared female students for inappropriate occupations. Women's colleges in particular faced a dilemma: should they help their students to gain access to the professions or encourage them to devote their lives to the roles of wife and mother? The *Smith College Weekly* in 1919 disputed the assumption that it was "fixed in the nature of things that a woman must choose between a home and work": it added, "there must be a way out, and it is the problem of our generation to find the way." But if these women were ambivalent, most other women students, as well as the public, believed there was no doubt which goal was more important.[26] Education with a material rather than a cultural motive was accepted only for men. Even if educated, the woman belonged in the home.

For middle-class and lower-middle-class Americans, the decision to send their sons and not their daughters to college was an equally clear-cut choice. As the sociologist Robert Angell observed in 1928, "Parents would be more willing to send a boy to a university to earn his way than a girl, not only because of the feeling that the female is the weaker sex but also because a college career is considered much less essential to a girl's happiness in life and therefore not to be undertaken in the face of hardships." When the Depression added more hardships, female attendance dropped 9.5 percent while male attendance fell only 7.5 percent.[27] The patronizing, if not antagonistic, attitudes of ambitious male educators reflected the normative sexual stereotypes of the 1920s. But more than that, they recreated and strengthened traditional sexual social patterns as part of their aggressive efforts to seek new and modern functions for their institutions.

Family Background

A young man's socioeconomic background largely determined his expectations of college attendance in the 1920s and 1930s. In Middletown, the Lynds found that a family's financial status was "potent among the determining factors" that led to enrollment. A 1927 survey showed that the median parental income of college students' families was substantially higher than the national average. The patterns of educational expectation found by W. Lloyd Warner and his colleagues in Hometown and Yankee City were typical of those reported by researchers between the wars: upper-middle- and lower-upper-class young people planned to go to college at rates about twice as high as their lower-middle-class peers and more than three times higher than lower-class students. Similarly, a study of Milwaukee public high school graduates in the late 1930s revealed that the gap between college-going rates among students from different economic classes was not narrowed during the Depression: whereas 100 percent of those from families with an income level of $8,000 or above went to college, only 44 percent of the high school graduates from families with incomes of from $2,000 to $2,999 and only 26 percent of those from families with incomes of from $1,000 to $1,499 did so.[28] While these figures suggest that more young people of all classes were going to college between the two world wars, they also indicate that the bulk of those who participated in the unprecedented enrollment boom following World War I came from middle- and upper-middle-class families.

An upper-middle-class young man, probably the son of a moderately successful businessman or professional, was perhaps more than twice as likely to attend college as the son of a semiskilled machinist in the 1920s, and perhaps as much as ten times more likely to attend college during the Depression. Even more important, the proportion of middle-class students who went on to college was still far greater than that of equally talented lower-class students. By the late 1930s, the increasing disparity in educational opportunity became a subject of great concern. "While nearly all the high school seniors believed in the democratic idea of equality of opportunity for all, the results belie this idea," reported one social scientist. "The poor boy does not have equal opportunity to attend college and compete on equal terms later." Consequently, much of the enrollment boom in the interwar period can be attributed to a rise in the number of mediocre middle-class young people attending college.[29] Rhetoric about the democratic nature of the collegiate student body before World War II appears self-serving at best and deliberately manipulative at worst, since a young person's opportunity to attend college and take advantage of the economic and social possibilities it offered was often based not on merit but on his parents' ability to pay for this privilege.

Furthermore, the higher the prestige of an institution, the greater the overrepresentation of students from more privileged socioeconomic backgrounds. To determine overrepresentation, experts divided the proportion of students of a defined background by the representation of that group in the relevant census population. The first such study was O. E. Reynolds' investigation of the economic and social backgrounds of students, completed in 1924 and published in 1927. Table 3 shows that the proportion of sons of proprietors, professionals, and farm operators who attended prestigious state universities and private colleges and universities was significantly greater than their proportion of the public high school enrollment of the day. Further analysis also demonstrates that the proportion of upper-middle-class students was even greater at men's colleges than at private colleges and universities generally; 32.76 percent and 22.24 percent of the students at men's colleges were the sons of proprietors and professionals, respectively.[30]

Similarly, a decade later, Walter J. Greenleaf compared the data on the living fathers of college men with 1930 census data and found that businessmen's and professionals' children were overrepresented by three times while the proportion of manufacturing workers' children in college was less than half that of manufacturing workers among men over the age of thirty-five in the work force. Agricultural and other non-white-collar workers' children were also underrepresented in America's best colleges.[31]

The overrepresentation of upper-middle-class children at the nation's most renowned private liberal arts colleges was unmistakable during the 1920s and 1930s. In a 1931 article in the Harvard alumni magazine, an anonymous graduate criticized his alma mater for matriculating a caste of young men of moderate or more than moderate wealth; indeed, about two-thirds of Harvard's 1923–24 freshman class had fathers who were proprietors or professionals, a figure twice as high as Reynolds' for men's colleges in general. Although Amherst's president interpreted the data as indicating "a rather healthy and diversified condition of student origins," approximately 60 percent of the Amherst student body in the late 1920s were the sons of businessmen and professionals. At Carleton, about half of the student body in the period just before World War I came from businessmen's homes; by the late 1920s, about 85 percent did.[32]

Table 3. Percentage of students enrolled in public and private high schools, junior colleges, and colleges and universities, 1923–24, by father's occupation

Father's occupation	High schools		Junior colleges		State universities	Private colleges and universities
	Public	Private	Public	Private		
Proprietor	19.8%	42.7%	19.1%	29.5%	24.4%	26.0%
Professional	9.4	31.0	14.0	15.3	15.1	20.9
Manager	16.5	11.5	16.3	9.4	10.9	9.0
Salesman	9.5	9.0	9.3	6.9	6.9	7.0
Clerical worker	5.8	2.1	3.8	1.1	1.4	2.5
Farm operator	2.4	0.7	14.2	26.9	26.8	20.8
Artisan	4.2	1.3	2.8	1.7	1.1	1.4
Manual laborer	29.1	0.3	15.6	6.7	11.3	10.9
Unknown	3.3	1.4	4.9	2.4	2.1	1.5
All occupations	100.0%	100.0%	100.0%	99.9%	100.0%	100.0%

Source: O. E. Reynolds, *The Social and Economic Status of College Students* (New York, 1927), pp. 12, 14.

The predominance of the upper middle class at Dartmouth was well documented. In the class of 1913, there were 25 sons of farmers, 26 sons of artisans, 17 sons of doctors, 29 sons of manufacturers, and 16 sons of engineers; in the class of 1930—Nelson Rockefeller's class—there were but 12 farmers' sons and 27 artisans' sons, while the number of sons of doctors, manufacturers, and engineers climbed to 39, 57, and 27, respectively. This dramatic increase in the number of sons of businessmen, lawyers, physicians, and engineers continued throughout the 1930s while the number of sons of farmers, artisans, educators, and clerks declined. The class of 1939 included 655 students, 423 of whom were the sons of businessmen, 60 the sons of lawyers, and 56 the sons of doctors—over 82 percent of the class came from these three privileged groups alone. Looking back, Dartmouth professor Herbert D. Foster recalled that there had been very few students of any means in his class of 1885; in the 1920s, he found the student body "far more well-bred" but not so intelligent.[33] As the next chapter will show, highly regarded private liberal arts colleges took advantage of the upper-middle-class rush to the campus to draw well-heeled students from around the country. These personable and comfortable young men often replaced poorer local students.

State universities had more diverse student bodies than the prestigious private liberal arts colleges, but even there the children of the upper middle and middle class predominated, particularly in states without a strong tradition of private higher education. In the mid-1920s there was one student with a professional father at the University of Minnesota for every 21 professionals in the state of Minnesota, while there was only one child of a clerical worker for every 185 clerical workers and only one laborer's child for every 1,583 laborers in the state. A 1940 study at Kansas University produced similar results: the index of representation—defined as the proportion of fathers in the student body divided by the proportion of male employed workers over forty-five years of age in the Kansas labor force—was 3.20 for professionals' children and 2.55 for proprietors' children, but only 1.29, 0.78, and 0.16 for the children of clerical, skilled, and unskilled workers, respectively.[34] Though the state universities permitted greater access to higher education, the children from less privileged socioeconomic backgrounds were still terribly underrepresented there.

By the late 1920s, as the number of farm families declined and farm prosperity ended, urban youngsters dominated the state universities.

As the proportion of children of farmers and unskilled workers declined at the University of Illinois between the two world wars, the proportion of children of businessmen, scientific professionals, government workers, and skilled laborers increased. A 1938 study at Indiana University revealed that only one-eighth of its students hailed from farms and over half came from the state's metropolitan areas. A *Boston Globe* reporter who covered the opening of the school year at Massachusetts Agricultural College in the fall of 1930 discovered that half of the largest freshman class in the college's history came from metropolitan Boston, nearly one hundred miles away from rural Amherst. "Somebody has told them that behind its 'hick' name, Aggie offers as strong courses in chemistry and economics, in landscape architecture and in the sciences required for medical school as anyone needs," he observed. "Most of these freshmen would laugh at the idea of raising cows or chickens. They come for chemistry and commerce." Yet the image of the state university as a stepping-stone primarily for rural young people died hard in people's minds.[35]

As better-off children went to more expensive and more prestigious private colleges, public institutions, particularly in states with a strong private sector, attracted significant numbers of the children of teachers, storekeepers, and skilled workers seeking training in the burgeoning while-collar, middle-class occupations. The *Boston Globe* reporter observed—as did the annual reports of the presidents of the Massachusetts Agricultural College in the 1920s and 1930s— that a majority of the students were working their way through college. Tuition there was $60 a year when the nearby prestigious colleges were charging $400. "Had there been more money at home," he conceded, "they might have gone to Harvard or to Boston University." During the 1920s and 1930s, with but few exceptions, the rivalry between the private and public sectors for the children of the upper middle class ended.

Large urban universities also came to reflect much of the diversity of their locales. These schools lost their traditional upper-middle-class clientele to the prestigious liberal arts colleges. About one-third of the University of Pittsburgh's students in 1925–26 had foreign-born parents; only 7 percent had professional fathers and about two of every five students' fathers were skilled or unskilled laborers. Public urban institutions included even greater proportions of ambitious lower-middle- and lower-class students. At the College of the City of New York in 1934, while less than 4 percent of the students' fathers were lawyers, doctors, dentists, and teachers and about 5 percent were manufacturers, one of four students' fathers was a factory worker and an additional one of five was a tailor.[36]

Young people with college-educated fathers were the most likely to attend college, and the overrepresentation of this group at prestigious institutions actually increased in the 1920s and 1930s. In the early 1920s, Reynolds found that over one-quarter of the students at men's colleges and about 10 percent of those at state universities had fathers who had graduated from college at a time when only about 2 percent of their age cohort had done so. At the University of Chicago, 18.6 percent of the entering class of 1924 had college-graduate fathers; the figure increased to 23.6 percent by the class of 1931; and in the fall of 1938, nearly one-third of the entering class had college-graduate fathers. Similarly, the proportion of college-graduate fathers rose from about one-fifth of the class of 1915 to one-third of the class of 1932 at Dartmouth. By the mid-1930s, since the proportion of students with college-educated fathers at the public universities remained fairly constant, the private liberal arts colleges had over twice the proportion of college-graduate fathers as their public counterparts did. A 1952 study of the demographic backgrounds of college graduates of the first half of the twentieth century concluded aptly, "Of all the people who want their children to attend college, the college graduates seem to want it the most—and to be best able to afford it."[37]

Pricing policies exacerbated these trends. Tuition was perhaps the most flexible source of revenue for a private college, and most schools took advantage of the enrollment boom to increase their fees. Market forces permitted the most prestigious schools to raise their prices even faster than the others. By the mid-1920s, without significant institutional financial assistance programs and in the absence of government support, less privileged students found it more and more difficult to attend the more prestigious liberal arts colleges. The median tuition fee at twenty Methodist colleges, for example, absorbed just 6.3 percent of the annual earnings of a middle-class family during the war-torn 1918 term, but by 1926 tuition swallowed up over 10 percent of its income. While only 8 percent of the college students in the entire country had family incomes of $10,000 or more, even given their privileged backgrounds, over two-thirds of Williams College's and nearly one-half of Yale's student body came from such upper-middle-class homes. Only 40 percent of the students at the University of Chicago in the late 1920s earned any portion of their way through college; at the Massachusetts Agricultural College at the same time, nearly 80 percent did so.[38] The need for some students to work their way through college sharpened class distinctions on the campus, since the working student had less time and money to devote to fraternity and other activities to raise his social standing.

Every segment of American society participated in the enrollment boom between the two world wars, but the bulk of the increase in attendance in the 1920s and 1930s was attributable to young men from better-off and nonethnic homes. Despite the growth of public and urban institutions and the subsequent achievements of their graduates, their well-deserved reputation as "Harvards of the proletariat" constituted a pyrrhic victory of social democracy. Indeed, the democratization of American higher education was made possible, in part, by the flight of the upper middle class to the more expensive and so-called selective liberal arts colleges.

The Myth of Democratic Education

Between the two world wars, institutions became differentiated in accordance with the socioeconomic backgrounds of the students they attracted. Institutions that were essentially similar on the eve of World War I attracted rather different student bodies by the end of the 1920s. The higher the status of an institution, the more it drew its student body from privileged classes in American society; indeed, an institution's public and self-image was dependent on its ability to attract, if not restrict its student body to, members of the upper middle and upper classes. The children of college-educated and financially comfortable fathers were dramatically overrepresented at the so-called flagship public institutions as well. The children of the upper middle and upper classes, those already at the upper reaches of American society, had an unmistakable advantage in college-going in the 1920s even if they had less ability than their less privileged peers. Once in college, there was further discrimination on the basis of socioeconomic background in the selection of student leaders and fraternity brothers. During America's first era of mass higher education, during a time when college attendance first became a critical criterion of economic and social mobility, equality of opportunity remained an elusive, if not ignored, ideal. But then, as Raymond

Hawes observed in 1930, "college life is no more and no less democratic than life in any other American community."[39]

That American higher education reflected the shortcomings of its host society cannot diminish its successes. The value of higher education lay as much in its symbolism as in its specific content; nearly all parents, including many lower-middle-class immigrants, inculcated in their children an intense desire for higher education as a badge of economic and social status. Given a helpful push by a high school teacher or coach, many poor students did go to college somewhere, perhaps with one of the few scholarships provided by private liberal arts colleges, where they prepared themselves for a professional career, learned preferred social skills, and maybe even married above themselves. This was the other side of college life, where students missed meals to conserve their financial resources as they struggled to fulfill their families' and their own ambitions to become professionals. Attendance even at a low-prestige, access-oriented institution, such as an urban denominational school or rural teachers' college, suggested to these students a possible end run around the social establishment to a career and adult success.[40]

Economic and social changes caused "the man who worked his way through college" to supplant "the self-made man" as an ideal type in the 1920s. This new social idol had all the traditional virtues—determination, honesty, and the like—but was clothed in a football uniform. A Boston newspaper columnist applauded the efforts of mothers who "with clear vision . . . saw that America could reach her greatest glory only when her boys and girls were trained to be broad-minded, honorable citizens." Encouraged by his family, this self-supporting college student was hard-working, intelligent, and amiable, not all that different, of course, from the self-image of the predominantly middle-class clientele of American colleges and universities of the 1920s. Unfortunately, while college presidents and students liked to characterize the typical American college student as poor, serious, and democratic in spirit, few actually were.[41]

"Even at the zenith of its growth, higher education in the United States was restricted to a definite segment of the population—the middle class and its immediate satellites," the radical student leader James Wechsler observed in 1935. "The favorite illusion of our democracy, that the workingman's son goes to college with the youthful Du Ponts, has long been exploded." Workers' children did not comprise much of the nation's student body; rather, those who did swell the college ranks in the 1920s were "the offspring of Babbitt, the sons of small businessmen, shop-keepers, life-insurance dealers, and the like."[42] The evidence—if not the official rhetoric—confirms this view. The enrollment boom was fueled by the desire to keep up with the Joneses in educational attainment among already privileged families. While the colleges' growth raised the possibility of enhancing the intellectual level of professional, business, and cultural discourse in the society, certainly a function of the institution of higher learning in a technological age, parents and students viewed college as a social experience. Students devoted their attention to maintaining an unoriginal campus life, a replica of their parents' middle-brow world, with but a dash of youthful energy and pranks.

Modern America's rush to the colleges manifested both its faith in and its ambivalence about the culture of aspiration. Since the early decades of the twentieth century, higher education has evoked the democratic promise among all segments of the American people. During the decade following World War I, the provision of a college education for one's son "became a normal duty for all middle class parents" and, much to the surprise of a British educator, even an "attainable ambition of the working classes." The United States, with three times the total population of Great Britain, had twenty times more university students; even as enrollment in institutions of higher education in France and Germany doubled in the 1920s, the proportion of American youth in college was more than three times greater than in either European country.[43] As disdainful as its class, sexual, and racial biases were, its inclusiveness was nothing less than remarkable. Yet between the two world wars, particularly at the most prestigious colleges and universities, enrollment was restricted to the upper middle class. More often than not, less privileged Americans who had only their intellectual aptitude and social ambition to offer had to wait their turn. Upper-middle-class Americans, idealistic and reform-minded though they could be, first took care of their own children.

7 / Discrimination in College Admissions

In the decade following World War I, a relatively small but critical number of liberal arts colleges enjoyed the luxury of selecting their student bodies for the first time. During this period of unprecedented enrollment expansion, they chose to limit the size of their classes and to seek a national and upper-middle-class student body at the expense of local and more diverse students. New admissions procedures were instituted to select those young people whose backgrounds suggested they should appropriately assume positions of leadership in American society after graduation. Despite the increasing heterogeneity of the American population, the growing importance of education and training in the economic structure of the country, and the emergence of the college student as a cultural ideal, these schools sought deliberately to become bastions of the Protestant upper middle class and to confine their student bodies to young men from socially desirable socioeconomic backgrounds.

Racial and ethnic bias flourished in the American college of the 1920s and 1930s. Restrictive admissions policies could have dictated the selection of students on the basis of their intellectual potential alone, but social class rather than achievement was central to the selection of democratic America's elite college students between the two world wars. Faced with the self-consciously determined opportunity and challenge to prepare a generation of leaders for a technological age, college officials and alumni—predominantly white Anglos-Saxon Protestant (WASP) and often anxious about the loss of status and power of "native" American stock in American society in general—created the model student in their own image. The object of these colleges' affection was the son of the WASP businessman or professional, the alleged twentieth-century spiritual heir to New England ministers' and farmers' sons. The target of these colleges' attention was the son of Eastern European immigrants, and the Russian Jewish student in particular, who was not considered worthy of the economic and social privileges to which his college degree would have entitled him.

Restrictive admissions quotas were developed to solve what was described often as "the Jewish problem."[1] Although Catholic and black applicants also faced discrimination, their numbers were too small to command the attention focused on Jewish students. Surely, anti-Semitism was rampant among the WASP upper middle class and its allies, including many German Jewish Americans. But the establishment of these quotas at the nation's best colleges was more than merely a case of anti-Semitism. Larger questions were at issue: Should America's elite be larger and more heterogeneous than it had been before? Should America's private elite colleges be responsive to democratic ideals in student selection? In the 1920s and 1930s, American higher education witnessed the emergence of the national elite liberal arts college, but it was a selective institution rooted in class and ethnic prejudice, not talent. Let us focus on the development of selective and restrictive admissions procedures at Dartmouth College, perhaps the nation's most popular school in the 1920s.

The Selection Process at the Small Liberal Arts College

Before World War I, institutions of higher learning matriculated essentially all interested young people. A potential student's parents or principal—or, more commonly, his headmaster—simply wrote the president or dean of a college about the student; the boy arrived at the college in September, took the school's entrance examination, and enrolled. The student inquired about only one college; there was no admissions office, no formal application process. As late as the second decade of the twentieth century, all American colleges were still seeking as many students as they could persuade to come, whatever their academic qualifications. The movement toward higher standards in admissions had only just begun at even the so-called best institutions on the eve of the war. In 1911, the founder of Oregon's Reed College studied the number of conditional students—students permitted to enroll with high school records that did not meet the formal entrance requirements—admitted to Harvard, Yale, and other schools and commented, "Oh, spirit of democracy, what scrambles for numbers and fees are performed in thy name." President James R. Angell of Yale later conceded, "The early university seems to have taught any one who appeared and could pay the necessary fee."[2]

By the end of the war, with the improvement in national transportation networks and the growth of the prosperous, mobile, and education-oriented upper middle class, the best American schools could engage realistically in a nationwide search for the most talented and socially desirable young men. Institutions that had formerly operated in similar but separate spheres now recruited students at the same rapidly expanding high schools of the country's metropolitan areas. "In no other civilized country do institutions of higher learning compete for students. Nowhere else are the allurements and advantages of the colleges' training so advertised," observed a 1911 Carnegie Foundation report. "College education in America is a commodity that is sold somewhat after the manner of life insurance and patent medicine."[3] Though their efforts were limited to New England and the Middle Atlantic states, officials of Dartmouth began to show lantern slides of life there at high school assemblies in 1915. Like those of other schools, Dartmouth's trustees and faculty reaffirmed their support for the "natural" enrollment growth of the college by liberalizing admissions requirements to attract students from the West as well as from the public high schools of the nascent eastern and midwestern suburbs.[4] The competition became fierce to convince young men not only of the value of college attendance generally but also of the special virtues of an individual school.

The rush to the colleges surprised even the most optimistic of educators. At Dartmouth, although the freshman class of 1918–19 had included fewer than 400 students, 698 young men were accepted to begin college in the fall of 1919—and Dartmouth officials were pleasantly shocked to find themselves rejecting 100 qualified applicants for fear of overcrowding. Within two years, Dartmouth became so popular that its acceptance list was completed in early February, and only half of the applicant pool was admitted. Faced with this unprecedented abundance of qualified potential students, Dartmouth officials realized that an alternative to the "first come, first served" admissions process had to be found. President Ernest M. Hopkins hired Dartmouth's first dean of admissions, E. G. Bill, and worked closely with him to develop one of the nation's first comprehensive selective admissions plans.[5]

Still, few institutions were overwhelmed by the growing interest in higher education in the early 1920s. A 1920 survey of forty of the most renowned colleges and universities showed that only thirteen of them were actually turning away any applicants at all: Dartmouth refused the most (1,600), Princeton was second (1,500), and Pennsylvania was third (750). Harvard rejected only 229 applicants, and Yale accepted all of the young men who fulfilled its entrance requirements. After years of deliberating whether to increase the size of the college or not, the Princeton trustees voted to limit enrollment to the approximately 2,000 students that could fit into the dormitories and eat in the dining halls, but other prestigious institutions were not yet fortunate enough to have this choice. At the University of Chicago, for example, a 1920 faculty committee refused to recommend an enrollment ceiling; it was not until 1923 that Chicago's president could report that an "increase in numbers was a matter of keen interest for many years, but has been decreasingly so for half a decade at least. We have now reached the point when it may properly sink into insignificance and be almost forgotten in comparison with our concern for the quality of our work."[6]

Less prestigious schools had no reason to alter their procedures. Only a few institutions were forced to turn away students because of a lack of facilities. A survey of Methodist colleges at the end of the 1920s pointed out that a student could show up two weeks after the semester began and still be admitted to most institutions. Further, the registrar alone passed judgment on an applicant's qualifications in two of every three of the schools studied; only twenty-five of the thirty-five schools required the filing of a formal application and even fewer requested a personal recommendation, an interview, or an intelligence test score.[7] The lack of admissions standards and formal selection procedures was common at all but a handful of schools between the two world wars.

Yet in the 1920s, several American colleges did choose not to pursue a policy of indefinite expansion and to seek instead the development of a small, carefully selected student body. The opportunity to select and limit students raised the possibility of an intellectual renaissance at many colleges. Frank Aydelotte took over the reins of Swarthmore College in 1921 hoping to attract a small group of highly motivated students and to provide them with a suitable academic environment. Insisting that "quality rather than quantity is the great need of education today," he urged successfully the creation of complementary selective admissions and honors programs. In 1922–23, 800 students applied for the 170 places in Swarthmore's freshman class; in 1926–27, just under 1,500 applied for 150 spots. To Aydelotte, the clearest sign of educational progress was that Swarthmore could point with pride "to the multitude that we turn away."[8] Though the number of such schools was insignificant in comparison with the panoply of American institutions of higher education, their influence was great.

As at other institutions, the decision to pursue a policy of selection and limitation was unprecedented at Dartmouth. In October 1919, a faculty committee on admissions proposed that admissions standards be raised to alleviate the problems caused by the sharp increase in qualified applicants, but the committee also favored expanding Dartmouth's facilities and faculty so that any interested young man who could meet the new standards would be able to enroll. The trustees rejected the latter recommendation and discussed the possibility of limiting enrollment. Hopkins convinced the majority that the number of interested and qualified applicants would probably continue to run well above the 500 young men the college could admit. The elder statesman of the board was pleasantly skeptical about the rapid turn of events since the end of the war; Hopkins recalled his reaction some years later:

> When I got done, Mr. Streeter leaned over and said very seriously and without the slightest intention of being humorous, "Mr. President, do I understand rightly that you seriously propose sometime in the future to decline the application of somebody who really wants to enter Dartmouth? . . . Well, now I guess this is all right and I'll probably vote for it, but, by God, I've got to have a little time on it after forty years of watching Dartmouth grab and hogtie every prospect that wandered inadvertently into town with a hazy idea of sometime going to college somewhere."[9]

Mr. Streeter's shock was understandable.

The Dartmouth trustees voted to limit admissions without conditions to those applicants in the top third of their high school class, but a faculty committee soon found it necessary to revise the plan to limit admission to those students in the top quarter of their class. At the time, the trustees did not believe that raising admissions standards would necessarily limit enrollment. But within two years, in 1921, the trustees decided to take further action to limit the size of the college and set attendance ceilings of 2,000 for the entire school and of 550 to 650 for each freshman class.[10] The opportunity to select and limit the size and composition of Dartmouth was welcome; though it ran counter to the value placed on expansion and growth in American economic life, it augured well for the future prestige of the college.

Hopkins' call for an "artistocracy of brains" in September 1922 became the most widely read statement about the advantages of selection and limitation of its time. He asserted that attendance at college was a privilege, not a right, and that college administrators had the responsibility to take great pains to determine just what young people were most deserving of its opportunities. "It would be imcompatible with all the conceptions of democracy to assume that the privilege of higher education should be restricted to any class defined by the accident of birth or by the fortuitous circumstance of possession of wealth," Hopkins declared, "but there is such a thing as an aristocracy of brains, to whom increasingly the opportunities of higher education ought to be restricted." Only then would higher education enhance excellence in American society.[11]

Hopkins' goal—and it certainly was an ideal of many other progressive educators—was to provide a valuable intellectual and social experience in a small community for those young people most capable of exercising leadership in society. He believed that economic and social progress was dependent upon the efficient use of the best young men democracy could produce, and he pledged to find those few talented future leaders, "whether these brains be found in the coal pit, on the farm, in the industrial plant, or among the professions."[12] He hoped his new selective admissions plan could bring such a student body together in rural New Hampshire.

Although Columbia University appears to have been the nation's first institution to use a formal application form, Dartmouth was the first to establish a comprehensive selective admissions process. Hopkins' plan was designed to pick a student body that consisted of intellectual-oriented and yet well-rounded students from diverse socioeconomic and geographical backgrounds. He listed nine elements or principles of the process:

1. *Exceptional Scholarship,* which shall be considered sufficient basis for selection.

2. *High Scholarship*, which shall be considered *prima facie* evidence in favor of selection.
3. *Personal Ratings* by school officers and others acquainted with the applicant and distinctive abilities evidenced by *School Activities* submitted by the latter.
4. *Priority of Application*.
5. *The Principle of Occupational Distribution*.
6. *The Principle of Geographical Distribution*.
7. All properly qualified *Sons of Dartmouth Alumni and Dartmouth College Officers* [shall be admitted].
8. *Low Scholarship* shall be presumptive evidence of unfitness for selection.
9. The entire class will be selected on the basis of qualifications and no one allowed to enter simply because he has secured rooming accommodations.[13]

Dartmouth's evaluation process also required a personal application—including a candidate's personal statement—and an interview. Most colleges adopted these innovations but also continued to rely on the traditional method of entrance examinations by fields well after Dartmouth began to use its more flexible applicant review system.[14] Two years in the making, the plan was put into effect in 1922. Over sixty years and many college generations later, it still summarizes the guidelines for selective admissions processes widely followed today.

The rank order of the principles of the plan suggests Hopkins' own priorities. Above all, he wanted to reward those who possessed the intellectual potential to make the best use of the college's facilities and who he hoped would then make the best use of their privileged place in American society. "It is an attempt to winnow out from among the applicants seeking admission to Dartmouth College those men of intelligence and mental power who have the greatest promise of living usefully and helpfully among their fellows in the society of their time," Hopkins told groups around the country.[15] Intellect came first, but even at the outset Hopkins recognized that he, too, had to make concessions to alumni and to other strategic interests within the college community.

The Goal of Diversity

Of greatest significance in the Dartmouth selective admissions plan was Hopkins' frank articulation of the principle of proportionate selection in college admissions. From the outset he self-consciously decided that the composition of an elite student body could be determined neither by intellect nor by socioeconomic background alone. Time and again Hopkins noted that the college's classes could be filled with the graduates of New England preparatory schools, but he wanted to reach out to a variety of occupational and geographical constituencies. No more than twenty-five students could be admitted from any one school, a decision that rankled the preparatory schools. Preference was given to residents of New Hampshire, the South, and the West in an effort to diversify the student body. Hopkins even favored assigning quotas to regional alumni groups. As he informed his friend Felix Frankfurter, Hopkins hoped this plan would enable Dartmouth to accept more students from poorer backgrounds and prevent the student body from becoming "a concentrated extract of American middle-class businessmen."[16]

Hopkins and Bill were justifiably proud of Dartmouth's success at attracting a geographically diverse student body. Of the 552 young men in the first class accepted under the new admissions process, 399 were public high school graduates and represented 323 schools. Over one-fifth of the freshman class received full scholarships. In 1917, two of every five Dartmouth students came from outside New England; by the time of World War II, nearly two of every three did. On the basis of such statistics, Dartmouth was considered one of only ten "national" colleges in a 1931 study.[17]

A close examination of the results of the Dartmouth plan, however, suggests that Hopkins' aspirations for diversity went unrealized. The plan's supporters—which included *The New York Times*—applauded the principles of occupational and geographical distribution, but other pressures compromised Hopkins' democratic-elitist ideals. Critics asserted that the plan was a subterfuge to justify the selection of alumni children and athletes, even if Hopkins' initial proposal assigned them low priority.[18] In addition, Hopkins brought alumni into the admissions process, particularly in areas away from New England, and such men were less committed to a diverse, intellectual-oriented student body than in ensuring the admission of their own children or those others with whom they closely identified.

In time even Hopkins admitted the bias toward upper-middle-class WASPs implicit in the operation of his selective admissions plan. While the number of students from the middle Atlantic and midwestern states climbed throughout the 1920s and 1930s, the evidence indicates that these students were not appreciably different from their New England peers. "We have undertaken to insure the geographical distribution, which has been likewise ours since the men born in New England have begun to emigrate into remote parts of the country and to send their sons back here to college," he explained. "Likewise, in this day of the trend toward the cities, we wish to preserve at least some semblence of the old type country boy constituency from which most of the leaders in urban centers have sprung."[19] Indeed, Hopkins hoped that the composition of Dartmouth's student body and that of the national leadership would continue to remain essentially the same. The hometown could change, but the same socioeconomic background continued to be the only appropriate one. Thus the plan was not designed ultimately to attract much diversity. By the late 1930s, a decade later, the proportion of farmers' and laborers' children had fallen precipitously to 6 percent and 10 percent, respectively, while the proportion of businessmen's and professionals' children had grown to 43 percent and about 35 percent, respectively.

While Dartmouth was attracting students from across the country, DePauw University, a fine Methodist liberal arts college in rural Indiana, was trying to capture a larger slice of the midwestern market. Between the two world wars, DePauw recruited the children of the upper middle class, more and more often hailing from suburban areas, and more and more able and willing to pay the rapidly increasing cost of private higher education. In the 1920s, the number of bankers, doctors, teachers, insurance salesmen, and business executives among the fathers jumped by about 50 percent while the size of the student body as a whole increased by less than 19 percent. In 1920, well over four of every five students came from Indiana; by the time of World War II, only two of five did. The number of students from the suburbs of Chicago alone increased to nearly one-quarter of the student body.[20] Despite DePauw's efforts to continue to attract the brightest of Indiana's rural and small-town high school graduates—particularly through the Rector Scholarship program, one of the nation's largest—the college lost its Indiana and socially diverse tone. Each DePauw administration had misgivings about this trend, but chose to adapt its admissions policy to it nonetheless. In 1939, DePauw's president acknowledged that his school had become "cosmopolitan, nondenominational, suburban, rather than rural in its student body," and though for financial reasons he was pleased by the increasing number of well-to-do students there, he was concerned that the college had lost its traditional clientele. Discouraged, he noted that rural students now tended to attend public institutions since the liberal arts college was "a luxury to many."[21] Yet these developments were essential elements in the popularity of DePauw and other schools.

The decisions to limit enrollment, recruit widely, and raise tuition were all fundamental to the effort to develop a high-quality, small, but national liberal arts college. This strategy was tried with varying degrees of success at nearly every liberal arts college, from Dartmouth and its competitors in New England to DePauw in Indiana to Pomona in California. At first, high hopes accompanied the effort to select top-notch student bodies; realistically, however, not every institution could expect to attract an intellectually oriented student body that could pay its own way. In addition, institutional concerns about financial and alumni sources of support appeared to intensify even during the prosperous 1920s. The suburban student market was tapped by schools for a combination of idealistic, financial, and social reasons, but most of all, selective admissions plans were created to project a sense of institutional prestige.

The decision to limit enrollment was thought to give a college a psychological advantage over its competitors. "The most desirable clubs, and the ones that are the hardest to get into, have the longest waiting lines," a DePauw professor observed. "The same is true of colleges." Efforts to appear selective were made even if there was no need for selection; even Harvard and Chicago, for example, having settled on the number of freshmen they would admit, failed to reach the target figure in the late 1920s. Chicago officials frankly conceded within their own community that their decision to limit enrollment had been made "with the hope that we shall thereby arouse students to apply in greater numbers." The enrollment ceiling was set at 750 freshmen, but only 676 students showed up.[22] Institutions were willing to try any policy that would entice upper-middle-class WASPs to apply in sufficient numbers, since they were considered the caretakers of prestige in American society.

The adoption of regional quotas by Dartmouth, Harvard, and other New England colleges was intended to make each school competitive in the hard-fought battle for upper-middle-class suburban WASPs from the Midwest and West. At first educators believed that such students would lead the intellectual renaissance of the American college. Almost immediately, however, educators at Dartmouth and elsewhere found that an emphasis on scholarship in the admissions process did not necessarily produce a student body with the social background considered suitable for the nation's future leaders. Since cultivating this constituency was so important, character soon replaced intellectual potential as the key admissions criterion. Increased attention was then paid to the socioeconomic background of an applicant, and the admissibility of socially undesirable young men, even if talented, was questioned.[23]

Regional quotas, originally intended to increase the diversity of the student body, soon became a tool for discrimination against socially undesirable young men. At Harvard, for example, a faculty committee established by its Board of Overseers in 1923 at first repudiated the idea of a quota on Jewish students and reaffirmed the school's tradition of equality of opportunity. Rather than adopt a selection process that could be seen as a covert means to bar students of undesirable ethnic backgrounds, the committee recommended that all students in the top one-seventh of their high school graduating class be automatically admitted to Harvard College. This strategy would increase the proportion of rural and noneastern students, thereby encouraging regional diversity. But the Harvard plan—and others at similar schools—did not produce the desired social balance. Once it was discovered that Jewish students from urban areas, intellectually competent but socially undesirable, were being admitted in larger numbers than anyone had foreseen, the plan was modified to exclude them. Similarly, national scholarship contests established in the 1920s and 1930s at the major eastern colleges were designed in large part to substitute lower-middle-class WASPs from the Midwest and West for the poor ethnic students in their own backyards.[24] Despite the rhetoric about academic and democratic values, institutional prestige apparently depended on the social homogeneity of a school's student body.

From Selection to Restriction

In the 1920s and 1930s, selective admissions plans became restrictive admissions policies. Many of the nation's best-known colleges gave the appearance of being selective only because they chose to reject deliberately and systematically qualified but socially undesirable candidates in order to placate their alumni and other upper-middle-class WASPs. A critic in *The Nation* opposed regional quotas and proportionate admissions policies because they often led to the acceptance of less qualified but socially acceptable applicants: "An educational institution should not be representative of all people, but only of those with ambition and ability to do its work. . . . To tell a Cohen, whose average on the college board examinations was 90, that he cannot enter because there are too many Jews there already, while a grade of 68 will pass a Murphy, or one of 62 a Morgan, hardly seems in line with the real interests of the college."[25] But such quotas were indeed considered in the colleges' best interest. At such colleges as Harvard, Yale, Princeton, Columbia, and Dartmouth, essentially only the ethnic Americans, particularly the urban Russian Jews, were being turned away. Nearly everyone else, especially if he were in the top one-fifth of his high school class or from outside New England and the middle Atlantic states, was accepted without question to the school of his choice between the two world wars.[26]

That anti-Semitism became critical to a college's ability to call itself an elite school testifies to the rampant nativism in this era. Harvard's Lowell and Dartmouth's Hopkins were not alone in their disdain for most ethnic Americans. The immigrant's disloyalty to the United States was all but assumed: the raids ordered by Attorney General A. Mitchell Palmer were intended to arrest and deport immigrant radicals in 1920, and the decade-long ordeal of the Italian immigrants Nicola Sacco and Bartolomeo Vanzetti, denied a fair trial and later executed for a crime they may not have committed, symbolized Americans' distrust of immigrants. In 1916 Madison Grant's *Passing of the Great Race in America* was hailed as scientific support for widely held racist views on the baneful influence of eastern and southern Europeans on the future of Western civilization and the human race. Even the so-called liberals of the day, those who preached the predominance of environmental over genetic factors in the shaping of individual character, more often than not doubted whether the immigrants were capable of becoming full participants in American democratic life. It is no historical accident that the restrictive immigration laws of 1921 and 1924 were passed and signed into law—one *Los Angeles Times* headline called the latter bill a "Nordic victory"—at the same time that college administrators were looking for ways to limit, if not eliminate, unwanted Jewish and other ethnic students.

Fearful of the rise of the city, with its huge concentrations of ethnic Americans, fearful of the increasing number and visibility of the children of immigrants in American economic, political, and social institutions, many WASPs scrambled for the means to preserve their cultural hegemony. Higher education was not immune to this climate of intolerance. Before World War I, the presence of Jewish students was not a pressing issue, as their number was still relatively small and higher learning had not yet become necessary for social status. In the 1920s, once collegiate training had come to be viewed as a critical avenue of economic and social mobility, it became important to exclude from elite schools those individuals and social groups deemed to be of inappropriate background and character to take advantage of the opportunities and privileges afforded by a college degree. Like the framers of federal immigration legislation, educators first tried a literacy test of sorts—the College Board examinations—to keep Jewish students out. When that strategy failed dramatically, more blatant tactics were adopted.[27]

The presence of even a small number of Jewish students on a college campus sent shudders through the bodies of administrators and alumni. As early as 1910, students demonstrated at Williams College to protest the admission of any Jews; in that same year, E. E. Slosson reported that Princeton officials believed that if Jews were admitted, "they would ruin Princeton as they have Columbia and Pennsylvania." A Menorah Society was formed at Harvard in 1906, and later elsewhere, to bring Jewish students (generally of Russian heritage) together, a sign of the beginning of the social disintegration there.[28] A 1919 survey by the Bureau of Jewish Social Research indicated that with the exception of the colleges and universities located in New York City, Jewish students accounted for no more than 15 percent of the student body at any school: while CCNY was at least 80 percent Jewish, the proportion of Jews at New York University was less than 50 percent, at Columbia about 20 percent, at Western Reserve University and the University of Pennsylvania about 15 percent, at Harvard 10 percent, and at Dartmouth, Princeton, Amherst, and Williams less than 3 percent. While Jews accounted for 1.19 percent of the college students nationwide as late as 1924,[29] the fact that they congregated at the nation's most prestigious schools heightened anxiety about their potential influence in society.

Informal sanctions restricting the number of Jewish students admitted had been accepted practice at several schools before World War I. Without formal admissions procedures, however, the number of such students rose dramatically shortly thereafter. Jews already in attendance were generally accepted by their peers, but with the influx of applications, new questions arose: How would the increasing number of new Jewish students, with their distinctive socioeconomic background and intellectual interests, be assimilated into the predominantly WASP student culture? What if these Jews were successfully integrated into college life and then sought further access to the professions? College officials and their allies not only were uncomfortable in the presence of large numbers of Jewish students, they also felt threatened by those students' aspirations to full participation in American society's economic and social elite.

Limiting the number of Jewish students became an obsession with officials at the elite colleges in the 1920s. Citing the case of City College, the dean of admissions at Yale believed that Yale would become "a different place when and if the proportion of Jews passes an as yet unknown limit." For Yale that acceptable level was about 10 percent of the student body. Sensitive to the fact that his school's "position at the gateway of European immigration [made it] socially uninviting to students who come from homes of refinement," Columbia's dean favored restricting the proportion of Jews there to about 20 percent of the entering class.[30] Some public institutions also confronted the "Jewish problem" in the 1920s: the dean of Massachusetts Agricultural College felt compelled to assure a rural newspaper reporter and local parents that "there is as fine a crowd of good, old New England stock here as you'll find anywhere." A study of collegiate business education in 1931 chronicled what the authors considered to be the indiscriminate acceptance of ethnic students into commerce programs: "A school, like a country, can absorb so much that is different from its accepted pattern or mode," they added. "Beyond that point, only confusion and negation result."[31]

Harvard's Lowell insisted that he had the best interests of Jewish students at heart when he sought to restrict their enrollment in the 1920s. In a letter to *The New York Times* in June 1922, he observed that the amount of anti-Semitic feeling grew in proportion to the increase in the number of Jewish students, and he suggested that if each well-known school limited the number of Jewish students, then anti-Semitic sentiment would be diffused, if not eliminated entirely. The Harvard Student Council Committee on Education in 1926 also emphasized that "no college can admit unassimilables with impunity" when it recommended that Jewish students constitute no more than 10 percent of Harvard's student body. Students who favored a quota system at Harvard supported the concept of proportionate admissions for the nation as a whole, and insisted that Jewish students, conscientious as they were about their studies, destroyed the unity of the college by not mixing well socially. Despite Lowell's and his students' remarks, Heywood Broun and George Britt's 1931 study *Christians Only* found Harvard's restrictions moderate in comparison with those at Yale, Columbia, Cornell, the University of Virginia, and other schools.[32]

At an emotional meeting with Protestant campus leaders in 1922, Harry Starr, president of the Harvard Menorah Society, found out "that it was *numbers* that mattered; bad or good, *too many* Jews were not liked. Rich or poor, brilliant or dull, polished or crude—*too many Jews,* the fear of a New Jerusalem at Harvard" motivated supporters of a quota on Jewish students. WASP students argued that their Jewish peers could not "be prepared in all qualities of mind, character, and personality to assume positions of active, helpful leadership in the world" and did not demonstrate any interest "in the larger life of the college." But the truth was that Jewish students were threatening in large part because of their successful assimilation into undergraduate life, particularly in those programs and activities ushered in by the renewed interest in scholarship. "It is not the failure of Jews to be assimilated into undergraduate society which troubles them," Horace Kallen told *The Nation's* audience. "What troubles them is the completeness with which Jews want to be and have been assimilated."[33]

Kallen's perspective dramatizes the irony of the restrictive admissions policies. The culture of aspiration had proved to be too successful. Too many Jewish and poor students surpassed their WASP peers in intellectual potential and, furthermore, eagerly sought to become integrated into the predominantly WASP world of the college campus. Yet, allegedly for their own good, educators claimed their aspirations had to be restricted, their enrollment limited. Without a vast majority of students from the appropriate upper-middle-class WASP background, these educators and their allies contended, not only would the collegiate community suffer irreparable damage, but the future solidarity and stability of American society would be put in jeopardy. These fears, rampant among his school's competitors for about a decade, soon impelled Hopkins to institute a quota on the number of Jewish applicants accepted at Dartmouth in the winter of 1931–32.

Anti-Semitism at Dartmouth and Elsewhere

Until the late 1920s there was little anti-Semitism at Dartmouth. In 1920, for example, Hopkins instructed a dean to send admissions information to a Mr. Morris Altman, "who states that he is an Episcopalian—whatever that has to do with it." In a later memo to Dean Bill, he stated emphatically that "the diminution of the Jews never figured in the slightest way in the formation of our plans, nor in our practice" of the selective admissions process. Though he felt that "any college has a right . . . to protect its own individuality . . . if it were true that men of specified race or characteristics were likely to inundate it in such large numbers so as to exclude all others," Hopkins denied privately to Felix Frankfurter and publicly to newspaper reporters that Dartmouth's admissions procedures discriminated against Jewish applicants. Instead, he suggested the school's rural environment did not appeal to urban Jewish students.[34] Even as some schools sharply curtailed the number of Jewish students, the total enrollment of Jews at American colleges and universities climbed dramatically; one 1927 survey of 665 institutions indicated that Jewish students constituted 10.7 percent of the student body.[35] But Dartmouth was still little touched by "the Jewish problem." While Hopkins acknowledged that some undergraduate organizations were anti-Semitic, as late as 1930 a faculty member believed that "discrimination, if it exists, is kept under cover."[36]

"The Jewish problem" emerged suddenly at Dartmouth in 1931. Once other prestigious colleges put severe limits on the number of their Jewish students, the number of Jews applying to and enrolling at Dartmouth increased rapidly. While the classes of 1926 to 1933 averaged about 29 Jews, the class of 1934 (accepted for fall 1930) included 53 Jews and the class of 1935 75 Jews. Reviewing the composition of the class of 1935 in the *Dartmouth Alumni Magazine* in November 1931, Dean Bill noted that Jewish students comprised over 10 percent of the entering class and that the proportion of entering students indicating no religious preference—considered to be a smoke screen for Jews who wished to hide their backgrounds—had increased from 8 to 14 percent in a few years. Within the previous decade, the proportion of Jews had increased about five times. "This triumph of the chosen and heathen peoples seems to be a continuing process," Dean Bill concluded in a deliberately provocative remark, "and it will not be long before the above table [on the religious preferences of the freshman class] can be limited to just two or three items." Although the proportion of Jewish students was lower at Dartmouth than at such schools as Harvard and Columbia, even after those two latter schools had established quotas, Hopkins was concerned. "I *know* we have necessity upon us to do something drastic," he conceded to Dean Bill.[37]

On Christmas Eve of 1931, Hopkins proposed that Bill and a Jewish alumnus get together to discuss the imposition of a quota on the number of Jewish students. Echoing Lowell's argument, he considered a quota to be in the best interest of the Jewish students as well as of the college. "Within the last two years," Hopkins informed a sympathetic and influential Jewish alumnus, "[I have realized that] in allowing the percentage of Jews to increase rapidly, and in not being as exacting in regard to qualities of character and personality among Jewish boys as we were among others, we were really not doing justice to those Jewish boys whom we did accept nor to alumni such as yourself." The selective admissions process had put its highest priority on scholarship potential, but, simply put, too many Jewish students had been accepted on that basis. With the same rationale that he had used earlier to cut the proportion of New England students at the college, Hopkins instructed Dean Bill to reduce, "perhaps even drastically," the number of Jewish students admitted to the class of 1936.[38]

To carry out its quota plan, Dartmouth followed established practices to identify and reject Jewish applicants. Its 1932 application form contained three new questions on financial need, religious background, and racial inheritance. In addition, a photograph was required for the first time; it was said that those Jewish students who did not belong at Dartmouth were "of a physical type that is unattractive to the average Dartmouth student."[39] Unlike other schools, such as Columbia and Yale, however, Dartmouth did not use psychological testing to weed out Jewish applicants. The College Board examinations and the Scholastic Aptitude Test were originally tailored to fit the class bias of their designers; as the dean of Columbia told Yale's dean of admissions, "most Jews, especially those of the more objectionable type, have not had the home experiences which enable them to pass these tests as successfully as the average native American boy." But Hopkins was aware that this strategy had proved ineffective in the mid- and late 1920s.[40]

Dean Bill looked carefully—literally—at candidates' applications and photographs and at reports from secondary schools and from alumni who had interviewed applicants. A young man's character now received Dartmouth's close attention: did the applicant possess leadership qualities? did he have good manners? did he engage in "fair play," or was he too competitive? The "good mixer," the upper-middle-class WASP, scored high in these criteria, and unwanted Jewish applicants, those considered too "bookish" or ill-mannered to particpate fully in the Dartmouth community, could be ferreted out. "Wielding an ax rather than a fine tool," Dean Bill wrote in his *Dartmouth Alumni Magazine* report on the class of 1936, "the Jewish delegation, which was 75 last year, is back to normal." Slightly over 5 percent of the class was Jewish; the actual number of Jewish students accepted, thirty-seven, remained remarkably and assiduously constant each year for at least the rest of the decade.[41]

Not even the Depression could shake the resolve of the Dartmouth administration to continue the quota system. Throughout the winter of 1932–33, Dean Bill reported to Hopkins that it would be impossible to admit a class of 650 students for the following fall unless the quota were waived. In March, after refusing every Jewish applicant who had had an unfavorable report from an alumni committee and tentatively accepting every other applicant who appeared capable of surviving academically at the college, Dean Bill discovered to his surprise that he had managed to reach the 650 mark only by including no fewer than 90 Jewish boys. He informed Hopkins, "How I am going to throw away 50 or 60 of these boys and still have a class of 650 here in September is more of a problem than I can contemplate." After scribbling in long division on Dean Bill's memo to figure out that such a class would then be over 13 percent Jewish, Hopkins wrote Dean Bill the following day to state in no uncertain terms that he would prefer not to accept a class of 650 if it meant admitting such a high proportion of Jews. He urged Dean Bill to consider accepting a number of "just 'the plain, ordinary bohunks' such as [Dartmouth] used to do" to meet the admissions target figure. The two men also agreed that some offers of financial assistance should be cut sharply in order to discourage the matriculation of even those few Jewish students admitted.[42]

Despite the continued enforcement of a strict quota, and even though the number of Jewish matriculants in each entering class stayed essentially the same, the number of Jewish applicants to Dartmouth continued to rise until at least 1939. Hopkins denied that

his school discriminated unfairly against Jewish applicants throughout the decade, and he continued to insist that his policy was appropriate even after World War II. Yet, in an angry reply to a Jewish
father who had written him in 1939 to ask if his son had been rejected
because of his religion, Hopkins conceded, "It probably is a fact that
a boy of Jewish heritage has to have outstanding characteristics in
general that are not required of racial stocks a little less aggressive."[43]
The facts bear out more than that concession. At the end of the
1930s, when nearly three-quarters of the non-Jewish applicants were
accepted by Dartmouth, only about one of ten Jewish applicants was
admitted.[44] Dartmouth was still one of America's renowned selective,
elite colleges.

As at other institutions, predominantly upper-middle-class WASP
alumni influenced the tone and substance of Dartmouth's undergraduate life. They certainly influenced the implementation of the
admissions quota policy. Aside from their disdain for socially undesirable Jewish applicants, alumni were concerned that their own children might not be accepted under tighter admissions standards. According to Harvard's former president Charles W. Eliot, Lowell
resolved to restrict the number of Jews there in part because of alumni
pressure he encountered while on a fund-raising speaking tour in
1922. Yale's board of admissions voted in 1925 that any limitation
on enrollment would not exclude any son of a Yale graduate.
Dartmouth alumni also exerted this kind of pressure. Hopkins received vigorous support for the quota from alumni class agents at a
meeting in March 1932, as he did from the Board of Trustees. He
even heard from a friend in the Harvard Corporation who told him
he had thought Dartmouth was the only Anglo-Saxon college left in
America, and was disappointed and shocked to see so many Jews
there when he visited the campus. The number of Dartmouth alumni
sons accepted continued to increase throughout the 1930s.[45] Tradition and character counted.

It is important not to underestimate the support that Hopkins'
policy received from a group of sympathetic Jewish alumni and students. They agreed that it was best for Jewish students, as well as for
the college, that a quota be instituted. In the winter of 1931–32,
Jewish alumni offered to work with Dean Bill to weed out the more
undesirable Jewish applicants. The only disagreement came when a
Jewish alumnus asked that an exception to the quota be made for all
brilliant Jewish students from the public high schools; Dean Bill re-

sponded that the alumnus had no idea of how many of those students were already applying, and had to be rejected. An age limitation helped solve the problem. In a March 1933 memorandum, Hopkins reported the satisfaction of Jewish alumni that Dartmouth was admitting only "the better type of Jews rather than . . . the Brooklyn and Flatbush crowd."[46]

The Dartmouth experience confirms the prevalence of what was called the Jewish version of the *Mayflower* social tradition. Most German Jewish leaders in American society held themselves aloof from the Jews of Eastern European extraction who were struggling to become a part of the mainstream of American life. This differentiation between acceptable German Jews and unassimilable Russian and Polish Jews was shared by German Jews and nativists alike. Percy Straus, the only Jewish member of the board of trustees of New York University, agreed publicly to the desirability of a quota on Russian Jewish students there in 1922. During the debate at Harvard, another prominent member of the Straus family told former president Eliot that he viewed the increase in Jewish commuter students as a catastrophe.[47] Well-educated, upper-class Jews generally acquiesced, perhaps with misgivings, in restrictions on less refined applicants of immigrant stock, whether Catholic, Protestant, or Jewish. But the vast majority of these uncouth applicants were Eastern European Jews.

German Jewish alumni were worried about the Russian Jewish students' competitive values and poor manners; the Russian Jews, Hopkins insisted, were "of such aggressive race consciousness on their own part, and so assertive, that they detracted from the community of spirit." Not only were they often too intellectual, but their poverty also embarrassed their wealthier German coreligionists.[48] At schools with a large number of Jewish students, the conflict between German and Russian Jews was reflected, among other ways, in the establishment of separate fraternities. Many German Jewish students were in an awkward position, alienated from the Russian Jews, the "grinds," and yet not always fully accepted by the WASPs. A character in a novel about Harvard was described as a "Manhattan Jew of two generations' money, not clever enough to be taken in by the intellectual Jews, not strong enough to make athletic glory feasible, too fastidious to forgather with the poor Jews to commute from Roxbury and Dorchester, too unconfident of himself to use his wealth to make himself accepted." He sat alone in his room, interrupted only by a Boston aristocrat who wanted to buy his typewriter for less than its value.[49] In the 1930s, their fears roused by the rise of Hitler, German Jewish Americans became even more sensitive to the underlying current of nativism and anti-Semitism in the United States and supported admissions quotas in the hope that they would protect the so-called assimilable Jews and blunt any criticism of their economic and social status. Like non-Jews, German Jews were wary of too much mobility on the part of ambitious Russian Jews and other ethnic Americans.[50]

The WASP-dominated elite college was no longer prepared to heed its own call for the meritocratic selection of its students. Instead, it reinforced the social prejudice and the anti-intellectualism of an anxious American society. In 1922 Hopkins had issued his call for an "aristocracy of brains"; by 1926 he had modified his stand and expressed the hope that Dartmouth's student body would consist of "men who supplement mental capacity with social antennae"; and by 1932, when the quota on Jewish students was instituted, he felt that an applicant's personality was more critical than his potential for scholarship. After all, he conceded, "any college which is going to base its admissions wholly on scholastic standing will find itself with an infinitesimal proportion of anything else than Jews eventually." The *Yale Daily News* warned that if Yale did not institute "an Ellis Island with immigration laws more prohibitive than those of the United States government," then Yale would become "a brain plant" with too many Jewish students. In *Christians Only: A Study in Prejudice*, Heywood Broun and George Britt blamed anti-Semitism in American colleges on the fact that the Jewish student strove more passionately for a Phi Beta Kappa key than for a football letter.[51] Resentful of Jewish students' academic interests and performance, Hopkins and others resorted to emphasizing the beneficent qualities of collegiate activities that only a few years before they had lambasted as "side shows [which had] swallowed up the circus."

Opposition to this perceived Jewish intellectualism, widespread in the 1920s, became even more bitter in the 1930s, particularly as it was linked to the student radicalism of the Depression era. Open-mindedness toward, if not support for, radical causes exacerbated the tension between Jewish and non-Jewish students. Hopkins, for one, feared that "the unhappiness of soul and the destructive spirit of revolt . . . characteristic of the Jewish race at all times under all conditions" could destroy the spirit of Dartmouth; criticizing the "specious and superficial radicalism" of Jewish students in the 1930s, he insisted that "the jaundiced mulling of that small portion of our undergraduate body which loves to line up against the wailing wall is little indicative of the spirit which education is supposed to produce and is little representative of the traditions of the American college."[52] To Hopkins and others, the American college should train safe leaders; it could do so by preserving social continuity, not by providing a home for social criticism or cultural pluralism.

The private elite liberal arts colleges of the Northeast were not the only institutions that attempted to minimize the number and impact of Jewish students. Historians have pointed out that Jewish students from the urban Northeast migrated to private and public colleges across the country, but they were rarely welcomed. Though the University of North Carolina, for example, was long regarded as perhaps the most liberal southern campus, it instituted quotas on the number of out-of-state students and established differential tuition policies on the basis of a student's residence to keep the proportion of Jewish students low enough so that the predominant tone of the campus would not be changed. Administrators and alumni made the same careful distinction between their state's "native" Jews and the "foreigners" from the North as northern alumni and administrators did between German and Russian Jewish applicants.[53] The failure to limit sharply the number of socially undesirable young men, particularly Jews, damaged the reputation of a number of America's finest private urban universities, including Chicago, Columbia, Pennsylvania, and Western Reserve. Chicago representatives stressed that the university wanted "to avoid becoming a city college for day students"; the proportion of Jewish students was limited to the proportion of Jews in the Chicago area, since "the Jews do not want to go to a Semitic school [and] others won't go to one which looks like it tends that way."[54] These schools often sanctioned discriminatory admissions policies and segregated campus activities. Even so, each of these highly respected institutions found that the mere presence of poor, ethnic, and particularly Jewish students drove socially conscious WASPs, their traditional sources of students and support, to "more elite" schools.

Some prestigious colleges continued to use exclusionary admissions quotas as late as the early 1950s. A special Mayor's Committee on Unity in New York City concluded that the situation had worsened during World War II. Women's colleges and less prestigious men's colleges—such as Colgate, which apparently admitted no more than about 5 of its 200 to 300 Jewish applicants—followed the lead of Harvard, Dartmouth, and the others. Hopkins himself still vigorously defended the quota system in a 1945 letter published in a New York City newspaper: the quota still both maintained Dartmouth's tradition of racial tolerance and protected Jews from anti-Semitism. If it did not limit the number of Jewish students, Hopkins argued, Dartmouth would have to exclude them altogether. After all, he concluded little more than two decades after his school had been at the forefront of the intellectual renaissance of the American liberal arts college, "Dartmouth College is a Christian college founded for the Christianization of its students." The *New Republic* called the quota "one of the outstanding blots on American civilization today"; noting the ironic coincidence of Hopkins' public statement and the dropping of the first atomic bomb, it added, "President Hopkins proposes that we handicap ourselves by arbitrarily rejecting certain elements, no matter how high their intellectual capacities, on a basis of religion and (fallaciously assumed) race. We can no longer afford these obsolete myths of racial differentiation." In addition, until after World War II, Jewish scholars were perhaps even more victimized than Jewish students by racial prejudice; in nearly every case, they were prevented from receiving appointments to university faculties even in an age of rising standards and specialization. "Somewhere along the road to democracy," the executive director of the Mayor's Committee wrote in 1946, "American higher education got impeded by a burden of traditions inconsonant with the very ideals ostensibly perpetuated by these traditions—and the schools were left behind."[55] Public pressure mounted to try to force these elite institutions of higher learning to fulfill the promise of American democratic principles, and not merely to meet the interests of their upper-middle-class WASP constituency alone.

Black Students

The treatment of black students provides an even more dramatic example of how WASP educators and their traditional constituencies clung to their racist views. While the number of students at black colleges and universities leaped six times, from 2,132 in 1917 to 13,580 in 1927, the number of black students at predominantly white colleges increased barely at all. Of these schools Oberlin had the highest proportion of black students during this era—4 percent; but even at this famous school founded by abolitionists, a faculty member admitted, "it [was] impossible . . . to uphold old Oberlin's ideals because of student prejudice." Most white colleges refused to admit black students; the student council at Antioch, a leading progressive school, voted in 1925 that it was "a matter of expediency" not to admit a well-qualified black that year. In 1922, Harvard found itself on the front pages of the nation's newspapers not only because it was slapping a quota on the number of Jewish students admitted, but also because President Lowell refused to permit six black students to live in his school's dormitories. Although the Harvard Overseers and Lowell's own faculty overruled him six months later, Harvard, like most institutions, remained a segregated school until after World War II. The 1,500 blacks who did go to "integrated" colleges in the 1920s and 1930s were essentially pariahs: at some places they were not welcome in the dormitories, in the bathrooms, or at the annual school prom. Black football players were withdrawn from countless games because of "gentlemen's agreements" between schools if an opponent was offended by the prospect of playing against an integrated squad. Blacks were clearly more victimized than even the least desirable white ethnic student.[56]

Prompted by W. E. B. Du Bois's call for the education of the "talented tenth" of America's blacks, middle-class blacks crowded the underfunded black colleges in search of the same professional- and status-oriented education that attracted their white peers during the 1920s. E. Franklin Frazier, a 1916 Howard University graduate and a leading sociologist of his day, declared in 1924 that there was "too much inspiration and too little information" in the curricula of black schools. Students at Fisk University went on strike in 1924 to dramatize their desire to establish fraternities and participate in inter- collegiate athletics. Not unlike their white upper-middle-class peers, these black students were willing to surrender their identification with less fortunate blacks if the opportunity for a practical education and a middle-class social life became available. Rather than Marcus Garvey, the spokesman for black separatist nationalism, they wel- comed "the black rite of Horatio Alger" to their campuses. Most of those few blacks who did go to school had no choice but to attend black colleges, with their vastly inferior facilities and future pros- pects. By 1940, only 1.3 percent of the total black population had graduated from college, compared with 5.4 percent of white Americans.[57] Between the two world wars, the deck of mobility cards was stacked without question and without regret against young people from lower-class, ethnic, and black backgrounds.

Prejudice and the Pluralistic Vision

In the 1920s and 1930s, American institutions of higher education engaged in egalitarian rhetoric, but their performance was a mockery of American ideals. When an unprecedented opportunity for selection in admissions suggested an intellectual renaissance, character was stressed; when the opportunity presented itself to select a heterogeneous and meritocratic elite, America's best colleges chose openly the sons of native stock, even if they were less qualified. In a courageous speech at Amherst's centennial celebration in 1921, with that exemplar of 1920s political and social conservatism, Amherst graduate Calvin Coolidge, in the audience, President Alexander Meiklejohn spoke out against the perpetuation of what he called an Anglo-Saxon racial aristocracy there and at other prestigious schools and urged Amherst students and alumni to welcome ethnic Americans into the nation's colleges for the sake of the future of society:

> If we are not to have a racial aristocracy, democracy must have a dwelling place within our colleges. . . . We are an Anglo-Saxon college; and so in greater part we must remain. And yet we are American. We may not keep ourselves apart either from persons or from cultures not our own. We dare not shut our gate to our fellow-citizens nor to their influence. . . . And if they do not come, we must go out and bring them in.[58]

The American college should fuse the positive attributes of many cultures, Meiklejohn believed, in order to produce the economic growth and social progress of a distinctive twentieth-century American culture. This meritocratic and pluralistic vision fell mainly on deaf ears.

Critics of the colleges recognized that there was more at stake than the admissions policies of a handful of important schools or the lives of even a few thousand students. If the Jewish student was denied admission to the nation's most renowned colleges, a leading rabbi wrote, he was "defeated in a far more significant battle, namely the right to entrance into the higher spheres of the professions and commerce." Such discrimination was not merely anti-Semitic, then, it was un-American as well. There was something very disquieting, a public high school teacher added, when the colleges' "enthusiasm for democracy is so slight that they demand shelter from its perplexities and from its dangers." The colleges, he asserted, would lose more than they would gain by excluding the "eager, heterogeneous varied amalgam which is America."[59] And so did America's democratic promise. Sadly, between the world wars, by pursuing discriminatory admissions practices, the best American colleges more often than not embodied the worst prejudices and fears of an anxious America.

8 / The Junior College and the Differentiation of the Public Sector

Responding to the rush to the colleges between the world wars and yet wary of it, public institutions of higher education underwent a steady process of internal differentiation. Major state universities attempted to emulate the elite institutions of the private sector; despite the increasing disparity in the socioeconomic backgrounds of students at the private colleges and state universities during the interwar period, both types of institutions catered generally to young people from the middle and upper middle classes. The responsibility for offering the training sought by practical-oriented, lower-middle-class students—the new college students of the twentieth century—fell to new types of collegiate institutions expanded or created to meet the demand for mass higher education. Normal schools, for example, were transformed into four-year, access-oriented, regional teachers' colleges or state colleges. Most important, however, was the rapid development of the public junior college.

No segment of American higher education expanded so rapidly during the interwar period as the public junior college, a creation essentially of the 1920s. Although there were 85 junior colleges with 4,500 students in the country in 1918, they went unmentioned in the federal *Educational Directory* of that year. By 1940, there were 456 junior colleges scattered across the country with a total enrollment of 149,854. In 1918, only 1.9 percent of all undergraduates in the nation attended junior colleges; in 1938, 17.6 percent of the nation's college students were enrolled in two-year institutions. Nearly two-thirds of these students went to publicly controlled junior colleges.[1]

A new niche was created for the public junior college in an increasingly rigid, hierarchical educational structure: it provided mass higher education. At the outset, it was a stepping-stone for many students too young or too poor to attend four-year colleges immediately following high school. As early as the 1920s, however, educators deliberately altered the curriculum of the typical junior college from a program that prepared its students to transfer to four-year schools to one that emphasized training in semiprofessional fields that did not require additional higher learning. Just as the selective liberal arts colleges would choose the best young men, so the terminal junior colleges would produce the desired number of future semiprofessional college graduates. The junior college curriculum was designed to meet society's perceived needs, not students' expectations. During the interwar period, the junior colleges became known as the "people's colleges." But democratic equality of opportunity was a figment of educators' rhetoric, not their goal.

Public Universities and Mass Education

"None of the world's higher institutions of learning come as close to expressing the spirit of democracy as do our great state univerisites," education writer R. L. Duffus claimed extravagantly in 1936. Since the passage of the Morrill Act in 1863, when the federal government gave land to the states and existing territories for the promotion of agricultural and mechanical education, public higher education's future lay in the creation of institutions responsive to the growing demands for training and research. By the 1920s, finally, economic growth and social progress were attributed to the broad diffusion of education and the technical innovations and individual initiative it fostered. "In a great democracy like ours," the president of Ohio State University explained, "the State feels keenly that education and widespread intelligence are the safeguards of our perpetuity."[2] This philosophy promoted the recognition that higher education had to be viewed not merely as a privilege of the elite but as a right of all America's young people.

In the 1920s and 1930s, the public sector continued to measure its success by its service to more and more diverse segments of society. This notion of service had been firmly established initially in the state university of the Progressive Era, the heyday of the so-called Wisconsin idea. At first, with the University of Wisconsin as their model, state universities pursued agricultural and social research geared to the solution of local problems, but these efforts only laid the foundation for more extensive involvement in all spheres of society. In the next several decades, surveys of public higher education stressed that the state university should be "the state's center of inquiry and distribution of all forms of knowledge bearing on the health, material interests, the intellectual and social welfare of its citizens." "There is no intellectual service too undignified for them to perform," concluded Lotus D. Coffman, president of the University of Minnesota. Insisting that "no state university could survive in a sheer intellectual empyrean," he told a 1932 audience, "If they are faithful to their constituencies, the state universities will be dynamic institutions to which society will look with increasing frequency and pride."[3] And society did, particularly for training and research in fields only recently recognized as worthy of inclusion in an institution of higher learning.

A speaker at Massachusetts State College in 1936 echoed a well-worn theme when he claimed that public insitutions were "unhampered by any of the snobbishness, the undemocratic class-consciousness, so characteristic" of private colleges. At Alabama Polytechnic Institute, as at public institutions generally, admissions criteria were affected increasingly "by political considerations and by the popular belief (not necessarily erroneous) that the State owes everyone an education—or, at least a degree." Most such universities felt obliged to enroll as many students as they could hold. Harry W. Chase, president of the University of North Carolina in the 1920s, criticized the state legislature for permitting overcrowding and warned that the state, "as a believer in equality of opportunity," should not pursue any policy that would lead to a limitation on enrollment. As David Kinley, president of the University of Illinois, put it: "No man has any right under a government like ours to undertake to determine that only a few shall be permitted to get an education of higher grade. In a democracy the only proper course is to keep proper standards and welcome all who can meet them. In saying this, of course, I am speaking of a publicly supported institution." No group in society had the right to determine how many should attend college, Kinley insisted. Anyone who spoke on behalf of the doctrine of higher education for the few had "whether consciously or not . . . aristocratic feelings and leanings."[4] Most public educators proclaimed that there could never be too many people in college, even as they pursued policies that would free their institutions from the need to bear all of the burdens of democracy.

The spirit of democracy was often expressed in ironic defenses of the social beneficence of the mass education of America's often mediocre youth. Students at the state universities came generally from upper-middle- and middle-class homes; they sought a practical higher education, hoping for careers that differed little from those pursued by their peers at the more prestigious liberal arts colleges. "There was perhaps a time when higher education could be discussed predominantly in terms of training for leadership," Harry Chase argued when he assumed the presidency of the University of Illinois in 1930, but that time had ended. "I believe in the power of leadership, but I also believe in the necessity of a high general level of intelligence and culture for the future of America."[5] Chase in essence endorsed what Coffman called "education for intelligent followership." The public university should reach beyond the traditional conception of higher education and bring many mediocre young people, as well as the best young minds of the state, to its campus. Chase, Coffman, and others hoped that the public university would continue to absorb new functions and new students.

Conservative faculty members at several public universities charged that their schools were devoting too much attention to these mediocre students. Norman Foerster, a philosopher at the University of North Carolina, wrote, "If higher education is to deserve the name, it cannot be brought within the reach of the ineducable and the passively educable." To date, he felt, the state universities "have preferred the maximum numbers, the masses, which satisfy their American zest for magnitude and grandiosity, to the smaller numbers, the more fit, which would appeal to an imagination interested in excellence and magnanimity; and they have buttressed this preference by a pseudo-democratic idealism subversive of higher education and social stability." Foerster believed that public universities had to resist the notion that every high school graduate had a right to a university education; he proposed a return to the Jeffersonian concept of free public higher education for the few. Professor George F. Sabine of Ohio State University agreed; he called the idea that all high school graduates deserved admission to the state university "arrant sentimentality." Sabine wanted the state university to emulate the privately endowed university by emphasizing research and specialized training of high quality for talented students alone.[6] Such educators as

Foerster and Sabine were offended, not seduced, by the opportunities enjoyed by public institutions to tap new markets and attract new students. As fewer intellectual-oriented students arrived at state universities, more faculty joined the ranks of those who supported the differentiation of higher education within the public sector as well as between private and public institutions.

State surveys of public higher education between the two world wars promoted the differentiation of public higher education as the most efficient means to provide higher learning. Critics of the wasteful rivalries between ambitious public institutions urged such schools to regard themselves as mere instrumentalities of a larger agency dedicated to meeting the overall educational and informational needs of society. Duplication of courses was seen as the main culprit at schools in Washington, Iowa, and at least sixteen other states. Iowa's board of education requested a survey to determine, among other questions, whether Iowa State College of Agricultural and Mechanical Arts should have an education department, a journalism program, a psychology program, or even any liberal arts at all. The competition between the University of Iowa and Iowa State produced such tension that the survey report recommended the suspension of the annual football game between the two schools for at least five years. The experts who conducted the Iowa, Washington, and other surveys enunciated the concept of the "major-service theory," which reserved for the state university the prerogative to offer courses of study in the prestigious professions, including graduate work in education, and restricted the freedom of the land-grant college to offer nontechnical or nonagricultural courses and of teachers' colleges to offer noneducational-oriented programs.[7]

This emphasis on efficiency was motivated in large part by a desire to preserve the state university as a bastion of elitism within the public sector of higher education. Left to their own devices, public colleges and universities had pursued their individual ambitions to become self-contained units; this course struck the experts as not only wasteful but unwise. Numerous calls for the statewide coordination of higher educational institutions were heard from educators as well as from penurious state legislatures. "It is the purpose of the university to maintain itself as a school of higher training for professional work," the Board of Curators of the University of Missouri announced in 1926, "rather than as a direct competitor of the junior colleges, the teachers colleges, and the endowed colleges, for students of the freshman and sophomore ranks."⁸ This approach made sense, saved money, and made conservative state university faculties happy. By the early 1930s there was a variety of institutions within the public sector, their prestige corresponding roughly to that of their major curriculum responsibilities and the socioeconomic composition of their student bodies.

Teachers' colleges, in particular, were criticized initially for putting their desire for expansion and their students' ambitions ahead of a statewide determination of the appropriate division of labor among public institutions. The remarkable growth of the high schools—in the decade after World War I the proportion of children of high school age in school more than doubled, from 20 to 50 percent—increased the demand for more and better-educated teachers. The passage of teacher certification laws by most states and the enactment of the federal Smith-Hughes Act in 1917 encouraged prospective educators to stay in college longer. Normal schools, previously little more than glorified high schools, had by the mid-1920s matured into teachers' colleges and considered themselves first-class institutions. For many of these colleges, teacher training was only the beginning; a survey team noted that the Kirksville, Missouri, State Normal School offered "a sort of educational lunch counter where everything 'the people' wish may be had in portions suited to their convenience." Studies showed that most teachers' college students came from lower-middle-class backgrounds; they could afford only a local, low-cost school and they aspired to practical training in education or in some other field of similarly low prestige. At first the expansion of these schools created tension in the public sector, but by the 1930s the distinctions between research- and professional-oriented state universities and regional-oriented teachers' colleges—some now called state colleges—were sharpened, to the satisfaction of educators at institutions of both types.⁹

Coffman's own University of Minnesota was a visible battleground between elite and democratic forces in public higher education during the 1920s and 1930s. While Coffman urged all who would seek a college education to come to the university, the dean of the school's College of Science, Literature, and the Arts, John B. Johnston, led a counterattack against open admissions. Johnston pressed successfully for the establishment of the General College, a two-year program within the university, dedicated to the general education of those students believed to be unprepared for the more rigorous four-year program. Johnston asserted that the first duty of the state university was to educate the most gifted students of the state; less talented young people must be educated also, but not at the intellectual expense of the more able. To be effective, the university must separate "the thinkers from the learners." Although he conceded it would be difficult to convince the public that it was wasteful and unwise to offer all students the same educational program, Johnston hoped that four-year curricula at state universities would be selective in the future.[10]

The General College, opened in 1932, was the solution. Its curriculum consisted of survey courses; no foreign language instruction, laboratory courses, or advanced technical courses were offered. The General College was designed to fill the demand for higher education among young people whose abilities or interests differed from those of the traditional university student. By 1939 it enrolled more than 1,000 students, more than one-fifth of them the children of working-class immigrants.[11] In its cirriculum and in its lower-middle-class student body, the General College constituted a typical example of the public sector's efforts to broaden higher education without compromising the existent status of the capstone of its system.

Efforts to deepen the distinctions between types of institutions within the public sector accelerated during the Depression of the 1930s. Rising standards in the professions and business and the scarcity of employment opportunities encouraged college attendance through most of the decade. Faced with the devastating financial impact of the Depression, state governments did not choose to devote increased resources to the expansion of their state universities. Instead, local teachers' colleges and public junior colleges assumed more and more responsiblity for educating lower-middle-class students. The transformation of teacher's colleges into four-year state colleges, with a wider range of curricular offerings, and the continued support of public junior colleges were responses to the need for inexpensive educational opportunities within commuting distance of the homes of poorer students. Thus the growing acceptance of the idea of a right to public higher education was offset in part by the fact that such a right was exercised increasingly by privileged students at high-status institutions and by students from lower socioeconomic backgrounds at local schools of little prestige. Even within the public sector, the democratization of higher education was achieved by the expansion or creation of new types of low-status colleges rather than by the democratization of the institutions at the apex of the educational structure.

Public Higher Education in California

Nowhere was this trend more in evidence than in California. "There is more education to the square inch in California than in any other part of the United States," observed a writer in a 1902 article in *Sunset Magazine*.[12] Both the private and public sectors expanded rapidly during the first three decades of the twentieth century. Stanford University secured its place as a national institution and, during the 1920s, as the West's leading upper-class university as well. The creation of the Claremont Colleges complex constituted one of the nation's most successful efforts to recreate the atmosphere of the New England liberal arts college. In the public sector, California led the nation in the creation of junior colleges. The 1920s also witnessed the establishment of the so-called Southern Campus of the University of California, soon known as the University of California, Los Angeles.

Despite fierce opposition from Northern California legislators, a wary state Board of Control, and even the university itself, UCLA emerged gradually over a decade. In 1919 the Los Angeles Normal School became the Southern Branch of the University of California, but it continued to offer only two years of collegiate-grade work. In 1922 it was permitted to offer four years of teacher training, although it could still offer no more than two years of liberal arts. A four-year College of Letters and Sciences was opened in the fall of 1924. It took four more years and a move to the present campus in Westwood for "the normal school that thought it could be a university" actually to become one. The demand for university-grade public higher education in the Southland had been met.[13] In the booming California of the 1920s, rather than pursue this extraordinary expansion of educational opportunity in a helter-skelter fashion, state and local governments, educators, and businessmen worked together slowly but steadily to plan the development of their state's higher education system.

In the 1930s, California developed the nation's most highly structured state system of higher education. The state legislature asked the Carnegie Foundation for the Advancement of Teaching to organize a study of California's public sector in 1932, and some of the best-known educators around the country went west to examine the plethora of public colleges and universities already formed there. The Commission of Seven was chaired by Samuel Capen, a former federal expert on higher education and now chancellor of the University of Buffalo, and included Minnesota's Coffman, George F. Zook, and the dean emeritus of Columbia University Teachers College, among others. After twenty-five years "of extensive experimentation" and confusion, the team admitted, the state had to come to grips with the financial exigencies of the Depression. More important, the report noted, there was a noticeable lack of unity in the administration of the public sector and a lack of articulation between segments of that sector. The Carnegie Foundation's 1932 report on California's public higher education stands out as the clearest statement of the philosophy of the differentiation of American higher education as originally conceived by educators between the two world wars.[14]

The study suggested that the Regents of the University of California be given the power to coordinate all public higher education above the junior college level in order to base statewide planning on "a scientific anticipation of genuine educational needs." This move would wrest control of public higher education from the ambitious hands of local educational entrepreneurs and politicians. Thus order would replace chaos, and money would be saved. Most of all, a highly organized public system of higher education would avoid the unnecessary and unwise duplication of purposes and courses among different types of institutions. The senior colleges and professional schools of the University of California should be selective because "overproduction . . . may readily become a social and professional evil, as well as an unwarranted cost to the university and the public." The new state colleges should cater to regional needs and the junior colleges should be viewed as an extension of secondary education. With the substantial increase in the number of young people seeking higher education and the increasing range of their talents and interests, this differentiation of public higher education was the most efficient, and therefore essential, response to modern educational conditions.

The report's critical message was that social efficiency should dictate the structure of higher learning in California and elsewhere in modern America. "In the past, educational careers have been too largely determined by personal whim," the experts concluded in their discussion of young people's selection of a college and a course of study. "Now that experience and psychological investigation indicate that a specific educational or vocational interest is not a good index to the possession of ability in a specific field, we are compelled to take into account both ability and interest, the first for social efficiency and the second for personal happiness. Both of these are desirable social goals." Progressive educators wanted to democratize higher education, and they did make it more accessible—the Carnegie team recommended, for example, that tuition not be charged at California junior colleges or for the first two years at the state colleges and universities—but they also believed that individual initiative should be curbed implicitly in the public interest.

This formulation for matching students with institutions is not inherently unfair, but the Carnegie team's proposal of sharp lines of demarkation between types of institutions would limit the ability of young people to move up from one segment to another. The study recommended that only the University of California at Berkeley be given the right to grant doctorates, and that the Los Angeles campus grant no degree higher than a master's. Similarly, the teachers' colleges should grant masters' degrees only in the field of education. The California Polytechnic Institute at San Luis Obispo should be abolished altogether, as its courses could be and were offered elsewhere. The four-year public colleges and universities should not provide technical training for the minor professions, which were properly the province of the two-year junior colleges. Further, the junior colleges should restrict themselves to a semiprofessional curriculum even if historically they had provided the first two years of a standard four-year college course and continued to be popularly regarded as part of the higher or university education system. Finally, the State Council for Educational Planning and Coordination should determine the state's personnel needs in each profession and field and advise the Regents accordingly on the appropriate enrollment level at each institution and in each course of study.

In the name of social efficiency, then, young people would be channeled to certain schools and into certain fields. The state would take a census of the state's work force, with particular attention to its professional and semiprofessional occupations, and determine how many young people should go to college, and where. Local educational entrepreneurs would be held in check; similarly, ambitious students who blossomed late in life—after high school—would find it difficult to move up from their prescribed position in the educational hierarchy. Personal whim, as the experts called it, took a back seat to social planning in educational matters. As in American economic life, the free market had not proved efficient enough in education. Planning was in the best interests of everyone, students and their parents, educators, and the state alike, and it was pursued more earnestly in California than anywhere else in the 1930s.

Presiding over this system was Robert G. Sproul, president of the University of California. Sproul asserted his support for a public system of education that offered the opportunity for higher learning to all, but, equally important, he also believed that the state's educational system should and could replicate the natural distribution of talent and needs in the society. Insisting that "the university is primarily designed for one type of mind and the junior college for another," he concluded, "what we need is . . . not more colleges and universities of the traditional type . . . but altogether different institutions which will suitably train those students and get them in their lifework sooner." It was therefore the responsibility of the state to offer a variety of educational opportunities to its youth, and each segment of the public sector should cater to specific concerns. In the interest of this "natural" efficiency, the California junior colleges should restrict themselves to educating those individuals interested in postsecondary education but not equipped for the professions, which were properly the province of the state university.[15]

While the rapid development of the junior colleges was taking place, California educators were encouraging the planned growth of the state college system. In the early 1920s, several normal schools became state teachers' colleges in order to meet the demand for high school teachers in one of the nation's most rapidly growing states. But, as elsewhere, these teachers' colleges provided access and training for more than just the prospective teachers in their region. In 1935 the state designated seven of them as state colleges. The public colleges at Chico, Fresno, Humboldt, San Diego, San Francisco, San Jose, and Santa Barbara were now given permission to offer a bachelor's degree in any of the liberal arts. To the administrators, faculty, and students of these schools, such recognition was long overdue. After all, they pointed out, in California and elsewhere, the teachers' colleges' curriculum and the abilities of their students had differed little from those of the universities since World War I, if not earlier.[16]

Educators simply wanted to clarify and simplify the boundaries between types of institutions and to shift the emphasis in each segment by defining its functions more carefully, a statewide California administrator argued in a 1939 pamphlet. "The new challenge to Democracy and the differentiation and specialization of the democratic process" demanded no less. After their designation as state colleges, these schools faced the task "of finding their proper and permanent place in the educational life of the state." He suggested that the state colleges should not try to become universities; instead, recalling their tradition as teacher-training institutions, they should emphasize the liberal, but not the learned, professions. While universities and liberal arts colleges were interested in the "idea of 'Culture' with a capital C"—"which carries an unconscious implication of preparation for a life of leisure and detachment from the hurly-burly of the market place"—the state colleges should remain "more sensitive to the needs of democracy."[17]

In its constituencies and its objectives, then, the state college differed from the more prestigious university; as a result, its "method will be psychological rather than logical, functional rather than structural." Preparation for teaching, middle-level government service, home economics, journalism, library work, nursing, personnel work, police work, psychiatric social work, and other social welfare work should be provided by the state college, since each of these areas was peripheral to the proper concerns of a university. Furthermore, state colleges should not be steered away from their proper functions by the growing interest in research at universities. The foundation of the state college curriculum should be an integrated study of the economic and social order which showed the organic relationships of individual personality, the scientific method, the American democratic social pattern, and the training for these liberal professions. These student-oriented institutions, as they were called, should emphasize "cooperative thinking," not the creation of new knowledge. Nor should they cultivate leadership skills, of course, since other institutions with other students logically enjoyed that privilege and responsibility. Socialization was clearly the first priority of institutions at this level. The state college had an articulated market, in theory if not always in reality, which distinguished it from the university above and the junior colleges below.

The Evolution of the Terminal Junior College

Though familiar today, the view that the predominant function of the junior college was to train its students for semiprofessional careers emerged only in the late 1920s. World War I had prompted fears that existing institutions would be overwhelmed by the crush of students. It seemed only logical to support the expansion and creation of two-year institutions in remote areas of large states, such as California, to meet the demands of people too young or impecunious to go away to college. Yet, while students and their parents continued to view the junior college as a preparatory step to university life and a university-trained career, educators began to articulate a different role for the two-year institution in an increasingly rigid educational hierarchy. Students at state universities contributed to the leadership of their generation; students at public junior colleges should contribute to social efficiency. No longer conceived of as a preparatory institution, the public junior college was altered in the late 1920s and 1930s into a terminal institution where most young people of limited means and allegedly limited abilities and aspirations concluded their education by preparing for a semi-professional occupation.

The roots of the junior college movement can be traced to American educators' interest in the German educational system in the late nineteenth century. Influential university presidents noted that secondary schools offered two more years of general education in Germany than in the United States. The graduate then went directly into the university for advanced or professional education. In the 1880s a number of private and public universities, including the universities of Michigan and Pennsylvania, made overtures to high schools in an effort to create such an arrangement. In 1892 William Rainey Harper, the "Father of the Junior College," divided the University of Chicago into the Academic College and the University College. A decade later, working with the public schools in Joliet, Illinois, Harper encouraged the establishment of the nation's first public junior college.[18]

Several top universities pursued the division of the undergraduate years into senior and junior colleges in the first two decades of the twentieth century. The lower division was separated into a distinct unit dedicated to general education. There, following the lead of Chicago's Harper and Stanford's David Starr Jordan, professional-oriented students received a general education before they specialized in the field of their choice or went directly to a professional school. The junior college was also developed to help ease the adjustment of young people who graduated from the many substandard high schools of the early twentieth century. Columbia's Nicholas Murray

Butler supported the formation of Seth Low Junior College in Brooklyn, for example, because he believed it would relieve some of the pressure for admission to his college by providing the two years of collegiate education then considered necessary before entrance to schools that prepared students for the nonlearned professions.

After World War I sparked the unprecedented demand for more widely diffused, practical, and local postsecondary education, the modern junior college was born. In 1918, although there were eighty-five junior colleges in nineteen states, fifty-six of them were concentrated in the five states of California, Missouri, Virginia, Texas, and Illinois; there was no junior college east of Michigan and north of North Carolina and Kentucky. For twenty-five years before the war the number of collegiate institutions had remained fairly constant; during the 1920s, however, as the number of colleges increased sharply from 670 to 1,076, nearly half of the new institutions—196 of 406—were junior colleges. The number of junior college students climbed tenfold, to 45,000, between the war and the mid-1920s, and nearly tripled again by even the most conservative estimate between 1928 and 1938.[19]

While both private and public junior colleges experienced rapid growth between the two world wars, the public sector became predominant. Between 1922 and 1927, enrollment in public junior colleges jumped 217 percent as enrollment in private junior colleges increased (only) 102 percent. Six states had enacted laws that stipulated the conditions for state support of local junior colleges by 1926; eleven states joined them in 1927 and 1928. As late as the 1930s, well over three of every four junior colleges were still housed in high schools. In Creston, Iowa, the junior college occupied the second floor of the new high school building opened in the fall of 1926. Located, or "fortunately situated," sixty-five miles from the nearest four-year college, Creston Junior College drew 104 students from eighteen high schools to its modest offices, library, drafting room, and few classrooms. The junior college students shared the laboratory, gymnasium, and auditorium with the 570 high school students. Also typical of the explosive growth of the public junior college was Sacramento Junior College: between 1922 and 1928, enrollment skyrocketed from 198 to 1,378 regular students, the number of faculty climbed from 10 to 57, and the school's budget went from less than $51,000 to nearly $240,000. During the Depression, no doubt in part because of their low cost (tuition was even free in eight states), public junior colleges nearly tripled their enrollment and increased their proportionate share of the junior college market.[20]

The distribution of these early junior colleges shows that they were most successful in sparsely populated regions, particularly in the Midwest, Southwest, and West. More than 40 percent of the junior college presidents surveyed after World War I gave their geographical remoteness from the state university as the primary reason for their school's creation; far fewer mentioned vocational training as the top initial priority. A 1931 proposal to establish a network of nine junior colleges in Utah demonstrated this public sentiment. The study suggested that a mining region east of Salt Lake City, for example, where only one in four high school graduates attended college, was the sort of place that needed a junior college. More rural parents than urban parents reported that their children would attend a junior college if one were nearby. Furthermore, these parents and potential students were interested in a wide variety of liberal arts and professional courses of study, particularly in commerce, but did not suggest that these studies should be terminal.[21] As far as parents and students were concerned, the public junior college was to be an all-inclusive rather than a narrowly defined institution.

Liberal arts educators were divided about whether the extraordinary growth of the junior colleges constituted a threat to their own existence in the 1920s. As late as 1929, presidents of small liberal arts schools such as Illinois's Knox College were wary of the competition. However, speaking at the National Conference of Junior Colleges in 1920, a meeting sponsored by the federal Bureau of Education, George F. Zook observed, "It is becoming increasingly apparent that universities and colleges alike are beginning to regard the junior college as an institution of great possible usefulness in the field of higher education." The dean of Carleton College insisted that most students drawn to the junior colleges were "not from the class of those who otherwise prepare themselves for larger service in the wider fields of leadership, but rather from those many of whom would have attached themselves to the artisan class a generation ago." Among the junior college's most important functions, he added, was that of freeing the liberal arts college and university from the need to educate "the throng of immature pupils who, but virtue of interest, or intellectual limitation, have no concern for a liberal education."[22] Many of the weakest liberal arts colleges were converted to two-year schools during the 1920s, but the junior colleges' threat to the well-established schools was insignificant by the early 1930s.

President Ray L. Wilbur of Stanford University, later secretary of the interior in Herbert Hoover's cabinet, was a leading proponent of university–junior college cooperation. "Such schools become clearing-houses for the universities, culling out those unable to go further and stimulating and pointing right those for whom a university course is necessary and desirable," he wrote in 1916. With the development of the junior college, Wilbur hoped that Stanford could "see its way clear to becoming more of a university and less of a college." Until the mid-1920s, Wilbur envisioned a day in the not too distant future when Stanford could eliminate its Lower Division because it duplicated the efforts of the junior colleges and could concentrate primarily on university work.[23] Besieged by students from diverse backgrounds and with various interests, more and more four-year institutions looked to establish cooperative arrangements with junior colleges, particularly in such fields as engineering and commerce. A 1930 survey pointed out that about one-third of the graduates of these programs—sponsored by such institutions as Boston, Rutgers, and George Washington universities—transferred to a university. "From a pedagogical point of view," the federal commissioner of education concurred, "such an extension of the secondary schools is natural and justifiable."[24]

Even as more and more educators supported the concept of the terminal junior college, this so-called preparatory function remained central to the mission of the public junior college throughout the 1920s. Pushed by these educators on one side and by ambitious students on the other, many junior college presidents were concerned about the schizophrenic nature of the two-year school's identity. "Is its function to prepare boys and girls for life or to prepare them for the junior year in the A. B. college?" asked a junior college president in 1920. "I want to know whether I must build courses for the 90 percent or say 75 percent who are going no further, or the 25 percent who are going on to the junior year of the standard four-year college. Shall we take care particularly of those going out into life or those going on to college?" From his position as professor of secondary education at the University of Minnesota, Leonard V. Koos admitted in the first large-scale study of the junior college movement in the mid-1920s that the preparatory, or isthmian, function was the primary thrust behind the founding of public junior colleges. A review of the statements of purpose of these schools as late as 1930 pointed out that preparation for university work was emphasized more than vocational education in nearly two-thirds of the 343 catalogues studied.[25] Most schools tried to offer both. This strategy was satisfying to students but not to those educators convinced that the junior college's function was primarily to provide semiprofessional training.

Despite the opposition of parents and students and the success of university–junior college arrangements, the public junior college was reorganized by education experts, as Southern College president Arthur Davis put it, "on a twentieth-century basis" in the 1920s and 1930s. Progressive educators, including Koos and Alexis Lange of the University of California, believed occupational training of large numbers of young people enhanced society's economic and social efficiency and secured those students' occupational, and therefore personal, happiness. Lange insisted that "the rise and progress of the Junior College needs to be looked upon as an integral phase of a country-wide movement towards a more adequate state system of education; a twentieth-century system, made in America; a system that shall function progressively so as to secure for the nation the greatest efficiency of the greatest number."[26] Businessmen eager for trained young people also boosted this concept.

The terminal junior college was viewed as an efficient and democratic solution to the problem of adjusting American youth to a modern hierarchical economic and social structure. "The problem of sifting the fit from the unfit and of selecting those who should be guided into shorter curricula on the semi-professional level would largely be solved in the junior college," Zook concluded. Consequently, when they guided certain students toward the junior college, these educators insisted they were doing those young people a favor. But most educators were actually more concerned about steering undesirable students, even if talented, away from the traditional four-year colleges; A. Lawrence Lowell of Harvard admitted, "One of the merits of these new institutions will be [the] keeping out of college, rather than leading into it, [of] young people who have no taste for higher education."[27] While parents and students still focused on the cultural aims of junior college education, educators focused the attention of the junior college on purportedly nonintellectual students. The junior college would supplement, not supplant or compete with, the four-year collegiate sector.

The vocational junior college that emerged in the 1920s flourished during the Depression. A few junior colleges were established before World War I for vocational purposes, most notably Chaffey Union Junior College in California, founded largely to assist local agricultural interests, and Chicago's Crane Junior College, which provided advanced technical training of the sort offered in the city's vocational high schools. Typically, when new junior colleges were created in the 1920s, efforts were made to incorporate local vocational interests in the curriculum. In 1923, a survey of education in Massachusetts recommended that junior colleges be formed to offer "the first two years of college work in liberal arts and sciences and such other courses of study of two years of less in length as the needs of the community seem to demand . . . [which] may include vocational, technical, commercial, and home-making courses of study." After examining the catalogues of 500 two-year colleges, G. Vernon Bennett reported in 1928 that while support for vocational junior colleges was still in its "very earliest stage," training for twenty-eight minor professions was already available, mainly at such privately controlled schools as the Wentworth Institute in Boston, the Pierce School of Business Administration in Philadelphia, the College of Industrial Arts in Denton, Texas, and even the Lewis Tea Room Institute in Washington, D.C. He predicted that more occupational fields would be included in the curricula of public junior colleges as states began to use such schools to meet the anticipated need for workers.[28]

Given these efforts, it is not surprising that surveys in the late 1920s began to indicate a rapid increase in the number of students enrolled in junior colleges for purposes other than preparation for a university education. A survey of the curricula of nineteen public junior colleges showed that while the total of credit hours offered in the ancient languages declined 18 percent between 1920–21 and 1929–30, the total number of credit hours in the social sciences rose 59 percent, and the total number of credit hours in engineering and home economics climbed 230 percent and 243 percent, respectively. A survey of more than five-thousand urban high school graduates in the San Francisco–Berkeley area who intended to go to a junior college found that nearly twice as many students were planning to take commercial and business courses as were planning to enroll in general academic courses. This 1930 study also concluded that this interest in vocational junior college education did not lead to a decline in attendance at the area's four-year institutions.[29] Educators' efforts to foster the development of the vocational junior college had taken root. A new type of educational institution had been grafted successfully onto modern American higher education.

Educators and businessmen of the 1930s stressed the need for locally based schools of postsecondary education where students could be kept off the job market while they were trained for work at low cost. The number of high school graduates had doubled in each of the first three decades of the twentieth century and increased further from 667,000 to 1,210,000 a year between 1930 and 1940; this growth provided a vast reservoir of potential students ill prepared to enter the job market in the best of times, let alone during the Depression. Young people were encouraged to enroll at a junior college for vocational training in an effort to reduce the labor supply and ease the economic crisis of the 1930s a bit. "The junior college has a certain passive value that is of immeasurable importance," the editor of the *California Journal of Secondary Education* wrote, "for in this day of widespread unemployment if offers a haven where millions of unemployed youths may occupy themselves with worthwhile activities."[30]

Walter C. Eells's 1941 study *Why Junior College Terminal Education?* applauded the pervasiveness of the terminal junior college. An extensive survey conducted for this report showed that 79 percent of the educators and laymen questioned believed that the terminal function of the junior college was more important than its preparatory function. Eells attributed the popularity of the public junior college to the opportunities it offered young people for "greater economic competence, social usefulness, and personal satisfaction" than they could find elsewhere, particularly during the Depression. As recently as 1937 the philosopher Norman Foerster and commented that the junior college was still "vague or inconsistent in [its] aims, awaiting some decisive definition"; but the die was soon cast. Locally based, semiprofessional, terminal junior college education became the stated goal of the American Association of Junior Colleges; similarly, sensitive to the connections between education and the labor market, W. Lloyd Warner and the Educational Policies Commission of the National Education Association endorsed the concept of semiprofessional education for those between eighteen and twenty years old. In two decades, economic and social forces had created a public junior college that trained its students for as many as 106 semiprofessional fields.[31]

Yet the public did not endorse the terminal junior college as enthusiastically as educators did. It proved difficult to discourage their ambitions for their children. Local access to higher education of any kind—and not just to vocational education—was the primary reason for attendance at junior colleges throughout the Depression. Parents supported the creation or expansion of junior colleges because they wanted higher education brought closer to their homes for financial or social reasons. Surveys showed that the junior colleges played a critical role in facilitating access to higher education for poor and ethnic students generally, and not just for those among them interested in the semiprofessional fields. A 1929 study showed that the proportion of lower-class students in California public junior colleges was more than three times greater than their porportion at four-year institutions in the state.[32] Junior college students were not nearly so inadequately prepared or so unintellectual as most proponents of the terminal junior college alleged they were.

The junior college students who transferred to four-year institutions did quite well there. In 1919, a study found that two-thirds of public junior college graduates continued their education at a college or university. This proportion of transfers declined throughout the 1920s, but as late as the 1930s as many as one-quarter of all junior college graduates went on to four-year schools. Even after the idea of the terminal junior college had taken hold—at a time when, for example, President Sproul of the University of California asserted that only 2 percent, or one of fifty, of the public junior college graduates were capable of university work—a substantial number of public junior college graduates moved up the educational hierarchy.[33] In addition, studies at institutions across the country pointed out that junior college transfers did as well as their peers in their junior and senior years of college, even at such prestigious universities as Minnesota, Michigan, Chicago, California, and Stanford. In the mid-1930s, for example, junior college graduates at Stanford scored slightly higher on psychological tests and graduated in greater proportions than those students who entered Stanford as freshmen.[34] Although embarrassing, the presence of these talented but poor students at public junior colleges did not deter educators from espousing the concept of terminal junior college education with increasing frequency during the 1920s and 1930s.

The history of the California public junior college movement reveals how the junior college evolved into a local, vocational-oriented institution between the two world wars. Laws passed by the legislature in 1917 and 1921 specified the rules by which local districts could receive state and county funds to set up junior college programs. One of these schools, Chaffey Junior College in Ontario, became the model vocational public junior college: it not only offered courses in commerce, home economics, and mechanical arts, it also operated an 88-acre orchard for agricultural experimental purposes. Between 1922 and 1930, the number of students in California public junior colleges increased from 2,259 to 20,641. The proportion of junior college students (both years) to high school graduates tripled in the 1920s alone, from 16 percent to 54 percent.[35] For young people far from Berkeley and other well-known schools, the junior college constituted the first step up the ladder of higher education.

Yet, beginning in the 1920s, California educators saw the junior college as an extension of the high school, not as part of the university system. Sproul declared that efforts by junior colleges to expand into four-year institutions were "subversive of the best interests of democracy." Two-year schools stood simply for "further educational preparedness for the greatest number, for democratic continuity and completeness of educational opportunity," but not for university-level training and social leadership.[36]

The 1932 Carnegie panel of educational experts echoed these sentiments; it, too, asserted that a public junior college that emphasized its university preparatory function rather than its terminal vocational function was undemocratic. The team recited the litany of complaints against ambitious local educational entrepreneurs and parents and students. It sharply criticized local districts for their slavish imitation of "expensive, higher-type schools." The public junior college that catered to the so-called self-deceptions of local parents who wanted a college preparatory curriculum was not performing "its allotted social duty." Instead, the national panel urged that greater emphasis be put on "the proper development of completion curricula." "When junior college management looks upward to the university to discover its functions, its point of view, its procedures, and its social philosophy, it creates the largest possible gap between itself and the community high schools," the experts advised, "whereas it ought to be looking outward upon the community and its life to discover how all its unselected and different kinds of students may be educated to intelligent cooperation and useful membership in society." Labeling statistics on the significant number of junior college transfers as misleading, they urged the public junior college to grant only the Associate in Arts degree, which

was "not to be confused with the qualifying function of a junior certificate or any other title or document designed to attest fitness to enter a
senior college or a professional school."[37] Ironically, then, by the late
1930s, President N. H. McCollum of Lassen Junior College was speaking for the mainstream of American educational thought when he
proudly proclaimed the California public junior colleges to be "the
'people's colleges,' designed and organized to provide graduates with
marketable skills and knowledge that they may become self-supporting citizens of our American democracy."[38]

The Social Impulse behind the Junior College Movement

The emergence of the vocational-oriented public junior college
bears dramatic testimony to the social influences that guided the
transformation of American higher education between the two world
wars. As education became more important to economic growth and
social progress, the evolution of institutions of higher learning was no
longer left to chance. Progressives who had sought to regulate the
marketplace, however tentatively, now looked to organize higher education. Optimistically, they felt that all young people should have
access to higher education in order to fulfill their personal potential.
But even in a democracy, they believed, there were leaders and fol-
lowers, and they set out to replicate this distinction in an equally
"natural" and "efficient" differentiated system of higher learning
evocative of their view of a complex modern world. Faced with a
potential student body increasingly large and diverse in socioeconomic backgrounds and interests, and with a great concern for the need
for an increasingly white-collar work force, educators encouraged the
formation of a new type of postsecondary education devoted to semiprofessional vocational training. The transmission of knowledge—as
well as the aspirations and abilities of the affected students—took a
back seat to the so-called public interest.

The junior college movement, then, constituted a critical stage in
the dramatic explosion of educational opportunities. It resulted in the
rapid and broad diffusion of higher education. At the same time,
however, an increased emphasis on terminal junior college education
between the two world wars circumscribed the education and training of students. Students were there to start college; educators
thought they should be there to start and finish postsecondary educa-

tion. Certainly, a majority of young people at the public junior colleges of this or any subsequent era were not capable of or interested in university-level work, but the interests and needs of the many who attended the junior college to prepare for the university were frustrated by educators' elitist intentions.

The social prejudices of most educators compromised their idealistic efforts to foster equality of educational opportunity. Intent on introducing order as an educational priority, they established a rigid hierarchy of institutions. Convinced of an inequitable distribution of talent in the society, and, even more important, of their ability to determine fairly those who were destined to lead and those others who were destined to follow, educators delineated distinctions between different types of institutions, and particularly between four- and two-year colleges. As a result, the public junior college evolved into an institution geared to meet society's needs for a trained work force rather than an institution of higher learning designed to accommodate the interests of worthy but not well-off students. In doing so, the public junior college did provide access to the training that was a preliminary step toward economic and social mobility for its students; yet, by leaving higher learning to four-year institutions, it also limited the opportunities available to those students. Reflective of the democratic possibilities brought about by educational expansion, the junior college movement also revealed the limitations of conservative American reform.

9 / Higher Education during the Depression

American higher education fared better than most social institutions during the Depression. The value of higher education was rarely questioned. While students and faculty suffered countless hardships, few institutions actually closed. Except during 1932–34, attendance edged upward during the decade. Academics hailed the seriousness of the student body. Moved by the pleas of able but underprivileged young people and worried college presidents, as well as by the increasing number of unemployed young adults, the federal government created a work-study program to enable a limited number of disadvantaged students to remain in school. This unprecedented peacetime project permitted many poor students—particularly the children of immigrants—the opportunity to attend college and to begin to move up the economic and social ladder. Public policy recognized education as an integral part of the economic structure of the troubled nation: campus protests, chiefly in support of the peace movement, marked the emergence of the student body as a critical social conscience for the country. In the face of adversity, then, American higher education consolidated and even strengthened its position in modern American society.

"Registration has stood up amazingly well," a professor remarked in the September 1933 issue of *Forum,* "[but] to send a girl or boy to college or to a school of collegiate grade this year will involved desperate sacrifices for many people. If they still insist on making such sacrifices, it will mean that the college idea has taken such firm root in the public imagination that it cannot be eradicated."[1] Did an 8 percent decline in enrollment between 1932 and 1934 indicate that the

American college had lost its popularity? Or did it show that the number of those who could not afford to go to college was far greater than the number of those who were determined to attend? Did those who enrolled do so because of their belief in the value of higher learning or because they had no better place to go to wait for the economy to improve? The dramatic vignettes of individual students' efforts to remain in school even at extraordinary sacrifice testify to American faith in higher education. Harry Chase told an Illinois audience in 1931:

> The current is too strong to be stemmed by any temporary depression, or by any criticism of the crowding of our colleges. . . . Almost unconsciously we have come to a point at which the prolongation of formal education up to the age of maturity has become the normal and accepted state of affairs. Never before in the world has this been possible for the average family. In times of depression it is one of the last opportunities to be surrendered.[2]

Even during bad times, it was still abundantly clear that college attendance enhanced one's hopes, if not one's actual possibilities, for economic and social mobility. On the whole, to paraphrase W. C. Fields, the comedic philosopher of the period, most students felt they would rather be in school.

The Depression did shake the confidence of American higher education. Though few colleges closed their doors in the 1930s, many were plagued by the constant fear of impending financial disaster. The federal Office of Education reported that the number of actual closings was small: between 1934 and 1936, for example, of 1,700 colleges and universities, 31 shut down and 22 others merged. Only three of these schools were four-year colleges, and nearly all were private.[3] Still, time and again, presidents of popular colleges felt compelled to deny rumors of the demise of their institutions. DePauw University's president responded publicly to the rumor that it would close for three weeks in the spring of 1933 because "at times of serious crisis, rumors, which under ordinary circumstances would be dismissed with a laugh, are given serious attention"; he assured the university community that the school was more solvent than most colleges. At the same time, an editorial in the Alabama Polytechnic Institute student newspaper predicted the school would close that fall because the state had not provided the funding appropriated to the

college by the legislature; the administration held meetings to reas-
sure the students that the school would remain open and to urge them
to press their local legislators to support the university. In 1936, even
as the school was put on probation by the Southern Association of
Colleges for its failure to provide adequate financial resources for the
library, faculty, and administrative expenses, more than 350 students
were turned away because of overcrowding.[4] Most less prestigious
institutions did not close, but they had to struggle to remain open.

Pressure on state budgets for employment and relief programs led
to the sharp curtailment of funds for public higher education. Between 1930 and 1936, public higher education's share of the states'
budgets dropped from 22.3 percent to 14.4 percent. Prestigious state
universities were not left untouched by the cost-cutting: in 1934, for
example, the University of Minnesota's appropriation was less than it
had been in 1921, although enrollment was 50 percent higher than it
had been a decade earlier. While enrollment climbed at the University
of California, the ratio of university appropriations to state expenditures declined 15 percent between the late 1920s and the mid-1930s.
The plight of Massachusetts State College was typical. Between 1930
and 1940, its state appropriation edged up 8 percent, the size of its
faculty increased 30 percent, and its enrollment jumped 54 percent;
the college witnessed an increase in attendance despite the administration's determination to limit its student body to the number specified by the state legislature because of financial considerations.[5]
Their relatively low cost made such institutions enormously popular.
Indeed, admission to Massachusetts State became so competitive that
its students' academic qualifications probably exceeded those of students at the well-known and purportedly selective private liberal arts
colleges nearby.

The desperate financial condition of most families put a severe
strain on the budgets of colleges and universities. In 1934, receipts of
all institutions were only 61 percent of the total receipts of four years
before, even though enrollment had dropped only slightly. The trustees of Pomona College authorized an increase in enrollment to make
up for lost income, but attendance declined. The student loan fund
was increased and a faculty committee was formed to handle requests
for credit from students, some of whom offered their families' proper-
ty as collateral; yet, even after the minimum room-and-board charge
was lowered to stimulate enrollment and faculty salaries were cut 15
percent, the college's deficits mounted until the middle of the decade.

Similarly, faced with a loss of 35 percent of its income from endowment and 18 percent of its income from student fees, the University of Chicago cut faculty salaries by as much as 20 percent, refused to replace retiring faculty, eliminated the school's fourth quarter, and made a wide range of other adjustments to the loss of liquidity.[6]

Colleges were willing to try nearly anything to retain students and thereby stay open. At least one of every seven private colleges and universities accepted personal notes in lieu of tuition payments. Carthage College in Illinois accepted coal in place of cash; at the University of North Dakota, farm produce sufficed. Colleges and their students turned to cooperative business ventures to remain in the business of higher learning: over 75,000 students in about 160 schools generated nearly $3 million in revenue annually from a wide array of businesses to help themselves and their schools.[7] But these efforts proved insufficient to keep an institution's financial picture even remotely bright, particularly before the federal work-study program got under way.

Institutions increased the amount of scholarship assistance available to students but this effort strained their budgets even further. In the prosperous 1920s, few colleges or universities had established significant scholarship or loan programs; indeed, the typical member of the prestigious Association of American Universities distributed loans to less than 1 percent of its students. In 1927–28, 402 institutions awarded 34,013 scholarships; by 1934—35, 674 colleges gave out 66,708 scholarships. Private and public institutions gave out 38 and 44 percent more loan money, respectively, in 1936–37 than in 1928–29. While these increases in scholarships and loans appear substantial, these funds were available at only a small proportion of schools and could help only a limited number of students. At the Case School of Applied Science, for example, only $5,000 had been set aside for the loan fund for the fall of 1932, yet even before registration there were requests for at least $9,800 in loans; by the end of the semester, loans totaling more than $20,000 were arranged, but they were restricted to juniors, seniors, and graduate students. The University of North Carolina and other colleges conducted special fundraising campaigns to increase the size of their loan funds.[8]

Thousands of students were forced to withdraw from school. Scholarships and loans were spread as far as possible—a Western Reserve administrator wrote, "In some cases, even a twenty-five dollar gift has proved to be the slender thread that has kept the hope of getting an education from fading completely"—but institutions could not meet students' needs for funds. While education was one of the last places where families economized, the number of students withdrawing from college climbed as the Depression deepened. Over 60 percent of the freshmen who left the University of Chicago in the fall of 1931 did so for financial reasons. Only 54 percent of those who entered Stanford in 1930–31 graduated four years later, the highest attrition rate since World War I. National surveys showed that the decline was proportionately greater among upperclassmen than among entering freshmen throughout the 1930s.[9]

Furthermore, it was not so easy as the popular myth suggested then, as now, for a student to work his way through school. The number of part-time students increased, but decent hours and pay were the exception, not the rule. In addition, college officials were often accused of misleading students about the possibilities of work-study projects. A working student complained, "Working one's way through college sounds wonderful but work is scarce and few of the majority of students who can get work are really capable of doing enough part-time work to earn sufficient money to pay for most of their necessities and still do good work in their studies." A study of student "mortality" at twenty-five colleges and universities pointed out that attrition increased during the Depression and that those who dropped out for financial reasons ranked higher in ability than those who left for other reasons.[10] Despite their best efforts, thousands of talented students could not work and stay in school.

Financial hardships aside, trends in attendance patterns established in the early 1920s continued, but at a much slower pace. The Depression dampened but did not extinguish Americans' desire for practical higher education. Although there was a lag of about two years, enrollment fell and rose in accordance with the business cycle. As late as 1932, enrollment edged upward slightly at some schools because students were still drawing on family savings. Then, as economic conditions worsened, undergraduate programs, particularly in professional fields, witnessed a sharp downturn. While universities lost less than 6 percent and liberal arts colleges about 3 percent of their enrollment between 1929 and 1934, professional and technical schools and teachers' colleges lost nearly 12 percent. Urban institutions were especially hard hit: an estimated 10,000 of the almost 13,000 students in New York University's engineering, commerce, and teaching programs left school; more typically, Worchester Polytechnic Institute in Massachusetts lost one-fifth of its student body during 1932–34. "The prevailing political philosophy has tended to cast doubt on technological enterprise, to weaken public faith in the integrity of industrial leaders, and to call into question the social enlightenment of the professions from which they are largely drawn," the president of the Case School of Applied Science explained, but the real truth was that public faith in higher education was largely dependent on the availability of jobs for college graduates, and enrollment followed the business cycle accordingly.[11]

Even if its performance was still erratic, the American economy improved sufficiently in the late 1930s to stimulate a substantial increase in enrollment. The campus atmosphere changed for the better as employers returned to the colleges after a three- or four-year hiatus: feeling more optimistic about their futures, students remained in school. First-generation and poor students, attracted to practical college courses as a short-cut to economic and social status, had been the first to be forced not to attend or to drop out of college for financial reasons; with the demand for engineers, middle-level managers, and teachers improving somewhat in the late 1930s, and with modest federal assistance, these students came back to school. Attendance at liberal arts colleges climbed 13 percent between 1934 and 1939, and enrollment in professional and technical schools and teachers' colleges leaped by over 37 percent and 40 percent, respectively, during the same period.[12]

By the end of the 1930s, then, most educators believed conditions had returned to normal. Stanford's experiences during the 1930s reveal the ups and downs suffered by even the most prestigious schools during the difficult decade. Seeking to reverse a decline in enrollment, the trustees voted to admit additional freshmen in the spring of 1932 with the understanding that admissions standards would not be compromised; yet in the next few years, all qualified men were admitted and even the strict quota on the number of women admitted was waived as well. In his 1936–37 annual report, President Ray L. Wilbur noted that while faculty salaries and institutional income were still below pre-Depression levels, the admissions situation and students' spirits had regained their 1920s form. In addition, Wilbur was convinced that the Depression had taught parents, faculty, students, and others alike that "the changes in business, industry, and the professions all require more university training for those who expect to occupy places of responsibility and training."[13] Not only had the confident rhetoric of the 1920s reappeared, but so had the students.

The Shift toward the Public Sector

With its relatively low cost and sensitivity to the practical concerns of parents and students, the public sector continued to grow at a faster rate than the private sector during the 1930s. Alabama Polytechnic Institute, for example, after struggling to keep its engineering, agriculture, and business programs alive earlier in the decade, enrolled nearly as many freshmen in the fall of 1940 as it had students in all four classes in 1934.[14] As a result of the rapid expansion of public junior colleges, public colleges and universities enrolled more students than private institutions of higher learning for the first time in the nation's history in 1933–34. By the end of the decade, public four-year institutions alone had drawn nearly even with their private counterparts (see Table 4).[15] The importance of access to the public sector cannot be overstated: in nearly every state, local teachers' colleges and public junior colleges suffered less during the early years of the Depression than other types of institutions and grew faster during the latter years of the 1930s because of their appeal to financially strapped students perhaps interested in, but certainly unable to afford, more prestigious schools.

The growth of the four-year public sector was modest in comparison with the extraordinary expansion of the public junior college. While every other type of institution, public and private, saw its attendance decline between 1929 and 1934, attendance at the na-

Table 4. Number of and percentage increase in students at public and private four-year colleges and universities, 1933–40

Type of school	1933–34	1935–36		1937–38		1939–40	
		Number	Percentage increase	Number	Percentage increase	Number	Percentage increase
Public	400,598	476,018	19%	555,815	17%	628,230	13%
Private	518,578	586,724	13	653,441	11	688,928	5

Sources: Biennial Surveys of Education: 1932–34, vol. 1, chap. 4, pp. 34–35; *1934–36,* vol. 2, chap. 4, pp. 38–39; *1936–38,* vol. 1, chap. 4, pp. 46–47; *1938–42,* vol. 1, chap. 3, pp. 14, 34–35.

tion's junior colleges increased by over 20 percent. During the decade as a whole, enrollment skyrocketed 76 percent. Not only did enrollment in the public junior colleges rise from about 56,000 to over 107,000 between 1934 and 1940, but the number of public junior colleges also increased from 152 to 217. The emergence of the terminal junior college widened the junior college's appeal, attracting young people interested in one of the semiprofessional fields, at the same time that a substantial number of young people who might have gone away to college chose to attend school near home for financial reasons. By 1940, one of every ten college students in the nation was enrolled in a junior college, a type of educational institution barely a generation old.[16]

This shift toward the public sector was attributed to the class bias of those in the elite private sector of American higher education. Ethnic and poor Americans were still kept out of more prestigious institutions by admissions quotas and high tuition, even in this time of financial exigency. Nearly two-thirds of the student body at a typical state university, but only about 15 percent of the students at a typical eastern elite institution, worked their way through school; a report by the American Association of University Professors blamed this disparity on selective admissions processes.[17] Indeed, the economic crisis seemed to dramatize the snobbishness of students at elite institutions. Their indifference to the plight of less fortunate Americans led the British political scientist Harold Laski to write an article titled "Why Don't Your Young Men Care?" published in Harper's Magazine in July 1931. Class divisions existed at state universities as well: the film critic Pauline Kael and others noted the distinctions and conflict between the poorer students working their way through the University of California at Berkeley and elsewhere and the schools' well-to-do fraternity and sorority members.[18]

The new president of Harvard, James B. Conant, conceded that private colleges and universities were competing fiercely for the children of the less than 5 percent of American families that had incomes of over $5,000 while brighter youngsters from poorer families were forced to forgo college or to attend less prestigious public schools. While most prestigious liberal arts colleges were able to maintain their pre-Depression enrollment levels, they were forced to sacrifice their admissions standards to do so. Without question, the proportion of mediocre students from upper-middle-class families admitted to such colleges as Dartmouth, Yale, and Chicago rose substantially as institutions chose deliberately to accept less qualified but paying customers. A Dartmouth memorandum on financial policy in 1935 stated baldly that "the College has adopted the definite policy of encouraging only a limited number of men who are dependent upon financial aid from us to enter each year." The president of Wesleyan University bewailed the presence of "white dullards" in college and admitted that Jewish and black students had to be two and ten times, respectively, as bright as their peers "to open the doors which the native white finds wide open before him."[19] The political and cultural clout of the WASP upper middle class, particularly in the East, also contributed to the austerity in public higher education, which further limited the opportunities for underprivileged young people to attend public institutions.

The largest losses in enrollment came in the eastern and north-central regions of the nations. While attendance at junior colleges and teachers' colleges in the West climbed even during the worst years of the Depression, attendance in the eastern and north-central states continued to decline until 1934–35. Some eastern urban universities benefited when more students chose to stay at home and commute to school, but the gains these schools made came at the expense of well-established rural residential colleges. The East had fewer public institutions to pick up the slack—the middle Atlantic states combined had fewer junior colleges than Iowa alone—and enrollment even at the state universities there was severely restricted by financially strapped state legislatures. The junior and teachers' colleges of the West, in contrast, did provide a means for poorer students to go to college; as one contemporary Colorado commentator noted, a student could get two years of college education at a nearby teachers' college or junior college for about the cost of railway fare from his home to a private college of similar caliber across the state.[20]

Disillusionment

By the winter of 1932–33, most institutions had begun to suffer from losses in income and attendance. Middle-class students found their checks from home had diminished; the radical student leader James Wechsler noted the steady and irresistible decline and fall of the middle-class members of "collegiate country clubs" across the nation. Poorer students were truly engaged in a life-and-death struggle to stay in school. As early as 1930, the college employment office at CCNY reported it could not find part-time jobs for needy students; within a few years, Wechsler observed, "scores of students there [were] under-fed [and] emaciated." At Kansas University, a student was found living on a quart of milk and one sweet roll a day. Students took any kind of job to keep themselves fed and clothed; a few even hunted each night for cockroaches to sell to a biological company for a penny apiece. Numerous students suffered from malnutrition, nervous breakdowns, or both.21

Graduates were not much better off. Bitter and unemployed youth denounced educators for promises made but not kept. Later the federal Office of Education commented that the worst effect of the economic crisis had been the deep discouragement felt by the large number of students who had worked their way through college only to find that no jobs awaited them. No more than three of eight Harvard graduates in the spring of 1932 had found work by the following fall, but even fewer graduates of other schools—about 15 percent—were so fortunate. The DePauw University student newspaper predicted that only one of eight 1933 graduates would get a job. It was suggested that graduates be given a hot dog instead of a diploma—it would be of more use to them. Students sang an "Ode to Higher Education":

> I sing in praise of college,
> Of M.A.s and Ph.D.s,
> But in pursuit of knowledge,
> We are starving by degrees.

Undergraduates implored college administrators to recognize the hollowness of their rhetoric and to admit that the training they were providing was worthless. "The world welcomed [the graduates of the 1920s] with open arms, absorbed them into industry, into professions," remarked a Dartmouth commencement speaker in 1935. "Now our college graduates are liberally sprinkled among the long, drab lines of unemployment in every state in the Union." Even when the college graduate did find a job, he enjoyed little of the prosperity his predecessors did: the average graduate of the class of 1934 at the University of Minnesota earned $1,200, $800 less than the average graduate of Minnesota's class of 1928. Robert and Helen Lynd, among others, wondered if such widespread disillusionment could end Americans' blind faith in the promise of higher education.[22] They were quickly proven wrong, but in the years between 1932 and 1934, a sense of betrayal permeated many a college campus. As with other economic and social institutions, it soon became apparent that only the federal government could alleviate the social tension that hung like a Dust Bowl cloud over American higher education.

The Government Steps In

In the final months of his administration, President Herbert Hoover called for a Conference on the Crisis in Education. Meeting in January 1933, the conference came to the not so startling conclusion that since institutions of higher learning furnished "conclusive proof of the reality of the equality of opportunity in American life" and educated a large proportion of the leaders of the country's economic and social life, higher education deserved to remain a high priority during what was considered the temporary economic setback. Its report urged the states to continue their support for public higher education in order to avoid any unnecessary reduction in educational opportunity. No specific recommendations were made.[23] The Hoover administration offered platitudes, not assistance. No doubt here, as in nearly all other policy matters, the president was a prisoner of his own past and his philosophy. After all, he had worked his way through Stanford University years before; now, from the White House, he could not, or refused to, see the "Hoovervilles" springing up on the outskirts of cities and the starving students who were unable to find even the meager jobs that had once propelled young men like Herbert Hoover to fortune and fame. Direct relief for persons or social institutions, if approved at all, was the prerogative of the individual states and local communities. In the bleak winter of 1932–33, educators and students, as well as the American people in general, waited for a New Deal.

In August 1933, after the frenzied "first hundred days" of Franklin D. Roosevelt's presidency, college and university presidents were invited to Washington to meet with officials of the newly created Federal Emergency Relief Administration (FERA) to discuss the possibility of establishing work-study projects on college campuses. In the early years of the Depression, for the first time, colleges had had to find substantial loan and scholarship money or risk bankruptcy;

most institutions, therefore, were eager to participate in any kind of reasonable program of federal assistance. Among those in attendance was Chicago's Hutchins, who brought with him a plan for a national student loan program. He gave the plan to President Roosevelt at a White House meeting, but the administration had already decided to set up an experimental work-study plan that fall at the University of Minnesota. Responding to the thousands of appeals from students and anxious college officials, the FERA announced its intention to support the concept of federal financial assistance for work-study programs nationwide if the Minnesota plan worked out well. It did; and in the spring of 1934 the program was extended to 65,000 students across the country.[24]

From the outset, in rhetoric and effectiveness the FERA work-study program was reminiscent of the SATC during World War I. The FERA plan was hailed as its generation's "greatest go-to-college recruiting campaign." Its primary stated aim, like that of its predecessor, was to maintain the supply of trained persons necessary for economic and social progress. By the early 1930s, educators could make an even stronger case for higher education's importance to modern society. With a little federal money, they argued, the nation's schools would be saved, needy students would be assisted, corporations and professions would continue to have a supply of trained young people, and other sectors of society would not be burdened with inefficient youths. Despite the fact that only a limited number of students was involved in either experiment, both plans effectively broadened the colleges' democratic base and helped to provide the trained work force wanted by other sectors of society.[25]

Like the SATC, the FERA work-study program gave the nation's colleges and their students a needed boost, legitimizing their functions. Along with the Civilian Conservation Corps (CCC), the FERA work-study plan sent a message to parents and young people that the federal government was willing to commit unprecedented funding to programs that might alleviate the pain of the present economic situation and at the same time enable young people to keep a hopeful eye on the future. Besides, the government should take care of American youth, Massachusetts Senator David Walsh advised, lest it become "demoralized and disheartened, and thus constitute a dangerous addition to the discontented and radical minded elements."[26] The FERA program recognized the increasing importance of formal education not only to America's structure but also to its people's faith in the promise of individual mobility.

Not surprisingly, the program was hailed by most students and college officials. An editorial in the DePauw student newspaper called the plan a lifesaver; "by helping college students," the paper added self-assuredly, "the state is building a better future for itself." The *Reserve Weekly* sounded the same themes: "It behooves us to register our heartfelt appreciation of the unselfish and thoughtful attitude expressed in the FERA. Evidently the government believes that education shall not be sacrificed upon an altar prepared by forces far removed from the halls of learning. It is gratifying to see that promising careers will not be stifled on account of lack of lucre." It was "a ray of hope . . . to many hopeless young Americans," remarked William H. Cowley, director of the program at Ohio State University. If the program had not been created, thousands of young people would have been left at home, "probably stagnating mentally and looking for an elusive job." Most educators recognized that the work-study plan enabled students to stay in college who otherwise would not have been able to do so. It increased the number of students, improved the quality of campus life, and raised student and institutional morale.[27]

While educators agreed it provided a life jacket to floundering students and colleges alike, its most important function may well have been to keep young people out of the job market. One of President Roosevelt's favorite college presidents, the liberal Frank P. Graham of the University of North Carolina, observed that the New Deal's relief and recovery program was aided in this respect by the college work-study plan. The FERA project became the centerpiece of the New Deal's "youth policy." By encouraging young people to stay in college, it reduced the number of untrained and unemployed youth, as well as the number of young people on relief, at the same time that it raised the level of educational attainment in American society. Indeed, Roosevelt emphasized the noneducational benefits of the program when he transferred it to the National Youth Administration (NYA) in June 1935. Despite protests from the National Education Association and the federal commissioner of education, he ordered the bureaucratic switch because it was primarily the relief problem that justified federal support for a program so largely educational.[28]

In the eight years of its existence the NYA spent over $93 million to assist more than 620,000 college students, but they constituted only the tip of the iceberg. At its peak in the late 1930s, the work-study program aided about one in eight college students, yet youth unemployment ran between 20 and 30 percent of the college-going age cohort throughout the decade. In 1935–36, for example, when work-study funds were allotted to institutions on the basis of 12 percent of their enrollment of the previous year, nearly one-third of white male youth between 15 and 24 years of age were unemployed and 14 percent of these young men were on relief. Even with the program, young people were entering the labor force faster than they could be absorbed; no wonder, then, that the NYA received the enthusiastic support of organized labor. Its influential leader Sidney Hillman proposed that formal learning be extended for as long as ten years beyond high school.[29]

Yet the establishment of.the NYA ensured that the level of educational attainment continued to rise during the Depression. As nearly twice as many high school students as college students received assistance from the federal agency, the pool of potential college students increased. In 1920, 17.3 percent of young men 18 and 19 years of age were in school; in 1930, 26 percent were; in 1937, over 30 percent of this age group were still in high school or college. With the development of the public junior college and the help of the work-study program, the proportion of high school graduates going on to college increased slightly each year of the Depression but the worst.[30] The work-study program enlarged upon the achievements of the SATC.

As with the SATC, federal support aided other activities at the nation's colleges and universities. Between 1933 and 1936, federal loans and grants totaling $71.4 million were made available to the colleges for building construction. In addition, the federal government used college personnel to develop correspondence courses for the CCC, to staff "emergency colleges" attended by about 15,000 people in cities across the country, and to conduct research through the Project in Research in Universities program, founded in 1936. By 1935–36, the proportion of the schools' funds for current purposes received from the federal government had reached 8.8 percent, nearly double what it had been a decade earlier.[31] Federal assistance allowed institutions to restore projects and services eliminated during the early years of the Depression. It stimulated the physical expansion of American higher education, as well as its growth in enrollment and in public acceptance, even if its pace had been sharply curtailed.

It is important to stress, however, that the work-study program was not intended to meet the needs of all students frustrated in their attempts to receive a college education. Charles Taussig, a leading New York City philanthropist and Roosevelt confidante, had urged that the program aid 20 percent of the nation's college students, but the project was still set up to assist only 12 percent of them. Time and again NYA officials showed that well over half of those denied work-study assistance did not enter or remain in college. Most schools were besieged by two or three times more applicants than their quotas; one urban university reported it had 1,160 applicants for 161 positions. Colleges tried to spread their allocated resources to as many students as possible—although students could receive up to $15 a month, the average student earned about $13 a month, so that more students could be aided—but many qualified students were not given the opportunity to work their way through school.[32]

Furthermore, work-study recipients constituted the truly selective portion of the student body at most schools. At Ohio State University, for example, well over a third of the aided students scored over the ninetieth percentile on the entrance aptitude test; their average was 77, while the university's average was about 50. Despite the long hours of work, the aided students generally surpassed their nonaided peers in the classroom. In 1935 the average grade of the first group of FERA-aided students was higher than or equal to that of non-FERA students at thirty-six of thirty-nine institutions. A typical performance could be found at the University of Illinois, where 15 percent of the aided students but only 9 percent of the nonworking students made the school's honor roll. The NYA reported that the academic records of aided students were above average at more than four of five colleges nationwide.[33] Only federal support could guarantee that poor and talented young people would be able to go to college, and the stunning academic achievements of the NYA students suggested to many educators and liberals that more federal support was both desirable and necessary.

The work-study program was still attacked by conservatives eager to dismantle the New Deal. Growing opposition to the New Deal forced sympathetic government officials to scramble for even limited funds as enthusiasm for federal relief programs dwindled in the late 1930s. At its peak in 1937, the federal work-study program had helped just 140,000 students: the number of aided students declined thereafter. While youth unemployment continued to hover around 20 percent, the proportion of the nation's college students to be supported was cut back to less than 10 percent and then to as low as 4 percent between 1937–38 and the plan's termination in 1943.[34] Defense preparedness took precedence in the latter years of the program, but the NYA work-study project was never more than a modest access program.

Several institutions refused to participate in the work-study program from its inception. In its first full year, only 1,466 of about 1,700 eligible institutions distributed work-study funds. Though the number of participating institutions climbed steadily throughout the decade, there were some well-known holdouts. Well-endowed liberal arts colleges such as Williams and Swarthmore, controlled by conservative trustees, declined federal assistance as a matter of principle. Swarthmore's Frank Aydelotte objected strenuously to the cultural philosophy on which he believed so many of the New Deal programs were based. "We see on every hand efforts to get as much as possible from the Government and to give as little as possible in return," he said on behalf of his board of managers. "This tendency, which threatens the very foundations of democracy, can only be checked if those institutions and individuals who are by any possibility able to care for themselves undertake to do so and refuse longer to allow themselves to be a charge upon the public revenue."[35] For most schools, the plan was a windfall essential for survival; for a few, it smacked of dangerous government-sponsored socialism. Work-study money was refused because acceptance would have indicated approval of "lavish federal Santa Clausing" and would have permitted the federal government to exert some subtle control over educational policy. Some conservative educators also criticized the program because it encouraged too many young people, particularly the poor, to go to college.

Some institutions that disapproved of the concept of federal student financial assistance still accepted the work-study largess. The head of Dartmouth's faculty committee on scholarships and loans complained that poor students looked upon the college "as an easy mark, due I am quite sure to the general Rooseveltian philosophy that the world owes an individual something even though the particular individual does not make any effort himself to contribute his share." At Princeton it was sanctimoniously said, "The president and trustees hold political beliefs which might promise something less than a cordial reception for New Deal economics, but they were interested in the needy undergraduates; they accepted the money and kept clear of politics." Similarly, the Harvard Corporation first refused to take part in the program, but later also reneged on its principled opposition to it.[36] For these biased conservatives, a poor—and often ethnic—student, working as much as twenty hours a week for 30 cents an hour and still outperforming his more financially comfortable peers in the classroom, was still suspect.

When slightly improved business conditions in the late 1930s opened up part-time work possibilities outside the federal umbrella, interest in the work-study program waned on the college campus as well as on Capitol Hill. At many schools, even students felt that since the federal aid had been offered as an emergency measure, it should be eliminated once economic stability had been restored. "There can be no reasonable denial of the fact that government aid to college students during the more difficult days of the depression was a necessity," editorialized the DePauw University student newspaper. "But its one-time worth is no good excuse for its continuation. . . . Youth must again accept the responsibility of making its own way rather than having its way made for it."[37] Middle-class students were no less conservative than their elders in the body politic.

In its ten years the FERA and NYA work-study programs helped over two million young people, including more than 600,000 college students. In an emergency, it had enabled many of the best students of their generation to attend college, yet it died a quiet death. The program's limitations confirmed that the preservation of economic and social privilege remained a higher priority than the principle of access in American higher education policy in the 1930s. Educational benefits in the 1930s—like the benefits provided veterans after World War II—were justified not as a tool to increase access to prestigious occupations and professions, but as a means to limit unemployment. Only in the 1960s did the federal government recognize that broad-based student financial support was essential to the democratization of American higher education.

Toward a More Heterogeneous Student Body

Still, they came to college: often traveling by subway, the children of immigrants and the poor arrived by the hundreds of thousands at college campuses, seeking to take that all-important first step up the economic and social ladder. The Depression was a time of great expansion in the educational attainment of children of fathers with low-status occupations and of first-generation Americans. Whereas none of the General Social Survey's children of operatives who were of college age on the eve of World War I went to college, by the late 1930s, fourteen of the eighty-seven in this group did acquire some college education. The proportion of children with fathers in other lower-middle-class and lower-class occupations also showed signs of an increase in educational attainment. The improvement among the children of immigrants was even more pronounced: only three of the twenty-two immigrants' children of college age surveyed attended college in the mid-1920s; in the late 1930s, twelve of thirty-one immigrants' children of college age had some college education.[38] Despite the obstacles, ethnic students became a larger presence on the college campuses of the 1930s.

The student body of most American colleges and universities became more heterogenous during the Depression. When admissions quotas kept them out of the elite private liberal arts colleges, poor and ethnic students turned to public—and not always local—alternatives. A national faculty committee noted the increase in the number of students from homes of lower occupational and social status at public institutions around the country; many Jewish students, for example, despite curbs on their enrollment wherever they went, fled successfully from the Northeast to universities elsewhere.[39] Many other first-generation students went to local denominational institutions or state teachers' colleges, which were sensitive to students' financial and social status and their desire for practical training. In the 1920s it was observed that upwardly mobile Jews sent their children to college earlier than other ethnic groups; in the 1930s, Catholic ethnic groups began to close this gap.

Catholic Students

Commentators in the early 1920s had attributed the low number of Catholic students to cultural and economic factors. They noted that Catholic culture did not stress the benefits of education unless a young man were preparing for the priesthood. The curriculum of most Catholic colleges was generally "too ecclesiastical." Furthermore, even in the few cities where Catholic colleges were located near large Catholic populations, they cost more than public institutions.

As a result, most of those few Catholics who went to college in the first two decades of the twentieth century went to nondenominational institutions.

By the mid-1920s, as the link between educational attainment and adult success became more apparent in the society as a whole, and as ambitious young people became increasingly ambivalent about their ethnicity, there were sharp divisions within local Catholic communities between those who wanted to expand Catholic higher education and those who hoped to enhance the number and presence of Catholic students at secular colleges and universities. Despite the differences in strategy, the two groups agreed on the need to propagandize the cause of higher education among the Catholic young and their parents. The National Catholic Welfare Council ran a campaign to encourage enrollment in Catholic colleges, but the themes it emphasized knew no denominational boundaries. In a series of newspaper advertisements, it proclaimed that college graduation led to "leadership and success," and that American society needed more Catholic lawyers, doctors, engineers, and businessmen. On the last day of the campaign, the president of a Chicago bank warned Catholic parents not to let their children enter the job market without a college degree. This message, which had been delivered to WASP middle-class parents for a decade or more, now finally resonated in Catholic ears as well. While these efforts were somewhat successful in the 1920s, when the growth of urban Catholic schools followed the rapid expansion of urban institutions generally, it was not until the 1930s that Catholics first attended American institutions of higher education in significant numbers.

During the 1930s, college attendance rose more rapidly among Catholics than among Americans as a whole, and perhaps equally important, the proportion of Catholic students who went to secular schools also increased. Whereas there were about 174,000 Catholics in college in 1930, in 1940 Catholic enrollment had climbed to 260,000. In sharp contrast to Jews, who generally rejected the idea of creating their own schools, Catholics continued to foster the expansion of their own denominational colleges, but the growth of Catholic colleges was marked by the same type of curricular innovations that their less expensive secular competitors had adopted. The proportion of Catholic students at Catholic institutions actually fell from about 60 percent at the outset of the decade to about 45 percent on the eve of World War II.[40]

Access became the top priority for Catholic colleges, as for other denominational institutions seeking to survive. The introduction of practical courses of study and lay faculty altered the tone as well as the substance of Catholic college life. Symbolic of efforts to liberalize the Catholic college and move it toward, if not ahead of, other institutions was the directive issued by Father Robert I. Gannon, president of Fordham University, to the deans of Fordham's various schools in August 1936 in an effort to end the long-standing understanding that black Catholics were not welcome there.[41] The ideal of the conservative Catholic college curriculum and its limited institutional focus on the priesthood was compromised time and time again as urban Catholic universities in particular seized the opportunity to meet the increased demand for higher education among its increasingly large middle-class and lower-middle-class clientele between the two world wars, especially in the 1930s.

Activism and Conservatism on the Campus

In a speech in 1937 the president of the University of Colorado said, "There has never been a time in my experience when students have been so eager, so earnest, and so hard-working as now." Many other educators similarly noted that the students of the 1930s burned more midnight oil and less gasoline than their predecessors of the 1920s. Certainly the Depression had much to do with this development, but the increased presence of poorer and ethnic students on college campuses around the country accounted in part for this change in tone. A faculty committee at Massachusetts State College remarked that the average student was now an ethnic student "of serious demeanor, conscientious, ambitious, and possessed of a rather high sense of moral responsibility," who expected the school to help him make his way in upper-middle-class life. Unlike the previous college generation, a significant number of 1930s students did not come to campus with money and social status already in hand. A NYA study found that the median annual family income of its work-study recipients was $1,124; these students came from the homes of clerical workers, craftsmen, laborers, farmers, and the unemployed.[42] If their backgrounds were humble, their dreams were not.

The poor and ethnic students drawn into the colleges in the 1930s shared most of the values and ambitions of their 1920s peers. As one

University of California student put it, "13,500 out of 14,000 students came here only to make money." But by any and all criteria, the intense desire of those new college students to improve their status also improved the quality of academic work in American colleges and universities. While Depression-era students were more intellectually curious than any comparable group in American history, in 1936 *Fortune* accurately characterized them as cautious, subdued, and unadventurous, adding, "security is the *summum bonum* for the present college generation."[43]

Ironically, poor and ethnic students were resented for their alleged ties to radical movements. These new students were considered too crude, too serious, too ungrateful, and too radical by a generation of college presidents and faculty that might have applauded their intense intellectual interests and social conscience if only their socioeconomic backgrounds had been more appropriate. Public perceptions of the radicalism of the students of the 1930s were exaggerated then, as perhaps they remain today. Radical students congregated at only a handful of schools; few schools had an "Alcove A," as CCNY did, where students debated socialist politics and ethics. Elsewhere—at the University of Illinois, for example—radical students comprised less than 1 percent of the student body; even at the most popular protest of the decade, the 1935 Strike for Peace rally, only about 2 percent of the student body showed up. It was the fact that urban and Jewish students were overrepresented among the radical factions at Illinois and other schools that provoked bitter denunciations of Jewish activist students.[44]

James Wechsler, who attempted to rally his peers on the college campuses to press for reform, if not revolution, essentially conceded defeat to personal ambition and social inertia. His book *Revolt on the Campus* chronicles skirmishes on such issues as the expulsion of the editor of the Columbia student newspaper for criticizing his college and the continuation of mandatory drill at several land-grant colleges in the Midwest. Wechsler sharply contrasts the students of the mid-1930s with their blasé, sophisticated predecessors of the 1920s, but he admits that "although there are large and highly significant numbers involved in these events, there are thousands more in American colleges only remotely connected with them." "The crucial number . . . have still not adopted any decisive stand," Wechsler lamely explains. "They are adrift in the middle, cajoled by their administrators to remain inert, incited by the Vigilantes to join the foray against the 'Reds,' still unwilling to dedicate themselves to the task of social revision."[45] The hard-working student more often than not proved to be too complacent by his standards.

The one cause with any substantial support on the college campuses of the 1930s was the peace movement. During the 1920s, sporadic protests had led to the elimination of mandatory ROTC drill or to the termination of ROTC altogether at sixty-four colleges and univerisities; at most schools, ROTC units were not revived until World War II, even though the Supreme Court ruled in 1934 that the Regents of the University of California had the right to compel participation in military training. Attention was then focused on the so-called Oxford Pledge, a statement approved by the Oxford University Union in Great Britain in 1933, whose student signatories pledged to refuse to fight in any war.

Beginning in 1934, one day in April was set aside for a student strike for peace. Only 25,000 students left their classrooms on April 13, 1934, mostly at eastern elite schools. The Socialist party leader, Norman Thomas, spoke to a small crowd at Yale; at Williams a senior named Carl Rogers (not yet distinguished as a psychologist) joined President Harry A. Garfield on the rostrum. An estimated 15,000 students, or about 60 percent of the protesters nationwide, crowded the New York City demonstration. The following year, about 175,000 joined protests on at least 150 college campuses, including a few in the South. Although more schools participated in peace programs in April 1936 and 1937—the total number of students involved in 1937 was estimated at 350,000 to 500,000—the peace movement failed to develop much of a following outside of its active cadres of supporters at such institutions as City College, Oberlin, Reed, and Milwaukee State Teachers College. Later some students turned out to voice their opposition to war and the fascism spreading throughout Europe, particularly in Spain. But the protesters of the 1930s did not press for a radical alteration of American society. Indeed, at City College, reputed to be the most radical of all schools (it was one of the few to experience any violence), a student insisted that less than 10 percent of students were involved in the protests because "few foreigners absorbed democratic views more readily and became better Americans than the Jews of that time."[46]

The college campus remained a bastion of conservatism in the 1930s. In a 1932 straw vote, Herbert Hoover won a decisive victory over Franklin Roosevelt, 50 percent to 31 percent. The chapter of the

Liberty League, an anti–New Deal organization, at the University of Pennsylvania was larger than that school's various leftist groups combined. A University of Chicago newspaper editorial criticized the "militancy and reactionary trends of state colleges," and Wechsler called the nation's Catholic universities "fortresses of retreat." Contrasting the students of Catholic schools with the "avowed atheists and pacifists" at City College, a church official boasted, "You will find no picketing, no communistic rebellions on the campuses of Fordham or Notre Dame." Peace protests were often accompanied by counterdemonstrations: at Temple, the football team pelted a rally with eggs, tomatoes, and bags of flour; three burning crosses appeared on the UCLA campus, along with handbills that called for students to "unite and drive off the menace of Communism." These forces for reaction were encouraged by such educators as the DePauw University official who referred to the National Student League—a socialist student group active in the peace movement—as "a bunch of neurotic Jews" and by such public officials as Martin Dies, the first chairman of the House Un-American Activities Committee, who in 1939 called the pro–New Deal American Student Union a Communist front. Consciously or unconsciously, the vast majority of American college students took the advice of Walter Lippmann, once a leftist student leader and now a conservative columnist, who counseled that the American student should not "let himself be absorbed by distractions about which as a scholar he can do almost nothing."[47]

Too Many Students?

The American college campus of the 1930s was a microcosm of its society. The cheerful optimism and self-confidence of the 1920s gave way to the struggles for institutional and personal survival during the Depression; yet few institutions were closed. Though the cost of college attendance remained high, access to institutions of higher learning was boosted by the federal work-study program and by the continued expansion of certain portions of both the public and private sectors. Everywhere there were increasing signs that higher education was even more essential to economic and social advancement than it had been in previous decade. And Americans' faith in education rarely wavered.

Yet increasing enrollment—particularly among children of the lower economic and social classes—during this decade of economic depression fostered much anxiety about the potential overproduction of college graduates in the United States. In 1933 one writer took American parents to task, asking, "Why do you, as a parent, aid and abet the over-production of white-collar alumni?" The all but universal desire for a white-collar job spurred the enrollment of an ever-broadening range of students with more varied and heightened expectations. Parents and experts alike worried that there were just not enough good jobs to absorb all the college graduates. If the saturation point had been reached in many professions, were students' hopes for individual mobility jeopardized? At the end of the 1930s, with ever more graduates and little economic growth, supply, they feared, had exceeded demand.[48]

Within a generation American higher education was confronted by social expectations radically different from those faced by even the most extravagantly optimistic educators of the early twentieth century. By the late 1930s, more and more young people were taking a fling—and a serious one, at that—at higher learning; experts insisted that two years of postsecondary education were rapidly becoming a normal part of an American teenager's plans. These new students were unfamiliar to most educators, and their numbers, socioeconomic backgrounds, and interests presented unprecedented philosophical and practical problems. The college "has never been traditionally a particularly democratic institution: it has felt a responsibility not to all youth, but to the selected few, to the 'potential leaders of tomorrow,' to use a popular phrase," one academic observed at the time. "Now it is puzzled how to treat the newcomers."[49] Economic and social changes between the world wars, which stimulated and in turn were accelerated by the promise of individual mobility, prompted increased pressure for the democratization of higher education.

Experts and educators boasted rightly that higher education facilitated a greater degree of economic and social mobility in the United States than in other countries. As evidence of America's commitment to democratic higher education, however, they could point essentially only to the expansion of new types of institutions. Elite schools generally did not expand or alter the composition of their student bodies in order to encourage equality of educational opportunity. The federal student assistance program helped to increase the number of poor and ethnic students, but its impact was sharply curtailed by widespread opposition to the New Deal's social programs, including federal aid to education. In the 1930s, then, American higher education was faced with increasing demands for its services while its resources dwindled.[50] A differentiated system of higher education emerged to resolve this social paradox.

While access to the apex of American higher education continued to be limited for the most part to the children of privilege, new types of institutions suggested the possibility of individual advancement to less fortunate Americans. Yet at each level of higher learning, the opportunity for economic and social mobility was indeed made available to some worthy but poor students. The complex organization of American higher education in the 1930s replicated American ambivalence in the face of the nation's traditional democratic values. Was higher learning for the intellectually gifted few or for the ambitious many? Was it a privilege, reserved primarily for the sons of the already privileged, or a right to be extended to the talented of any background? The anxious generation between the two world wars grappled with these questions, and we continue to struggle with them today. Looking back, we can see that educators—and American society in general—took some small strides forward during the 1920s and 1930s, steps that made possible the giant leaps of the post–World War II era.

10 / Is Higher Education a Privilege or a Right?

American higher education expanded remarkably between 1915 and 1940, but its democratic promise remained unrealized. Poised between its traditional function of transmitting past culture and its modern function of occupational and social training, it was confronted by a wide array of interests and opportunities. Though the proportion of young people who attended college more than tripled and faith in the value of education took on the fervor of a secularized religion, there were danger signals as well: gender and racial discrimination were accepted practices; admission to high-prestige institutions was based on an applicant's background, not on his ability; the most rapidly growing sectors of higher education were those at the lowest rungs of an increasingly differentiated educational ladder; and access to higher education in general was more dependent on a young person's socioeconomic status than on his talent. By the end of the 1930s there was a new sense of urgency to the question: Should higher education be a privilege or a right?

American educators did take some steps to enhance educational opportunity between the world wars. Following economic trends, pressures for professionalization and democratization escalated during this period. More trained young people were needed to fill the growing number and range of white-collar occupations. As a result, traditional conceptions of the institution of higher learning were often modified; as the president of the University of Illinois put it in 1928, "we have chosen, if one cares to view the matter that way, to give a higher education to a larger number of mediocre talent as well as to those of greater talent because we have believed that only by establishing a high minimum standard of education and intelligence was our democracy secure."[1] All but a few schools admitted any student who could pay the tuition, and once enrolled, he could study almost anything. The growth of local state, teachers', and junior colleges confirmed the increasing importance of technical education to modern America.

Institutions of higher learning were encouraged to adjust themselves to capture a larger or smaller share of the educational market by establishing and maintaining a clear sense of identity and purpose. Since, as one educator surmised, "neither the democratic ideal of democratic education nor the scholastic ideals of standard colleges and universities seem likely to give way," most schools sought to place themselves somewhere between these two extremes.[2] An essential aim of education was to contribute to social efficiency; the differentiation of institutions of American higher learning was a beneficial accommodation to differences in individual abilities and interests. "I think we ought to welcome a differentiation among institutions," Harry W. Chase said in 1930. "With the new social importance which higher education has assumed, it is certainly a time when institutions should clarify their functions, but it is not a time when all institutions should seek to fulfill the same functions. For my part, I welcome variety in the educational field."[3] With diverse types of colleges available, Americans could reach their natural level and full potential. Yet, while the concept was honorable, its application fell far short of the ideal.

In the 1920s and 1930s, the differentiation of mass higher education did not eliminate class distinctions in American society; in fact, it heightened them. Differences between the private and public sectors discernible by the early 1930s worried many educators, including Parke R. Kolbe, a leading booster of private urban universities:

> On one side we have the tendency towards education of the masses, open to all. . . . On the other side is evident the tendency of the older and stronger private institutions to choose their entrants with extreme care. . . . If this situation means the beginning of an educational class or caste system, it is fraught with grave danger to our democracy.[4]

The calls for an "aristocracy of brains" were manifested perversely in exclusionary admissions quotas at nearly all of the country's leading private liberal arts colleges and many highly regarded state universities. Rapidly increasing tuition charges in the 1920s and limited scholarship and federal financial assistance in the 1930s precluded even further the enrollment of significant numbers of worthy but poor young people. The ambitions of those less privileged students able to attend college, while greater than their elders', were too often limited to the study of less prestigious subjects at less prestigious schools. Frustration mounted with these glaring examples of the inequality of educational opportunity as higher education became more central to America's culture of aspiration.

The Rising Cost of Higher Education

The optimistic view of the differentiation of higher education was challenged by an increasing number of experts and citizens during the Depression. While discriminatory admissions quotas were left essentially untouched until after World War II, the larger question of access to any higher education at all received attention. More poor young people were going to college, but the disparity in educational attainment based on students' socioeconomic backgrounds continued to widen. And the stakes were getting higher. By the end of the 1930s, as the economy seemed to stabilize and as privilege seemed entrenched in educational institutions, Americans' faith in the democratic promise of education was far greater than the higher education system's ability or even willingness to meet it.

Pricing policies in both the private and public sectors made it more difficult for the poor to attend college, exacerbating the impact of the Depression. Studies conducted in the 1920s had shown that families' ability to pay was the most critical determinant of the rate of college-going; still, tuition, in relation to the general price level, continued to climb steadily throughout the interwar period. According to a General Education Board survey, private liberal arts colleges raised their fees by 26 percent, private universities by 15 percent, and state universities by 47 percent between 1928–29 and 1936–37. Between 1932 and 1934 eight state universities, including those of California and Wisconsin, charged tuition or fees for the first time. After tuition increased from $60 to $100 for state residents and from $180 to $300 for out-of-state students at Massachusetts State College, the 1936 student commencement speaker warned, "If the tuition is raised again, we should be in danger of losing our own individuality and becoming a younger brother of the rich men's colleges of New England." Student strikes to protest tuition hikes were held at such different schools as Brooklyn College and San Antonio Junior College. By the middle of the Depression the federal Office of Education conceded, "The time-honored American boast that education is free from the kindergarten through the university seems not to be as true as it once was." Indeed, in 1939 the president of Ohio University admitted that the gradual increase in tuition struck at the very heart of the concept of equality of opportunity, and was "eating away at the principles of the founders" of public higher education in the United States.[5]

Similarly distressing was the widening gap in educational attainment among young people of different socioeconomic backgrounds. As early as the mid-1920s, studies showed that while there were differences in intelligence scores among the children of fathers in different occupational categories, those differences were not nearly so significant as the overrepresentation of higher socioeconomic groups in college generally, and particularly at high-prestige institutions. A Pennsylvania study pointed out that a quarter of the students in college there had lower test scores than over half of those who went directly to work after high school because they could not afford to begin college. Even in a state with a leading public university, Minnesota, five of six students in the top fifth of their high school graduating classes who did not go to college did not do so because of insufficient financial resources. "Pathetic as it is for hundreds of young people to go to college who could employ their time at things for which they are better fitted," commented an official of the access-oriented University of Pittsburgh in 1928, "it is even more pathetic that so many who ought to go on do not."[6]

Surveys in diverse states came to the same conclusion: the talented poor were greatly underrepresented in American higher education, and the Depression made matters worse. A 1935 study of Pennsylvania students with intelligence test scores of 110 or above demonstrated that while 93 percent of the young people from above-average socioeconomic backgrounds graduated from high school and 57 percent attended college, only 72 percent of the students with comparable test scores from below-average socioeconomic backgrounds graduated from high school and only 13 percent attended college. In Milwaukee, although 94 percent of the students with IQs of 117 or above and family incomes of $5,000 or above were in college, only 20 percent of the students with the same test scores but with family incomes of less than $500 were in college. Even in a study titled *Democracy Enters College,* R. L. Duffus conceded that it was difficult financially and socially for the poor and the children of immigrants to go to college. "We prate of free schools; we give more free schooling than any people; we do not, however, have freedom of opportunity for all children alike," the president of Wesleyan University added. "We have social barriers in education, too. We still 'give to him that hath.'"[7]

"It would seem that society's first job is to change the nature of 'equality of opportunity' from that of a noble jingle to an established and effective reality," asserted Howard M. Bell, author of a 1938 American Youth Commission study on the young people of Maryland. Bell's work testified to the promise of higher education, but also to its contemporary shortcomings. A college graduate's income was growing more rapidly than a high school graduate's. In addition, while college was increasing its value as an opportunity cost investment, fewer lower-middle-class individuals could afford to attend college. Some of America's most exciting success stories were being written about working college students, Bell commented, but such students were the exceptions rather than the rule. One-fifth of the children of Maryland professionals graduated from college, but only 6 percent of the children of sales personnel and less than 2 percent of the children of skilled and unskilled laborers were so fortunate. Even more dramatic, Bell found that while the children of professionals accounted for just 1 percent of the elementary school graduates in the state, they accounted for 58.9 percent of its college graduates. Other social scientists, including W. Lloyd Warner, confirmed that a college education in the 1930s was reserved primarily for the children of privilege; one report found that the sons of men in the highest census occupational category were more than ten times as likely to go to college as their equally talented but poor peers.[8]

Critics dismayed by the cumulative impact of the increasing cost of higher education, the limitations of the federal work-study program, and rising attrition in the 1930s proposed programs to encourage college attendance by qualified but poor students. John B. Johnston, founder of the University of Minnesota's General College, suggested that tuition be adjusted to a student's academic performance; honors students would be exempt from all fees. Helen Goetsch, author of a study of Milwaukee youth, recommended free tuition at all public junior colleges and four-year municipal institutions, the exemption of tuition costs from federal and state taxes, and the expansion of current scholarship, loan, and work-study programs. Efforts by the National Youth Administration and various commissions to expand the NYA's work-study program were frustrated by Congress's attention to other matters, chiefly preparations for America's impending involvement in World War II, but also by in-fighting within the educational establishment. The highly regarded Educational Policies Commission, for example, proposed in October 1941 that student financial assistance be made available at all times (through the states, not to students directly), but its plan faded from public view after the attack on Pearl Harbor less than two months later.[9]

Above all, the American public was not yet prepared to accept the public policy implications of the assertions that the future health of the American economy and indeed of American democracy was dependent on broad access to higher education. Still struggling to keep its collective financial head above water, the nation had more pressing matters on its agenda. Widespread opposition to the growth of the federal government and the centralization of power and authority played a critical role in curbing public interest in federal aid to education. Even "Dr. New Deal" was skeptical of increased federal involvement. "I am sick and tired of having a lot of long-haired people around here who want a billion dollars for schools, a billion dollars for public health," Franklin D. Roosevelt declared in 1939. "Just because a boy wants to go to college is no reason we should finance it."[10] Finally, most Americans were still dubious about the "Americanness" of the nation's ethnic population and therefore indifferent, if not antagonistic, to efforts to help the socially unacceptable but talented student. It was not until after World War II that prejudice and ideological constraints gave way to public recognition of the right to higher education as the foundation for a successful postindustrial democratic society.

Postwar Developments

Suddenly, once again, a world war accelerated the expansion of American higher education. In 1947 President Harry S Truman's

Commission on Higher Education pronounced itself satisfied with the twentieth-century development of American higher education, but it also reported that colleges and universities had not kept pace with changing social conditions. The overwhelming response of veterans to the educational provisions of the G.I. Bill of Rights revealed that the public's belief in the personal and social benefits of education was years ahead of public and educational policy. America's emerging predominance on the world stage, symbolized by the atomic bomb, created a new sense of the urgency of preparing young people for the jobs opening up in an increasingly technocratic economy, and of providing them with more general education as well. Echoing the words of educators of previous decades, the commission announced that higher education's "most important role is to serve as an instrument of social transition, and its responsibilities are defined in terms of the kind of civilization society hopes to build."[11]

But there were differences, too, differences that demonstrate the tremendous leap in what the public had come to expect of the educational establishment. The 1947 commission found the record of growth of the 1920s and 1930s "encouraging," "but we are forced to admit nonetheless that the educational attainments of the American people are still substantially below what is necessary either for effective individual living or for the welfare of society." Citing economic barriers, regional variations, a restrictive curriculum, and racial and religious discrimination, the commission issued the following indictment in boldface: **"One of the gravest charges to which American society is subject is that of failing to provide a reasonable equality of educational opportunity for its youth."**[12] World War II, its technological triumphs and its human horrors, challenged the United States to realize its own democratic rhetoric.

The commission's six-volume report, titled *Higher Education for American Democracy,* emphasized the need both to expand and to equalize educational opportunity. It noted that "too many of our citizens have tacitly assumed that the ladder of opportunity for education was equally accessible to all children and youth," when in fact, "for the great majority of our boys and girls, the kind and amount of education they may hope to attend depends, not on their own abilities, but on the family or community into which they happened to be born or, worse still, on the color of their skin or the religion of their parents."[13] Those who had not gone to college were wrong to blame themselves; what had failed was an educational system and a society that condoned economic inequality and social prejudice. Above all, the commission lashed out at the "commonly practiced" quotas directed primarily against blacks and Jews.

These exclusionary admissions policies were not only un-American, they were "European in origin and application." "We have lately witnessed on that continent the horrors to which, in its logical extension, it can lead," the commission stated in an obvious reference to Nazi Germany's planned extermination of Europe's Jews. "The quota system denies the basic American belief that intelligence and ability are present in all ethnic groups, that men of all religious and racial origins should have equal opportunity to fit themselves for contributing to the common life." The most "outstanding example" of this barrier to equality of opportunity was the segregation of black students in black colleges, but the quotas that discriminated against Jewish students at the nation's best undergraduate and professional schools were also described and attacked at length.[14]

In the Cold War environment, the United States simply could not afford an undereducated people, nor could it tolerate economic or social tension. On nearly every page the commission drew a sharp contrast between democracy and totalitarianism, and it challenged educators to "undertake to effect democratic reconciliation, so as to make of the national life one continuous process of interpersonal, intervocational, and intercultural cooperation."[15] Colleges and universities must meet the ever-growing aspirations of the American people, or the new postindustrial society would shake on its foundation. The growth and democratization of higher education in the 1920s and 1930s had only whetted the American appetite.

In 1915, less than one in twenty young people went to college; the 1947 commission insisted that free and universal access to at least two years of postsecondary work be a major goal. Ignored until after World War I, the nation's junior colleges were highlighted in this report; indeed, they were renamed community colleges to stress their potential for service to nontraditional students. These schools' primary task was to eliminate geographical and economic barriers to college attendance. To that end, the commission recommended that all public higher education be tuition-free through the fourteenth grade and that federal financial assistance be provided to competent students who needed it to ensure their attendance through that level.[16]

By 1960, it was hoped, the number of young people in college would double to about one in three of the college-going age cohort.

By the end of World War II, then, there was increasing dissatisfaction with the American higher education of the prewar years. Now it was claimed that only one-third of the qualified young people were going to college on the eve of Pearl Harbor; furthermore, after decades of silence, those institutions that discriminated against blacks and Jews came under heavy attack. States were criticized for their penury, since the cost of attendance at public colleges had increased as much 30 percent in the previous decade.[17] Exceeding all expectations, the crush of veterans who returned to the colleges under the G.I. Bill had established a most successful model for the future. The commission's thrust was clear: the economic and social health of modern American society depended on a commitment by higher education and the federal and state governments to meet the increasing demands for college education and training, and for the upper-middle-class occupations and status they promised. After years of debate, of progress and frustration, the triumph of the culture of aspiration seemed within reach.

The Elusive Goal of Equal Opportunity

Despite the self-congratulatory rhetoric of the interwar period, *Higher Education for American Democracy* could not have been written with any conviction a decade before. In the 1920s and 1930s, educators spoke of the right of young people to a college education only to dismiss the notion. Charles Van Hise, president of the University of Wisconsin, asserted that "it is accepted doctrine that the right of the boy to secure the highest education in the land shall not depend upon the amount of money which he may possess, but upon his inherent capacity, moral and intellectual"; but, he added, "if this is attained, it will be a new thing in the world." Similarly, the philosopher Jay Hudson believed that if Americans wanted to ensure equality of educational opportunity, "a new heaven and a new earth" would be required, "as well as a new college." Rather than affirm their faith in the future of democracy, Horace Kallen argued from a more radical perspective in 1933, educators and college graduates "confirm, by transmitting as social heritage, the spirit of caste presently incarnate in the industrial establishment."[18] American society could not bring itself to support this "new thing," equality of educational opportunity.

Even as an increasing proportion of young people attended college between the world wars, the goal of universal access to higher education remained elusive. In these decades the attainment of higher learning was a distinctive form of consumption available to increasing numbers of Americans, but it still connoted class status. For every student for whom a college education promised a step up the economic ladder there were many more for whom it constituted insurance against a step downward. Worse yet, young people from socially undesirable backgrounds were excluded systematically from most of the prestigious schools, even if their ability surpassed that of their more privileged peers. In 1939 Homer P. Rainey, head of the American Youth Commission, grudgingly recognized education's contribution to social stratification; he observed that "the striking concurrence of social and economic forces tends to freeze social groups into a sort of perennial status quo." It was time, Howard Bell said, "to break up the conspiracy of forces" that barred underprivileged youth from higher education.[19] But the continued imposition of admissions quotas, the manipulated differentiation of educational institutions, the dramatic increase in the cost of attendance in both the private and public sectors, and the absence of a more significant federal financial assistance or work-study program demonstrated that American society lacked the will to fulfill the principles of its political and social rhetoric, as well as the aspirations of many of its citizens.

Then, as now, American higher education embodied the ambivalence of a culture torn between the ideals of democracy and equality of opportunity and the all too human realities of status concerns and class, gender, racial, and religious discrimination. In the 1920s and 1930s, from the establishment of the Student Army Training Corps to the formation of the National Youth Administration work-study program, the public applauded—cautiously—federal policies that recognized higher education's potential contribution to economic and social mobility. With the creation and expansion of new types of institutions of higher learning, most notably practical-oriented urban universities and widely dispersed junior colleges, the foundation was laid for more innovative reforms and further explosive growth. Still, even as higher education expanded in both conception and fact, it reinforced its society's limitations on individual mobility. While its progress was not only laudable but in many respects remarkable, on the eve of World War II the scale was still tipped toward privilege, not toward a young person's right to education. Since then, the debates have continued and the doubts have remained, but American society has chosen wisely to risk the rewards of its democratic promise.

Notes

Archival sources are cited as follows:

AC   Amherst College Archives
API   Alabama Polytechnic Institute Archives, Auburn University
CCNY   Archives and Special Collections, College of the City of New York
CWRU   Case Western Reserve University Archives
DC   Dartmouth College Archives
DPU   Archives of DePauw University
EU   Special Collections Department, Robert W. Woodruff Library, Emory University
HBS   Archives and Manuscript Department, Baker Library, Harvard Graduate School of Business Administration
UC   Department of Special Collections, University of Chicago
UI   University Archives, University of Illinois
UM   Archives of the University of Massachusetts
UNC   The Carolina Collection and the Archives of the University of North Carolina

In the interest of clarity, the *Biennial Surveys of Education* issued by the Bureau (later Office) of Education, Department of the Interior, will be cited according to the years of the surveys rather than according to the dates of publication; the references section lists each survey's full citation.

Preface

1. Paul Fussell, "Schools for Snobbery," *New Republic,* October 4, 1982, p. 25.

1 / Introduction

1. Rosemary Stevens, *American Medicine and the Public Interest* (New Haven, 1971), p. 24.

2. Laurence R. Veysey, *The Emergence of the American University* (Chicago, 1965), p. 338.

3. Burton J. Bledstein, *The Culture of Professionalism* (New York, 1976). The literature on professionalization at the turn of the century is voluminous. The most important contemporary work remains Abraham Flexner's *Medical Education in the United States and Canada*, Carnegie Foundation for the Advancement of Teaching Bulletin no. 4 (New York, 1910). See also, for medicine, Paul Starr, *The Social Transformation of American Medicine* (New York, 1982); Stevens, *American Medicine;* E. Richard Brown, *Rockefeller Medicine Men* (Berkeley, 1979), esp. chaps. 1–3; and Gerald E. Markowitz and David K. Rosner, "Doctors in Crisis: A Study of the Use of Medical Education Reform to Establish Modern Professional Elitism in Medicine," *American Quarterly* 25 (1973):83–107. On legal education, see Jerold S. Auerbach, *Unequal Justice* (New York, 1976), and Laurence M. Friedman, *A History of American Law* (New York, 1973), esp. pp. 525–97. For a specific discussion of disciplines, see Thomas Haskell, *The Emergence of Professional Social Science* (Urbana, 1977); Daniel Kevles, *The Physicists* (New York, 1978); Roy Lubove, *The Professional Altruist: The Emergence of Social Work as a Career* (Cambridge, Mass., 1965); Bruce Kuklick, *The Rise of American Philosophy, 1860–1930* (New Haven, 1977); William J. Goode, "Encroachment, Charlatanism, and the Emerging Professions: Psychology, Medicine, and Sociology," *American Sociological Review* 25 (1960): 902–14; Monte Calvert, *The Mechanical Engineer in America, 1830–1910* (Baltimore, 1967); and several essays in Alexandra Oleson and John Voss, eds., *The Organization of Knowledge in Modern America, 1860–1920* (Baltimore, 1979). On education, see Lawrence A. Cremin, *The Transformation of the School* (New York, 1961); Raymond E. Callahan, *Education and the Cult of Efficiency* (Chicago, 1962); Diane Ravitch, *The Great School Wars* (New York, 1974); David B. Tyack, *The One Best System* (Cambridge, Mass., 1974); Michael B. Katz, *Class, Bureaucracy, and Schools* (New York, 1971); Rush Welter, *Popular Education and Democratic Thought in America* (New York, 1962); David Tyack and Elisabeth Hansot, *Managers of Virtue: Public School Leadership in America, 1820–1980* (New York, 1982); Joel H. Spring, *Education and the Rise of the Corporate State* (Boston, 1972); and Merle Curti, *The Social Ideas of American Educators* (New York, 1935), esp. chap. 6. Finally, two recent sociological interpretations of the process of professionalization are Magali Sarfatti Larson, *The Rise of Professionalism* (Berkeley, 1977), and Randall Collins, *The Credential Society* (New York, 1979).

4. See Robert H. Wiebe, *The Search for Order* (New York, 1968), for a leading interpretation of the Progressive Era. Monographs and interpretive works on this period abound.

5. James Bryce, "American Revisited: Changes of a Quarter Century," *Outlook*, March 25, 1905, pp. 736–38.

6. Carnegie Foundation for the Advancement of Teaching, *Papers Relating to the Admission of State Institutions to the System of Retiring Allowances of the Carnegie Foundation* (New York, 1907); Flexner, *Medical Education;* Morris L.

Cooke, *Academic and Industrial Efficiency* (New York, 1910), pp. iv–v; W. Bruce Leslie, "Localism, Denominationalism, and Institutional Strategies in Urbanizing America," *History of Education Quarterly* 17 (Fall 1977):235–56; Ellen C. Lagemann, *Private Power for the Public Good: A History of the Carnegie Foundation for the Advancement of Teaching* (Middletown, Conn., 1983).

7. Quoted in James C. Stone and Donald P. De Nevi, eds., *Portraits of the American University, 1890–1910* (San Francisco, 1971), pp. 171–73.

8. In a 1908 graduation speech, for example, Stanford's David Starr Jordan warned that "the very usefulness of the college, its popularity, its respectability, all growing by leaps and bounds, are sources of danger" (Stone and De Nevi, eds., *Portraits*, p. 12).

9. Laurence Veysey, "Stability and Experiment in the American Undergraduate Curriculum," in Carl Kaysen, ed., *Content and Context* (New York, 1973), p. 9.

10. Jay W. Hudson, *The College and New America* (New York, 1920), pp. 72–73. Martin A. Trow, "Reflections on the Transition from Mass to Universal Higher Education," *Daedalus,* Winter 1970, pp. 1–42, discusses the conflict between the public and autonomous functions of American higher education.

2 / The Colleges Go to War

1. Hudson, *College and New America*, pp. 3–4.

2. Parke R. Kolbe, *The Colleges in War Time and After* (New York, 1919), pp. 25, 21.

3. *Case Tech,* December 11, 1918, p. 2.

4. "The American College" (editorial), *New Republic,* October 5, 1922, p. 5.

5. Kolbe, *Colleges in War Time,* pp. 128–29, 171; *Biennial Survey of Education, 1916–18,* pp. 48–49; William W. Sweet, *Indiana Asbury–DePauw University: 1837–1937* (New York, 1937), p. 216; Louis R. Wilson, *The University of North Carolina, 1900–1930* (Chapel Hill, 1957), p. 270; Thomas D. Clark, *Indiana University: Midwestern Pioneer* (Bloomington, 1973), 2:229–30.

6. Ernest M. Hopkins to Lyman P. Powell, August 1, 1917, Hopkins Papers, DC.

7. Reports of the President and Other Officers of Western Reserve University, 1917–18, pp. 10–11, 16, CWRU; Kolbe, *Colleges in War Time,* p. 37. The Emory College circular can be found in EU.

8. *Biennial Survey of Education, 1916–18,* pp. 48–49.

9. Edgar O. Lovett, president of Rice Institute, in Rice Institute Pamphlet 5 (October 1918):184.

10. Frederick C. Ferry, quoted in Edward D. McDonald and Edward M. Hinton, *Drexel Institute of Technology: 1891–1941* (Philadelphia, 1942), p. 61.

11. Kolbe, *Colleges in War Time,* pp. 49–50; Reports of the President and Other Officers, 1917–18, p. 16, CWRU; see also Samuel P. Capen, "The Effects of the World War, 1914–18, on American Colleges and Universities," *Educational Record* 21 (January 1940):40–48; Kevles, *Physicists,* p. 137.

12. Capen, "Effects of the World War," pp. 42–46; Ernest M. Hopkins to Secretary, Committee on Education and Special Training, January 24, 1919, Hopkins Papers, DC. The remark by the dean of the University of Kentucky is quoted in James Wechsler, *Revolt on the Campus* (New York, 1935), p. 14.

13. Reports of the President and Other Officers, 1918–19, p. 8; Kolbe, *Colleges in War Time*, pp. 69–81; and for the best historical treatment, see Carol S. Gruber, *Mars and Minerva* (Baton Rouge, 1975).

14. Rice Institute Pamphlet 5 (October 1918):183; Kolbe, *Colleges in War Time*, p. 75.

15. Chancellor's Report, 1918–19, EU, p. 2; Annual Report of the President to the Trustees, *1918–19*, p. 2, API; President's Report, 1917–19, pp. 97–103, UC; Samuel E. Morison, *Three Centuries of Harvard* (Cambridge, Mass., 1936), p. 459.

16. Leon B. Richardson, *History of Dartmouth College* (Hanover, N.H., 1932), 2:763–64; Wechsler, *Revolt on the Campus*, p. 17; *Daily Illini*, October 1, 1918, pp. 1–2; Robert I. Gannon, *Up to the Present: The Story of Fordham* (Garden City, N.Y., 1967), pp. 153–55; Douglas D. Martin, *The Lamp in the Desert: The Story of the University of Arizona* (Tucson, 1960), pp. 132–33, 278–79.

17. Eileen Eagan, *Class, Culture, and the Classroom* (Philadelphia, 1981), pp. 25–26; 1918–19 Annual Report, Stanford University, p. 130; *Campus* (CCNY), October 23, 1918, p. 1; Wechsler, *Revolt on the Campus*, pp. 14–17; Gruber, *Mars and Minerva*, pp. 231–32.

18. Ralph B. Perry, secretary of Committee on Education and Special Training, to the presidents of SATC institutions, December 11, 1918, Hopkins Papers, DC; John S. Brubacher and Willis Rudy, *Higher Education in Transition* (New York, 1976), pp. 226–27.

19. Gruber, *Mars and Minerva;* Phyllis Keller, *States of Belonging: German-American Intellectuals and the First World War* (Cambridge, Mass., 1979); Earl C. Kaylor, Jr., *Truth Sets Free* (New York, 1977), pp. 202–4; Minutes of the Faculty of Emory College, September 16, 1918, and October 1, 1918, EU; and Carl A. Stephens, manuscript history of the University of Illinois, pp. 25–33, UI.

20. Quoted in E. Wilson Lyon, *The History of Pomona College, 1887–1969* (Claremont, 1977), pp. 177–89.

21. *Daily Illini*, October 2, 1918, p. 2.

22. Wechsler, *Revolt on the Campus*, p. 20; Kolbe, *Colleges in War Time*, p. 185.

23. *DePauw Daily*, October 23, 1919, p. 2; *Daily Illini*, October 15, 1919, p. 4. See also *The Class Book of the Class of 1919*, pp. 12–15, DC; *Massachusetts Collegian*, October 1, 1919, p. 10; Dartmouth College, *150 Years of Dartmouth* (Hanover, N.H., 1921), p. 129.

24. Reports of the President and Other Officers, 1915–16, p. 63, CWRU; Richard Hofstadter, *Anti-Intellectualism in American Life* (New York, 1962), p. 206; Kevles, *Physicists*, p. 67.

25. Godkin and Tocqueville are cited in Stephen Skowronek, *Building a New American State* (New York, 1978), pp. 3, 42; see, generally, pp. 3–18, 42–45;

Samuel P. Hays, "The Politics of Reform in Municipal Government in the Progressive Era," *Pacific Northwest Quarterly* 55 (1964):157–69; Sidney Fine, *Laissez-Faire and the General Welfare State* (Ann Arbor, 1965); Morton Keller, *Affairs of State* (Cambridge, Mass., 1977); Martin J. Schiesl, *The Politics of Efficiency* (Berkeley, 1977).

26. Hofstadter, *Anti-Intellectualism,* pp. 155–56, 191–95.

27. Quoted in ibid., pp. 209–10.

28. Kevles, *Physicists,* pp. 102–54; Hofstadter, *Anti-Intellectualism,* pp. 211–12; Gordon H. Gerould, "The Professor and the Wide, Wide World," *Scribner's,* April 1919; "The Demobilized Professor," *Atlantic Monthly,* April 1919; Paul Van Dyke, "The College Man in Action," *Scribner's,* May 1919; Robert Cuff, *The War Industries Board* (Baltimore, 1973).

29. Quoted in Lawrence E. Gelfand, *The Inquiry* (New Haven, 1963), p. 48.

30. See ibid., esp. pp. 23–27, 46–65, 100–108, 318. See also Paul Johnson, *Modern Times* (New York, 1983), p. 23.

31. *Higher Education and the State,* University of Missouri Bulletin no. 34 (December 15, 1933), p. 19.

32. Rice Institute Pamphlet 23 (July 1936):207; Thomas A. Krueger and William Glidden, "The New Deal Intellectual Elite: A Collective Portrait," in Frederic C. Jaher, ed., *The Rich, the Well-Born, and the Powerful* (Urbana, 1973), pp. 353–54; Hofstadter, *Anti-Intellectualism,* pp. 214–20.

33. *Biennial Survey of Education, 1916–18,* 1:12, 4:686; George F. Zook, "The Emergency in Higher Education," in *Addresses and Proceedings of the Fifty-eighth Annual Meeting of the National Education Association* (Washington, D.C., 1920), p. 232.

34. *Higher Education and the State,* pp. 28–31; George F. Zook, ed., *The Residence of Students in Universities and Colleges,* U.S. Bureau of Education Bulletin, 1922, no. 18, p. 21. See also Walter J. Matherly, "Present and Probable Future Needs for Collegiate Business Education," *Journal of Business of the University of Chicago* 4, pt. 2 (July 1931):49; James H. Bossard and J. Frederic Dewhurst, *University Education for Business* (Philadelphia, 1931), p. 36.

35. Garland G. Parker, *The Enrollment Explosion* (New York, 1971), p. 23; Annual Report of the President, 1919–20, Case School of Applied Science, p. 1, CWRU; President's Report, 1922–23, p. 5, UI; Merle Curti and Vernon Carstensen, *The University of Wisconsin: A History, 1848–1925* (Madison, 1949), pp. 202–4; the Chancellor Papers of Robert M. House, UNC; Edward F. Potthoff, "Enrollments in the Secondary Schools and Higher Institutions of Illinois" (Urbana, 1951), p. 54; E. C. Miller to Robert M. Hutchins, September 12, 1939, Presidential Papers, 1925–45, Special Collections, UC. The DePauw University figures can be found in annual reports in the university's archives.

36. The annual rate of attendance increase as a proportion of the college-age cohort was 0.35 percent between 1920 and 1940, 1.3 percent between 1940 and 1960. See *Biennial Survey of Education, 1930–32,* chap. 3, p. 13; Jerome Karabel and A. H. Halsey, eds., *Power and Ideology in Education* (New York, 1977), p. 110.

37. Elise Hatt and F. Dean McClusky, *A Study of Enrollment,* Studies in

Higher Education, no. 2 (Lafayette, Ind., 1926), p. 20; Elmer E. Brown, "Too Many College Students?" *North American Review*, June 1921, p. 750; Kaylor, *Truth Sets Free*, pp. 176, 262; *Biennial Survey of Education, 1938–42*, vol. 2, chap. 4, p. 4.

38. Clark, *Indiana University*, 2:314; *Massachusetts Collegian*, October 1, 1919, p. 10; *Daily Illini*, October 7, 1919, p. 1; Edward P. Cheyney, *History of the University of Pennsylvania* (Philadelphia, 1940), p. 382; Christopher Jencks and David Riesman, *The Academic Revolution* (Garden City, N.Y., 1969), p. 117.

39. *Biennial Survey of Education, 1916–18*, 1:8–9, 233–34; *1924–26*, p. 350; *1928–30*, pp. 464–65; and J. O. Malott, *Commercial Education in 1924–26*, U.S. Bureau of Education Bulletin, 1928, no. 4, p. 2. Elmer E. Brown estimated that as much as 75 percent of the postwar expansion in American higher education was due to the fact that "every industry and business is on its way to school" ("Too Many College Students?", p. 734).

40. *University of North Carolina Record*, December 1923, p. 1; Wilson, *University of North Carolina*, pp. 440–48.

41. The views of European visitors can be found in Stewart E. Fraser, ed., *American Education in Foreign Perspectives* (New York, 1969); see the views of Australian educator E. R. Holme in ibid., pp. 293–94. See also Arthur E. Shipley, *The Voyage of a Vice Chancellor* (New York, 1919), esp. pp. 37, 47, 54, 89, 147, and 181; Ramsay Muir, *America the Golden* (London, 1927), pp. 27–32; Delaye Gager, *French Comment on American Education* (New York, 1925), esp. p. 14.

42. Matthew Arnold, *Culture and Anarchy*, ed. J. Dover Wilson (Cambridge, Eng., 1932), p. 22. See also Sir William Ashley's speech to an audience at Rice University, in *Some Addresses from the Book of the Opening of the Rice Institute*, Rice Institute Pamphlet 3 (October 1916):238; Sir William Ashley, cited in L. C. Marshall, ed., *The Collegiate School of Business* (Chicago, 1928), p. 45; and Oleson and Voss, eds., *Organization of Knowledge*, p. vii.

43. Shipley, *Voyage of a Vice Chancellor*, pp. 179–80; Muir, *America the Golden*, pp. 33–35.

44. Harold E. Stearns, ed., *America Now* (New York, 1938), p. 334; Paul A. Schilpp, ed., *Higher Education Faces the Future* (New York, 1930), p. 137.

45. I. G. Wyllie, "The Businessman Looks at the Higher Learning," *Journal of Higher Education*, June 1952, p. 296.

3 / Business Goes to the Colleges

1. Charles H. Judd, *Problems of Education in the United States* (New York, 1933), p. 76; McDonald and Hinton, *Drexel Institute*, pp. 59–60.

2. *Harvard Crimson*, October 30, 1928, p. 2.

3. President's Research Committee on Social Trends, *Recent Social Trends in the United States* (New York, 1933), p. 269.

4. Wallace B. Donham, "Training for Business," February 26, 1929, Donham Papers, HBS. See also Alfred D. Chandler, Jr., *The Visible Hand* (Cambridge, Mass., 1977).

5. Quoted in Bossard and Dewhurst, *University Education for Business*, p. 9; David F. Noble, *America by Design* (New York, 1977), p. 169.

6. Irwin G. Jennings, "The Young Man and America's Opportunity," *Scribner's*, May 1917, pp. 628–30; Noble, *America by Design*, pp. 50–51.

7. Noble, *America by Design*, pp. 170, 24; Calvert, *Mechanical Engineer*; Parke R. Kolbe, *Urban Influences in Higher Education in England and the United States* (New York, 1928), p. 214; Walter J. Greenleaf, *Self-Help for College Students*, U.S. Bureau of Education Bulletin, 1929, no. 2, p. 39; Walter J. Matherly, *Business Education in the Changing South* (Chapel Hill, 1939), p. 99.

8. McMurtie is quoted in Oleson and Voss, eds., *Organization of Knowledge*, pp. 150–51. See also, pp. 269–72; Edward D. Eddy, Jr., *Colleges for Our Land and Time* (New York, 1956), pp. 172–74.

9. *Some Addresses from the Book of the Opening of the Rice Institute*, Rice Institute Pamphlet 3 (October 1916):242; Eddy, *Colleges*, pp. 172–74; Oleson and Voss, eds., *Organization of Knowledge*, p. 41; Kevles, *Physicists*, pp. 69, 94–95.

10. Oleson and Voss, eds., *Organization of Knowledge*, pp. 264–66; Judd, *Problems of Education*, p. 77.

11. Eddy, *Colleges*, p. 158; *Amherst Student*, October 16, 1919, p. 7; Glen L. Swiggert, *Objectives in Commercial Education*, U.S. Bureau of Education Bulletin, 1924, no. 16, p. 55.

12. Charles R. Mann, *A Study of Engineering Education* (New York, 1918); Society for the Promotion of Engineering Education, *Report of the Investigation of Engineering Education, 1923–29* (Pittsburgh, 1930).

13. "A Discussion of the Development of the College of Engineering" (1918), UI.

14. Eddy, *Colleges*, pp. 114, 124–26, 140–44, 132, 150–51, 174–80, 191, 200; Oleson and Voss, eds., *Organization of Knowledge*, esp. pp. 240–41.

15. Wilson is quoted in Richard Hofstadter and C. De Witt Hardy, *The Development and Scope of Higher Education in the United States* (New York, 1952), p. 43; Eddy, *Colleges*, pp. 116–17, 156–57; President's Report, 1934–35, pp. 5–6, UI.

16. Rita S. Halle, *Which College?* (New York, 1928), p. 31.

17. Bossard and Dewhurst, *University Education for Business*, p. 9.

18. Quoted in Veysey, *Emergence of the American University*, pp. 13–14.

19. Hofstadter, *Anti-Intellectualism*, pp. 233–71.

20. Frank A. Vanderlip, *Business and Education* (New York, 1907), esp. pp. 16, 22–28, 49–50; Noble, *America by Design*, pp. 199–200.

21. See Willard E. Hotchkiss, *Higher Education and Business Standards* (Boston, 1918), pp. 96, 106–8; *Enterpriser*, April 1922, p. 6, UI; Noble, *America by Design*, p. 243.

22. C. R. Dooley to Ernest M. Hopkins, October 18, 1922, Hopkins Papers, DC, expresses the thoughts of a businessman anxious to send his son to the "right" school.

23. Sinclair Lewis, *Babbitt* (New York, 1961), p. 73.

24. J. O. Malott, *Commercial Education in 1924–26,* U.S. Bureau of Education Bulletin, 1928, no. 4, p. 1.

25. Bossard and Dewhurst, *University Education for Business,* p. 53. See also Stone and De Nevi, eds., *Portraits,* pp. 182–92; an anonymous letter in the General Electric Company Bureau Correspondence, HBS; *The DePauw,* February 4, 1938, p. 2; Thyrsa W. Amos et al., *And so to College,* Radio Publication no. 41 (Pittsburgh, 1928), pp. 10–11. See Henry Fairchild, ed., *The Obligations of Universities to the Social Order* (New York, 1933), p. 268, for skeptical and negative references to the value of higher education by businessmen of the period.

26. *The DePauw,* November 11, 1929, p. 2; A. C. Neilsen to Wallace B. Donham, May 3, 1938, Donham Papers, HBS; Matherly, *Business Education,* p. 127; and Hofstadter, *Anti-Intellectualism,* p. 256. The quote from *The New York Times* was reprinted in *The DePauw,* April 1, 1925.

27. L. C. Marshall, ed., *The Collegiate School of Business* (Chicago, 1928), p. 9.

28. Quoted in Matherly, *Businesss Education,* pp. 40–41.

29. Edwin F. Gay, "The Founding of the Harvard Business School," speech at the dedication of the George F. Baker Foundation, June 4, 1927, HBS.

30. *University Training for Public Service,* U.S. Bureau of Education Bulletin, 1916, no. 30, pp. 57–58; John P. Dyer, *Tulane: The Biography of a University* (New York, 1966). A fascinating exception was a rejection by the local Chamber of Commerce of Jacob Schiff's plan to raise $500,000 for a school of commerce at the College of the City of New York in 1911. The chamber was unwilling to grant the CCNY trustees full control of the curriculum: could it have been wary of supporting CCNY's ethnic students? See S. Willis Rudy, *The College of the City of New York: A History* (New York, 1949), p. 326.

31. Quoted in Marshall, ed., *Collegiate School of Business,* p. 55.

32. Raymond A. Kent, ed., *Higher Education in America* (Boston, 1930), p. 78.

33. Bossard and Dewhurst, eds., *University Education for Business,* pp. 253–56; Marshall, ed., *Collegiate School of Business,* pp. 4–9, 210; Matherly, *Business Education,* pp. 71–88.

34. Kent, ed., *Higher Education in America,* p. 83; *State Higher Educational Institutions of Iowa,* U.S. Bureau of Education Bulletin, 1916, no. 19, pp. 97–98; Marshall, ed., *Collegiate School of Business,* pp. 13–14.

35. Quoted in Charles E. Widmayer, *Hopkins of Dartmouth* (Hanover, N.H., 1977), pp. 3–6.

36. Kolbe, *Colleges in War Time,* p. 101; *DePauw University Bulletin,* 3d ser., (May 1914):60–61 and 7 (May 1920):10–11, DPU; Clark, *Indiana University,* p. 215; the president of Grinnell College is quoted in Joan G. Zimmerman, "College Culture in the Midwest, 1890–1930," Ph.D. dissertation, University of Virginia, 1978, p. 89. See also Floyd W. Reeves et al., *The Liberal Arts College* (Chicago, 1932), pp. 240–43.

37. The history of Antioch College is well told in Burton R. Clark, *The Distinctive College* (Chicago, 1970), pp. 36–38; George C. Newman, "The Morgan

Years: The Politics of Innovative Change at Antioch College in the 1920s," Ph.D. dissertation, University of Michigan, 1978, esp. pp. 37–132, 157–84. For a contemporary view, see J. E. Kirkpatrick, *The American College and Its Rulers* (New York, 1926), pp. 174–87.

38. Marvin L. Frederick, "Personal Qualities Requisite for Success in Business," *Journal of Business of the University of Chicago* 4, no. 3, pt. 2 (July 1931):44; Walter V. Bingham, *Placement Service in American Colleges and Universities* (New York, 1926); *Reserve Weekly,* November 4, 1930, p. 2; Michael McGiffert, *The Higher Learning in Colorado: An Historical Study, 1860–1940* (Denver, 1964), pp. 176–77.

39. President's Report, 1915–16, UC, p. 70; Annual Reports of the President, 1918–19, p. 160, and 1921–22, p. 242, Stanford University; Associate Dean files, Hopkins Papers, 1919–20, DC; *Emory Alumnus,* March 1926, p. 9; Bingham, *Placement Service,* pp. 2–3. The president's talk to high school students may be found in *DePauw University Bulletin,* 3d ser., 13, no. 12 (December 1926):10.

40. Frederick, "Personal Qualities," p. 38; *The Plainsman* (student newspaper, Alabama Polytechnic Institute), March 26–27, 1925, p. 3, and April 17, 1925, p. 4; Matherly, *Business Education,* pp. 119–20; Zimmerman, "College Culture," pp. 102–14.

41. *Case Tech,* January 18, 1922, p. 2.

42. *Conference on Commercial Education and Business Progress* (Urbana, 1913), pp. 63–64.

43. Most college English departments introduced courses in "business correspondence" to remedy this problem. See Zimmerman, "College Culture," pp. 95–96.

44. Kirkpatrick, *American College,* pp. 6, 11, 88, 152–71; Curti and Carstensen, *University of Wisconsin,* p. 244.

45. Upton Sinclair, *The Goose-Step* (New York, 1922), esp. pp. 314, 23–25, 33, 320–22; Percy Marks, *Which Way Parnassus?* (New York, 1926), p. 5.

46. Barnard Barker, "The Sociology of Professions," in Kenneth S. Lynn, ed., *The Professions in America* (Boston, 1963), p. 16. For two views of the impact of Frederick W. Taylor's principles of scientific management on higher education, see Hotchkiss, *Higher Education,* pp. 45–65; Hofstadter and Hardy, *Development and Scope,* pp. 88–94. See also Samuel B. Haber, *Efficiency and Uplift* (Chicago, 1964).

47. Lynn, ed., *Professions in America,* pp. 19–24; Jencks and Riesman, *Academic Revolution,* pp. 204–5, 252–53; Marshall, ed., *Collegiate School of Business,* pp. 305–24, 358–61, 389–97; Gager, *French Comment,* pp. 25, 110–11. See also Fritz K. Ringer, *Education and Society in Modern Europe* (Bloomington, Ind., 1979), esp. pp. 2–8.

48. F. Lawrence Babcock, *The U.S. College Graduate* (New York, 1941), p. 70.

49. Hofstadter, *Anti-Intellectualism,* p. 261; Wyllie, "Businessman Looks at the Higher Learning," p. 296.

4 / Expansion and the Urban University

1. Dewey Anderson and Percy E. Davidson, *Recent Occupational Trends in American Labor* (Stanford, 1945), pp. 17–27.
2. Kolbe, *Colleges in War Time,* p. 1; Kolbe, *Urban Influences,* pp. 112–21; Matherly, *Business Education,* p. 12.
3. Quoted in Frederick P. Keppel, *Columbia* (New York, 1914), pp. 175–76.
4. E. E. Slosson, *Great American Universities* (New York, 1910), pp. 346, 361–63; Samuel Lipshutz, "Four Years of College," *American Mercury,* October 1929, pp. 131–35; Cheyney, *University of Pennsylvania,* p. 475; E. Digby Baltzell, *Puritan Boston and Quaker Philadelphia* (New York, 1979), pp. 258–68; Heywood Broun and George Britt, *Christians Only: A Study in Prejudice* (New York, 1931), pp. 72–76.
5. Reports of the President, 1919–20, pp. 23–24, and 1920–21, pp. 20–21, CWRU.
6. This and the following paragraph are based on *A Survey of Higher Education in Cleveland* (Cleveland, 1925), esp. pp. 190–93, 239–46, 79–84, 20, 48–50, 289.
7. *Some Addresses,* Rice Institute Pamphlet 3 (October 1916):231.
8. Kolbe, *Urban Influences,* p. 127; R. H. Eckelberry, *The History of the Municipal University in the United States,* U.S. Office of Education Bulletin, 1932, no. 2, esp. pp. 113–26, 170; C. R. Foster, Jr., and Paul S. Dwyer, *A Study of the Geographical Distribution of Students in 363 American Colleges and Universities* (New Brunswick, N.J., 1931), p. 22; Ellis M. Reeves, "Which College?" *Journal of Higher Education,* February 1932, p. 73. The proportion of students staying in state for college has remained at about 80 percent since World War I; see Jencks and Riesman, *Academic Revolution,* p. 155.
9. George F. Zook, "Is the Junior College a Menace or a Boon?" *School Review,* June 1929, p. 417.
10. "College Aims Past and Present," *School and Society,* December 3, 1921, pp. 499–509; John W. Evans, *The Newman Movement: Roman Catholics in American Higher Education, 1883–1971* (Notre Dame, Ind., 1980), pp. 9–10, 68; W. Bruce Leslie, "Localism, Denominationalism, and Institutional Strategies in Urbanizing America: Three Pennsylvania Colleges, 1870–1915," *History of Education Quarterly* 17 (Fall 1977):235–56.
11. Manuel P. Servin and Iris H. Wilson, *Southern California and Its University* (Los Angeles, 1969), esp. pp. 99, 112–13; McGiffert, *Higher Learning in Colorado,* pp. 179–81.
12. Robert Hassenger, ed., *The Shape of Catholic Higher Education* (Chicago, 1967), pp. 17–19, 34; Edward J. Power, *A History of Catholic Higher Education in the United States* (Milwaukee, 1958), pp. 47–48.
13. *Biennial Survey of Education, 1924–26,* pp. 7–8; Riesman's view can be found in Hassenger, ed., *Catholic Higher Education,* p. 4.
14. Kaylor, *Truth Sets Free,* pp. 176–242; Peter Per Person, "A History of Higher Education among Swedish Immigrants in America," Ph.D. dissertation, Harvard University Graduate School of Education, 1941, pp. vii–viii, 94.

15. Paul M. Gaston, *The New South Creed* (Baton Rouge, 1970), is the leading study of its subject. The data on professionals in the South can be found in Thomas A. Whitener, "Guidance of College Freshmen," master's thesis, University of North Carolina, 1924, pp. 3–4.

16. Quoted in William H. Crawford, ed., *The American College* (New York, 1915), p. 126.

17. I. L. Kandel, ed., *Twenty-five Years of American Education* (New York, 1924), p. 394.

18. Ibid., p. 390; *Bulletin of Emory University* 4, no. 2 (February 1918):2.

19. Henry M. Bullock, *A History of Emory University: 1836–1936* (Nashville, 1936), esp. chap. 13, provides background on the decision to locate Emory in Atlanta.

20. Mark Bauman, "Confronting the New South Creed: The Genteel Conservative as Higher Educator," in Ronald K. Goodenow and Arthur O. White, eds., *Education and the Rise of the New South* (Boston, 1981), pp. 92–113, is a synthesis of Bauman's longer study "Warren Akin Candler: Conservative amidst Change," Ph.D. dissertation, Emory University, 1975.

21. Chancellor's Report, 1917–18, p. 16, and diary of Ross McClean, fall 1919, both in EU; Thomas H. English, *Emory University: 1915–65* (Atlanta, 1966), p. 111.

22. Minutes, Executive Committee of the Board of Trustees, March 8, 1919, p. 76, EU; *Emory Wheel*, December 12, 1919, p. 1; *Emory Alumnus*, December 1932, p. 6.

23. *Emory Wheel*, October 29, 1925, p. 4; Goodrich C. White, commencement speech, Mercer University, May 25, 1934, in White Papers, EU. The region's difficulties in moving into the mainstream of twentieth-century America are explored by an eminent Emory University graduate, C. Vann Woodward, in *The Burden of Southern History* (Baton Rouge, 1960).

24. Eckelberry, *History of the Municipal University*, p. 170.

25. Ibid., pp. 128–36; Zook is quoted in Kolbe, *Urban Influences*, pp. 119–20.

26. Kolbe, *Urban Influences*, pp. 152–53.

27. W. J. Cooper, "Present-Day Trends in Our Colleges," *Current History*, June 1930, p. 518.

28. This and the following paragraph are based on Leslie L. Hanawalt, *A Place of Light: The History of Wayne State University* (Detroit, 1968).

29. George D. Strayer et al., *Report of a Survey of the Colleges under the Control of the Board of Higher Education of the City of New York* (Albany, 1944), chap. 2, p. 1 (CCNY); Rudy, *College of the City of New York*, p. 372.

30. Key contemporary sources include *Proceedings of the Board of Trustees of the College of the City of New York*, January 17, 1924, pp. 13–15, and *Proceedings of the Board of Higher Education of the City of New York*, March 18, 1930, p. 110, both in CCNY. See also Rudy, *College of the City of New York*, esp. pp. 382–88.

31. Rudy, *College of the City of New York*, pp. 397–98.

32. Strayer et al., *Report*, chap. 2, pp. 11–14; Sherry Gorelick, *City College and the Jewish Poor* (New Brunswick, N.J., 1981), esp. p. 195.

33. Quoted in Veysey, *Emergence of the American University*, p. 356.

34. Roscoe Pound, "The Place of Higher Education in American Life," *School and Society*, August 8, 1936, p. 161.

5 / Curriculum Reform between the World Wars

1. Hugh P. Baker, "80th Annual Report of the Massachusetts State College," *Massachusetts State College Bulletin* 35, no. 2 (February 1943):4–5; Crawford, ed., *American College*, p. ix.

2. Robert M. Hutchins, *The Higher Learning in America* (New Haven, 1936, rpt. 1961), p. 43.

3. Julian Park, "A Philosophy of Curriculum Making," *Journal of Higher Education*, April 1930, p. 233.

4. Thorstein Veblen, *The Higher Learning in America* (New York, 1918), pp. 6–11.

5. Ibid., pp. 23–25, 42–43, 101.

6. Ibid., pp. 27, 30–31, 204, 19–20, 196.

7. Max McConn, *College or Kindergarten?* (New York, 1928), pp. 17, 9, 38–49.

8. *The Students Speak Out!* (New York, 1929), p. 90.

9. Lotus D. Coffman, "Flexner and the State University," *Journal of Higher Education*, October 1931, p. 81.

10. R. Freeman Butts, *The College Charts Its Course* (New York, 1939), p. 359; Fairchild, ed., *Obligation*, p. 335; Robinson is quoted in Rudy, *College of the City of New York*, p. 381; Crawford, ed., *American College*, p. 97.

11. M. S. Noble is quoted in *University of North Carolina Record*, no. 161 (December 1918), p. 55; Willystine Goodsell, *The Education of Women* (New York, 1923), pp. 162–63; Gulick's views are in Fairchild, ed., *Obligation*, pp. 281–83.

12. McConn, *College or Kindergarten?* p. 109; Ross McClean diary, March 1, March 2, and May 10, 1920, EU; Jencks and Riesman, *Academic Revolution*, p. 14; Curti and Carstensen, *University of Wisconsin*, p. 615.

13. Daniel Bell, *The Reforming of General Education* (New York, 1968), p. 19; George W. Pierson, *Yale: The University College, 1921–37* (New Haven, 1955), pp. 315–32; Frederick Rudolph, *Curriculum* (San Francisco, 1978), esp. p. 214.

14. Nell Battle Lewis, newspaper column, *Raleigh News and Observer*, August 11, 1935, clipping in Vice Chancellor's Papers, UNC.

15. Leon B. Richardson, *A Study of the Liberal College* (Hanover, N.H., 1924), p. 190; James R. Angell in Fairchild, ed., *Obligation*, p. 21; Norman Foerster, *The American State University* (Chapel Hill, N.C., 1937), pp. 87–90.

16. Bell, *Reforming of General Education*, pp. 14–15; Frances Blanchard, *Frank Aydelotte of Swarthmore* (Middletown, Conn., 1970), pp. 126–28.

17. Ernest M. Hopkins to Secretary, Committee on Education and Special Training, Student Army Training Corps, January 24, 1919, in SATC folder, Ernest M. Hopkins Papers, DC; Richardson, *History of Dartmouth*, 2:784; Gruber, *Mars and Minerva*, p. 244; Rudolph, *American College*, pp. 236–38, 256; A. Lawrence Lowell, *At War with Academic Traditions in America* (Cambridge, Mass., 1934), p. 345; *The DePauw*, May 19, 1933, p. 2.

18. Reeves et al., *Liberal Arts College*, pp. 210–11; Carl M. Stephens, manuscript history of the University of Illinois, chap. 9, pp. 44–45, UI; "The Needs of Adelbart College: A Report by the Curriculum Committee," Western Reserve University, 1936, in FAS files, CWRU; William Leutner's view is in Reports of the President and Other Officers, 1919–20, p. 40, CWRU; Harold L. Butler, "The Fine Arts," in Kent, ed., *Higher Education in America*, pp. 243–61; Rudolph, *American College*, pp. 265–67.

19. Park, "Philosophy of Curriculum Making," p. 234; Matherly, *Business Education*, p. 211; Charles H. Haskins, dean of Harvard College, in Crawford, ed., *American College*, pp. 44–50. For an overview, see Dorothy Ross, "The Development of the Social Sciences," in Oleson and Voss, eds., *Organization of Knowledge*, pp. 107–38.

20. *Class Book of the Class of 1933*, p. 9, DC.

21. Rexford G. Tugwell and Leon H. Keyserling, eds., *Redirecting Education* (New York, 1934), esp. pp. 87–93, 125–32.

22. Slosson, *Great American Universities*, pp. 2–3; Floyd R. Reeves, "The Liberal Arts College," *Journal of Higher Education*, October 1930, p. 374; George P. Schmidt, *The Liberal Arts College* (New Brunswick, N.J.: Rutgers University Press, 1957), pp. 209–11.

23. Minutes, Board of Trustees, May 31, 1929, p. 78; Goodrich C. White, 1930 speech, undanted, in White Papers; and Annual Report of the President to the Trustees, 1930–31, p. 25, all in EU. For the views of a conservative educator at the University of North Carolina, see Addison Hibbard to———, January 27, 1928, "What of the A.B. Degree?" file, Vice Chancellor's Papers, UNC.

24. *Journal of Higher Education* editorial, January 1940, p. 43; Stephens MS, chap. 13, pp. 25–27, UI.

25. John Dewey, *The Way Out of Educational Confusion* (Cambridge, Mass., 1931), pp. 19–27 (italics in original).

26. John Dewey, *Democracy and Education* (New York, 1966), esp. chaps. 7 and 18; Kent, ed., *Higher Education*, p. 446.

27. Stewart G. Cole, *Liberal Education in a Democracy* (New York, 1940), p. 20.

28. Frederick Lewis Allen, *Only Yesterday* (New York, 1964), p. 197.

29. Schilpp, ed., *Higher Education*, p. 204; Oleson and Voss, eds., *Organization of Knowledge*, pp. 302–4.

30. Hudson, *College*, p. 74; see also Ernest H. Wilkins in Fairchild, ed., *Obligation*, p. 85; Report of the President to the Board of Trustees, January 18, 1927, p. 3, DPU; *Class Book of the Class of 1930*, p. 11, DC.

31. "The Trouble with the Colleges," *Forum*, December 1933, p. 348; Fraser,

ed., *Foreign Perspectives,* pp. 337–38; Hofstadter and Hardy, *Development and Scope,* pp. 103–6; George M. Baker, "Reflections on the American College," *Sewanee Review,* October 1927, pp. 420–21, 427–28.

32. William H. Kirkpatrick's review of Flexner's book can be found in *Journal of Higher Education,* October 1931, p. 357; Abraham Flexner, *Universities: American, English, German* (New York, 1930), pp. 3–4, 57, 222, 53, 149.

33. Flexner to Wallace B. Donham, June 1, 1931, Donham Papers, HBS; Flexner, *Universities,* pp. 5–6, 11, 62.

34. Flexner, *Universities,* pp. 23, 42; *Junior College Journal* 1 (May 1931):522; Rudolph, *American College,* p. 205.

35. Hutchins, *Higher Learning,* pp. 4–14.

36. Ibid., pp. 26–27, 33.

37. Lowell, *At War,* esp. pp. v–v11, 274.

38. *Harvard Crimson,* November 9, 1928, p. 2; November 13, 1928, p. 2; November 14, 1928, p. 2; September 19, 1930, p. 2; Morison, *Three Centuries of Harvard,* pp. 440–49, 476–79.

39. Richardson, *Study of the Liberal College,* pp. 17–20, 280–81; "Report of the Senior Committee," 1924, pp. 24–32, DC. The *New Republic* of July 30, 1924, carried an editorial on the student report.

40. The federal specialist in education, Arthur Klein, is quoted in *Biennial Survey of Education, 1922–24,* pp. 19–20. This discussion of Swarthmore's honors program is based on Swarthmore College Faculty, *An Adventure in Education* (New York, 1941), and Blanshard, *Aydelotte of Swarthmore,* pp. 188–238.

41. Schilpp, ed., *Higher Education,* p. 148; Clark, *Indiana University,* pp. 100–105; Brubacher and Rudy, *Higher Education,* p. 269; Widmayer, *Hopkins of Dartmouth,* pp. 88–89; Reeves et al., *Liberal Arts College,* p. 274.

42. Foerster, *American State University,* pp. 27, 59–60, 151–57, 170; Alexander Meiklejohn, *The Experimental College* (New York, 1932).

43. Zimmerman, "College Culture," esp. pp. 16–18, 77–94, 121–25, 255.

44. Reeves et al., *Liberal Arts College,* pp. 13–17, 49–50; Reeves, "Liberal Arts College," pp. 376–77; *Biennial Survey of Education, 1916–18,* 1:7.

45. *Amherst Student,* March 17, 1921, p. 2; *Students Speak Out!* pp. 15–16; *The Dartmouth,* November 18, 1937, p. 2; Clark, *Indiana University,* pp. 179–80.

46. James R. Angell, *American Education* (New Haven, 1937), p. 16; Angell in Fairchild, ed., *Obligation,* pp. 7–22.

6 / The Middle-Class Culture on the Campus

1. Halle, *Which College?* p. 3; *Emory Wheel,* April 12, 1928, p. 4.

2. Irwin Edman, "Richard Kane Goes to College," *Century Magazine,* October 1924, p. 723.

3. Robert C. Angell, *The Campus* (New York, 1928), p. 21.

4. Veysey, *Emergence of the American University,* p. 440; Bledstein, *Culture of*

Professionalism, pp. 292–94; R. L. Duffus, *Democracy Enters College* (New York, 1936), p. 76.

5. Harold S. Wechsler, *The Qualified Student* (New York, 1977), p. 77; *Harvard Crimson*, October 1, 1929, p. 2, carried the *New York Times* editorial on Butler's remarks; Angell, *Campus*, p. 145.

6. Committee on the Bureau of Personnel Research, "Report to the Trustees," January 4, 1927, pp. 1–2, in Hopkins Papers, DC; Mekeel's comments are in *Students Speak Out!* p. 64; *Daily Illini*, May 11, 1927. See also Fred H. Turner, "College—Just Ahead," typescript copy of article from *American Boy* magazine, September 1929, in Turner Papers, UI; Christian Gauss, dean of Princeton University, in Harold E. Stearns, ed., *America Now* (New York, 1938), p. 335.

7. The Association of American University Professors report was published as Malcolm M. Willey, *Depression, Recovery, and Higher Education* (New York, 1937), p. 223; Foerster, *American State University*, p. 62; Lovett's view is in Harold E. Stearns, ed., *Civilization in the United States* (New York, 1922), p. 89; W. Lloyd Warner, Robert J. Havighurst, and Martin B. Loeb, *Who Shall be Educated?* (New York, 1944), pp. 155, 67. In *Middletown* (New York, 1929), p. 28, Robert and Helen Lynd reported that when a housewife worked outside the home, she generally did so in order to earn additional income for her sons' education. See also McConn, *College or Kindergarten?* pp. 18–19, 25.

8. Percy Marks, *Which Way Parnassus?* (New York, 1926), p. 157; *Massachusetts Collegian*, October 8, 1919, p. 4; John P. Gavit, *College* (New York, 1925), pp. 301–3.

9. Fred H. Turner, "Like Father, Unlike Son" (1926), pp. 8–11, in Turner Papers, UI.

10. Annual Report of the Officers for 1936–37, DePauw University, pp. 47–48, DPU; McConn, *College or Kindergarten?* pp. 19–29.

11. Flexner, *Universities*, p. 69; Hutchins, *Higher Learning*, p. 29; H. L. Mincken in *American Mercury*, October 1929, p. 163.

12. James A. Hawes, *Twenty Years among the Twenty-Year-Olds* (New York, 1929), esp. p. 49; Reeves et al., *Liberal Arts Colleges*, pp. 385–86; Zimmerman, "College Culture," p. 162; *Amherst Student*, June 17, 1929, p. 6; *Massachusetts Collegian*, November 12, 1919, p. 5; Wechsler, *Revolt on the Campus*, esp. p. 37. The most complete critique of middle-class student life between the two world wars is Paula S. Fass, *The Damned and the Beautiful* (New York, 1977).

13. Fass, *Damned and Beautiful*, pp. 175, 423. David Riesman's reminiscences of his Harvard years in the late 1920s are in Seymour M. Lipset and David Riesman, *Education and Politics at Harvard* (New York, 1975), p. 298; see also Frederick Rudolph, *The American College and University* (New York, 1962), p. 461.

14. *Harvard Crimson*, October 14, 1929, p. 2; Angell, *Campus*, p. 5; Rudolph, *American College*, p. 378; David Riesman and Reuel Denney, "Football in America," *American Quarterly* 3 (Summer 1951):309–25.

15. Alexander G. Crawford's 1922 Campus Oration, Massachusetts Agricultural College, UM; Fass, *Damned and Beautiful*, esp. pp. 139–49.

16. George A. Weller, *Not to Eat, Not for Love* (New York, 1933), p. 56; Curti and Carstensen, *University of Wisconsin*, pp. 501–2; Marks, *Which Way Parnassus?* p. 129; Gavit, *College*, pp. 166–69; Arthur J. Klein, *Survey of Land-Grant Colleges and Universities*, U.S. Office of Education Bulletin, 1930, no. 9, pp. 510, 527–28; Stephens MS, chap. 9, p. 32, UI; Tugwell and Keyserling, eds., *Redirecting Education*, p. 120; Christian Association, "Survey of Religious Life and Work" (1925), pp. 12–13, CWRU. For the history of a student-led movement to create a Jewish fraternity at Massachusetts Agricultural College, see the Presidential Papers of Edward M. Lewis, box 3, UM. *The Dartmouth*, October 13, 1933, p. 1, and February 26, 1934, p. 2; and "A Survey of Social Life at Dartmouth College" (1935), 1:83, all document the class bias inherent in the fraternity system there.

17. Gavit, *College*, pp. 116–19; Weller, *Not to Eat*, p. 55; Wechsler, *Revolt on the Campus*, pp. 26–35, 46–47, 423–25; *Harvard Crimson*, September 28, 1929, pp. 4, 6; Harvard *Class Album*, 1931, pp. 198–99.

18. The rabbi is quoted in Paul Carter, *The Twenties in America* (Arlington Heights, Ill., 1975), p. 13; Cornelius H. Patton and Walter T. Field, *Eight O'Clock Chapel* (Boston, 1927), pp. 319–20.

19. Blanshard, *Aydelotte of Swarthmore*, p. 273; Angell, *Campus*, pp. 127–29; Sinclair, *Goose-Step*, p. 379; Stephens MS, chap. 9, p. 33, UI. One Harvard student said, "Intellectual prowess and social prestige are in inverse ratio" (quoted in Gavit, *College*, p. 120).

20. The term "other-directed" was given currency by David Riesman in *The Lonely Crowd*, written in collaboration with Nathan Glazer and Reuel Denney (New Haven, 1950).

21. Marion Talbot, *The Education of Women* (Chicago, 1910), pp. 19–28; Willystine Goodsell, in Kandel, ed., *Twenty-five Years*, pp. 336–38; Rosalind Rosenberg, *Beyond Separate Spheres* (New Haven, 1982), pp. 44–53; Rockwell D. Hunt, *History of the College of the Pacific* (Stockton, Calif., 1951), p. 128.

22. Patricia A. Graham, "Expansion and Exclusion: A History of Women in American Higher Education," *Signs* 3 (Summer 1978):759–74; Mary R. Walsh, *No Women Need Apply* (New Haven, 1978); Helen L. Horowitz, *Alma Mater* (New York, 1984); and Mabel Newcomer, *A Century of Higher Education for American Women* (New York, 1959) all address opportunities for women in early-twentieth-century institutions of higher learning. Barbara M. Solomon, *In the Company of Educated Women* (New Haven, 1985), is the finest survey of this subject.

23. Margaret Rossiter, *Women Scientists in America: Strategies and Survival to 1940* (Baltimore, 1982), esp. pp. 51–296.

24. Talbot, *Education of Women*, pp. 169–70, 176–77; Solomon, *In the Company*, p. 63, 143–44; Goodsell, *Education of Women*, pp. 26–28, 170–71; Annual Reports of the President and Other Officers, Stanford University, 1907–8, pp. 88–89, and 1909–10, p. 7; Reeves et al., *Liberal Arts College*, pp. 43–45.

25. Jordan's view is included in Stone and De Nevi, eds., *Portraits*, pp. 309–

10; *Harvard Crimson*, November 19, 1927, p. 5; Nielsen is quoted in *Harvard Crimson*, January 29, 1930, p. 2.

26. Solomon, *In the Company*, pp. 157–85, summarizes this debate.

27. Matherly, *Business Education*, p. 116; Angell, *Campus*, p. 174; Gavit, *College*, p. 288; *Biennial Surveys of Education: 1936–38*, chap. 4, p. 13; *1938–42*, chap. 4, pp. 12, 33; *1932–34*, chap. 4, p. 4.

28. Lynd and Lynd, *Middletown*, p. 185; O. E. Reynolds, *The Social and Economic Status of College Students* (New York, 1927), p. 22; Warner et al., *Who Shall Be Educated?* pp. 66–67; Helen B. Goetsch, *Parental Income and College Opportunities* (New York, 1940), p. 87; Jencks and Riesman, *Academic Revolution*, pp. 95–96.

29. Howard M. Bell, *Youth Tell Their Story* (Washington, D.C., 1938), p. 61; Noel P. Gist, C. T. Philblad, and C. L. Gregory, "Scholastic Achievement and Occupation," *American Sociological Review* 7, no. 6, pt. 2 (December 1942):761–62; Jencks and Riesman, *Academic Revolution*, p. 97. The quotation is from J. Edward Todd, *Social Norms and the Behavior of College Students* (New York, 1941), pp. 117–18.

30. Reynolds, *Social and Economic Status*, pp. 14–16.

31. Walter J. Greenleaf, *Economic Status of College Alumni*, U.S. Office of Education Bulletin, 1937, no. 10, p. 25.

32. "From a Graduate's Window," *Harvard Graduates' Magazine* 39 (March 1931):342; Leonard V. Koos, *The Junior College Movement* (Boston, 1925), p. 158; Claude M. Fuess, *Amherst: The Story of a New England College* (Boston, 1935), p. 342; Zimmerman, "College Culture," pp. 173–85.

33. *Class Book of the Class of 1913*, pp. 24–25; "The Class of 1930," pp. 27–28; and *Dartmouth Alumni Magazine* 28 (January 1936):20, all in DC; Patton and Field, *Eight O'Clock Chapel*, p. 332.

34. John B. Johnston, *The Liberal College in a Changing Society* (New York, 1930), p. 52; Mapheus Smith, "University Student Intelligence and Occupation of Father," *American Sociological Review* 7, no. 6, pt. 2 (December 1942):771.

35. This and the following paragraph are based on Matherly, *Business Education*, p. 306; Eddy, *Colleges*, p. 152; Reports of the Registrar, 1934–35, Table 14A, and 1939–40, Table 14A, in President's Annual Report files, UI; Clark, *Indiana University*, 2:281, 370; Annual Reports of the Massachusetts Agricultural College and Massachusetts State College (data on fathers' occupations and home residences) and clipping from *Boston Globe*, October 5, 1930, in University Historical Collection, UM; W. S. Hoffman, "Occupations of Parents of College Students," *School and Society*, January 2, 1932, p. 26.

36. The information from the University of Pittsburgh was gleaned from Ruth Crawford Mitchell's "Nativity Study" (1928), typescript copy in the University of Pittsburgh Archives, kindly provided to me by Leila W. Jamison. The data on CCNY can be found in Louis A. Millendorf, "A Study of the Vocational Choices of the Students of the College of the City of New York," master's thesis, CCNY, 1934, p. 17.

37. Reynolds, *Social and Economic Status,* p. 42; Edward F. Potthoff, "Who Goes to College?" *Journal of Higher Education,* June 1931, p. 297; Haven Hubbard, "The Relation of Social and Economic Factors to the Obtaining of the College Certificate by the Entering Class of 1931," master's thesis, University of Chicago, 1934, p. 53; Dean of Students' background material, May 1940 Trustees Report, in William B. Benton Papers, UC; Dartmouth Class of 1915 *Green Book,* p. 52, and Class of 1932 *Green Book,* p. 133, DC. For more data on the backgrounds of students at public institutions, see Angell, *Campus,* p. 231, on the University of Michigan; Sanford Winston, "Social Backgrounds of College Freshmen," *Southern Association Quarterly,* November 1938, in Carolina Collection, UNC, for a survey of North Carolina State College freshmen in the mid-1930s; Strayer et al., *Report,* chap. 2, p. 10 (CCNY); and Ernest Havemann and Patricia S. West, *They Went to College* (New York, 1952), pp. 15, 182.

38. Patton and Field, *Eight O'Clock Chapel,* pp. 310–12; Reeves et al., *Liberal Arts College,* pp. 526–27, 622–26; Reynolds, *Social and Economic Status,* p. 24; Hubbard, "Social and Economic Factors," p. 56; *Massachusetts Collegian,* November 1, 1930, p. 2.

39. *Daily Illini,* September 18, 1930, p. 4.

40. Warner et al., *Who Shall Be Educated?* pp. 36–37; Sinclair, *Goose-Step,* p. 442; Flexner, *Universities,* pp. 68–69; *New York Evening Post,* April 15, 1927, p. 4; Jencks and Riesman, *Academic Revolution,* p. 105.

41. *Daily Illini,* September 17, 1930, p. 4; Julia E. Deane, "The School Counselor," *Boston Herald* clipping, in Hopkins Papers, H. M. Tibbetts folder, 1919–20, DC; Edward K. Graham, "The Typical North Carolina Student," speech delivered October 11, 1913, in Carolina Collection, UNC.

42. Wechsler, *Revolt on the Campus,* p. 51.

43. W. H. G. Armytage, *The American Influence on English Education* (London, 1967), p. 57; Fritz K. Ringer, *Education and Society in Modern Europe* (Bloomington, Ind., 1979), pp. 148, 229, 52–65, 253.

7 / *Discrimination in College Admissions*

1. Harold S. Wechsler, *The Qualified Student* (New York, 1977), and Marcia G. Synnott, *The Half-Opened Door: Discrimination and Admissions at Harvard, Yale, and Princeton* (Westport, Conn., 1979), are the two most complete studies of discrimination in college admissions. See also Harold S. Wechsler, "The Rationale for Restriction: Ethnicity and College Admissions in America, 1910–1980," *American Quarterly* 36 (Winter 1984):643–67.

2. Burton R. Clark, *The Distinctive College* (Chicago, 1970), p. 100; Crawford, ed., *American College,* p. 184; Fairchild, ed., *Obligation,* p. 22.

3. Quoted in Hofstadter and Hardy, *Development and Scope,* p. 119.

4. James L. McConaughty, "Dartmouth College and the Secondary Schools," *School and Society,* December 18, 1915, p. 891; E. M. Hopkins to Craven

Laycock, March 1, 1918, Hopkins Papers, DC; Richardson, *History of Dartmouth,* pp. 674–75, 750.

5. Richardson, *History of Dartmouth,* p. 768; E. G. Bill to Hopkins, April 22, 1927, Hopkins Papers, DC.

6. Widmayer, *Hopkins of Dartmouth,* p. 63; Synnott, *Half-Opened Door,* p. 189; President's Report, 1922–23, p. xi, UC.

7. Reeves et al., *Liberal Arts College,* p. 361.

8. John Dugdale, "America's Mass Education," *Current History,* April 1930, p. 73; Clark, *Distinctive College,* pp. 186–91; Aydelotte is quoted in Robert L. Kelly, *The Effective College* (New York, 1928), p. 6.

9. Hopkins to Morton C. Tuttle, August 15, 1930, in Hopkins Papers, DC.

10. Laycock to Hopkins, October 1 and December 2, 1919, and Hopkins to Laycock, November 11, 1919, all in Hopkins Papers, DC; Richardson, *History of Dartmouth,* p. 768.

11. E. M. Hopkins, "Aristocracy of Brains," September 21, 1922; Theodore Groves to Hopkins, October 26, 1922, both in Hopkins Papers, DC.

12. Hopkins to Joseph Gollomb, October 5, 1922, Hopkins Papers, DC.

13. E. M. Hopkins, "A Selective Process," 1922, in Hopkins Papers, DC.

14. E. M. Hopkins, "Talk on the Selection of Students," 1925; Bill to Hopkins, February 1927, both in Hopkins Papers, DC.

15. E. M. Hopkins, *This Our Purpose* (Hanover, N.H., 1950), pp. 178–79.

16. Hopkins to Felix Frankfurter, February 26, 1923, Hopkins Papers, DC.

17. E. G. Bill, "The Class of 1926," p. 6, in Hopkins Papers, DC; Hopkins, *This Our Purpose,* p. 272. A national institution was defined as one that enrolled students from at least three-quarters of the states and enrolled less than 30 percent of its students from its home state. The ten were Antioch College, Asbury College of Kentucky, Sweetbriar College, Washington & Lee College, Wellesley College, Georgetown College, Smith College, Yale University, Dartmouth College, and Notre Dame University. See *Dartmouth Alumni Magazine* 24 (October 1931):29.

18. *The Dartmouth,* December 6, 1921, p. 1; Richardson, *History of Dartmouth,* p. 782.

19. Hopkins to Editor of *Louisville* (Ky.) *Post,* December 29, 1921, Hopkins Papers, DC. The geographical distribution of each entering class in the 1930s was presented in a table in each year's November issue of the *Dartmouth Alumni Magazine.*

20. *DePauw Daily,* May 5, 1922, p. 1; *Bulletin of DePauw University,* 4th ser., 16, no. 7 (September 1929):51; Annual Report of the Officers, 1939–40, pp. 51, 86, DPU; *Bulletin of DePauw University,* 3d ser., 7, no. 9 (1920):3.

21. President's Report to the Trustees, June 10, 1938, pp. 9–10, and November 3, 1939, pp. 2–4, DPU. See also George B. Manhart, *DePauw through the Years* (Greencastle, Ind., 1962), p. 329.

22. W. W. Carson, "The College and the Coming Years," *DePauw Magazine* 8, no. 3 (March 1927):32; Wechsler, *Qualified Student,* p. 226; David H. Stevens to Harold P. Swift, January 25, 1928, Presidential Papers, 1925–45, UC.

23. Heywood Broun and George Britt, *Christians Only* (New York, 1931), p. 108; *New York Times,* June 2, 1922, p. 1.

24. Jewish students constituted 42 percent of those accepted under Harvard's "top seventh" plan when it was first adopted; see Synnott, *Half-Opened Door,* pp. xvii, 92, 107, 110, 202. See also Stephen Steinberg, *The Academic Melting Pot* (New York, 1974), pp. 29–30; Lipset and Riesman, *Education and Politics,* pp. 147–48.

25. William T. Ham, "Harvard Student Opinion on the Jewish Question," *Nation* 115 (September 6, 1922):225–27.

26. In 1922 E. M. Hopkins told one alumnus: "I do not know whether it would be well to tell this to men who are selecting their college, but it is a fact that it is not so hard to get into Dartmouth College under the selective process as it is popularly supposed. Practically any chap who has a record of good character and good scholarship and has diverse interests, though he may not be an exceptionally good scholar, can gain admission" (Hopkins to S. S. Larmon, December 8, 1922, Hopkins Papers, DC).

27. Gavit, *College,* pp. 204–6; Synnott, *Half-Opened Door,* pp. 14, 26–57; Carey McWilliams, *A Mask for Privilege* (Boston, 1948), pp. 28–38, 68.

28. Slosson is cited in Synnott, *Half-Opened Door,* pp. 150–51, 174; Morison, *Three Centuries of Harvard,* p. 417.

29. Synnott, *Half-Opened Door,* pp. 15–16; Reynolds, *Social and Economic Status,* pp. 31–34.

30. Synnott, *Half-Opened Door,* pp. 154–55. At Yale, the classes of 1911–14 included 5.5 percent Jews; the classes of 1923–26 had 10.2 percent Jews; the class of 1927, 13.3 percent Jews; and each class thereafter, about 10 to 12 percent Jews. See also Wechsler, *Qualified Student,* p. 135.

31. The April 15, 1921, clipping can be found in the Historical Collection files, UM; Bossard and Dewhurst, *University Education for Business,* p. 558. See also Broun and Britt, *Christians Only,* p. 113, and *The Campus* (CCNY), October 28, 1930.

32. Events at Harvard are discussed in Steinberg, *Academic Melting Pot,* pp. 21–31; Lipset and Riesman, *Education and Politics,* pp. 144–46; Broun and Britt, *Christians Only,* pp. 89–90.

33. Starr is quoted in Synnott, *Half-Opened Door,* p. 75; Kallen is in Steinberg, *Academic Melting Pot,* p. 28.

34. Hopkins to Laycock, January 1, 1920; Hopkins to Bill, July 15, 1922; Hopkins to Frankfurter, July 15, 1922; Hopkins to *New York World,* April 30, 1926 (telegram), all in Hopkins Papers, DC.

35. Wechsler, *Revolt on the Campus,* p. 354.

36. Hopkins to Rabbi Harry Levi, November 21, 1922, Hopkins Papers, DC; Broun and Britt, *Christians Only,* pp. 120–21.

37. *Dartmouth Alumni Magazine,* November 1930, p. 22; November 1931, p. 99; and November 1932, p. 20; Hopkins to Bill, October 14, 1931, Hopkins Papers, DC.

38. Hopkins to Bill, December 24, 1931; Hopkins to Judge William N. Cohen, February 1, 1932, both in Hopkins Papers, DC. In a later memorandum to Bill,

dated March 7, 1932, Hopkins wrote: "I shrink from and abhor the whole necessity [but] in the last analysis there is no more reason why we should withhold from doing this than from letting the College become exclusively a rich man's college or exclusively a Massachusetts institution" (ibid.).

39. Bill to Hopkins, October 12, 1932, and January 3, 1933, Hopkins Papers, DC.

40. The dean of Columbia is quoted in Synnott, *Half-Opened Door,* p. 18, and see pp. 18–19 and 109–10; Reports of the President and Other Officers, 1926–27, pp. 61–62, CWRU; Sinclair, *Goose-Step,* pp. 357–59; Wechsler, *Qualified Student,* p. 159; and Steinberg, *Academic Melting Pot,* pp. 17–21, for more discussion of the testing issue. Even the Commission of the College Board agreed that the initial Scholastic Aptitude Test in 1926 was biased; see Claude M. Fuess, *The College Board: Its First Fifty Years* (New York, 1950), p. 107.

41. The number of Jewish freshmen remained at 37 or 38 for the rest of the decade; see the November issues of the *Dartmouth Alumni Magazine* each year in the 1930s. See also Herbert A. Wolff to Hopkins, April 14, 1932; Hopkins to Wolff, May 5, 1932, Hopkins Papers, DC; *Dartmouth Alumni Magazine,* November 1932, p. 20.

42. Bill to Hopkins, March 24, 1933; Hopkins to Bill, March 25, 1933, Hopkins Papers, DC. The following is an example of a favorable alumni committee report on a Jewish candidate, as reported by Bill to Hopkins, January 19, 1933: "I would very much like to see him come to Dartmouth, and if the well-pigmented Phibetes are to be reduced materially and a somewhat more gentlemanly lot from the same ethnic roots introduced, I know of no more suitable than Don Frank, Toledo, Ohio."

Hopkins expressed his willingness—owing to widespread support—to do whatever was necessary to keep the proportion of Jewish students down: "I have not yet heard one single reservation expressed in regard to the reduced proportions of Jews in the last class, and I have heard overwhelming satisfaction expressed even among some of the Jewish alumni and boys themselves. I think I would rather take the hazards of what appears to be a group of less scholastic promise, distributed among Anglo-Saxons, Hibernians, Scandinavians, and those from other outlying districts, than to let the Jewish proportion again rise above the admirable proportion that you established in this year's class" (Hopkins to Bill, February 20, 1933, DC).

43. Hopkins to Myer Segal, May 18, 1939, Hopkins Papers, DC.

44. Robert C. Strong to Hopkins, April 4, 1939, Hopkins Papers, DC.

45. Synnott, *Half-Opened Door,* pp. 58, 152; Hopkins to Bill, April 25, April 28, and June 24, 1932, Hopkins Papers, DC. See also the data on the increasing number of alumni children in the November issues of the *Dartmouth Alumni Magazine.*

46. Judge William N. Cohen to Hopkins, January 29, 1932; Bill to Hopkins, April 12, 1932; Hopkins to Bill, March 25, 1933, all in Hopkins Papers, DC.

47. Broun and Britt, *Christians Only,* pp. 50–53, 63–64, 111, 299; Synnott, *Half-Opened Door,* pp. 78–79.

48. Hopkins to Arthur Cohen, March 16, 1932, Hopkins Papers, DC; see also Synnott, *Half-Opened Door,* pp. 142–43.

49. Weller, *Not to Eat,* pp. 250–51, 6, 39, 47, 319.

50. Hopkins expressed this point of view as early as his lengthy March 25, 1933, memorandum to Bill: "The impulses and motivations which have led to Hitlerism and the Jewish pogroms in Germany will presumably not be allowed to get out of hand in other parts of the world but the will is sufficiently near the surface, even in a lot of our communities in America, so that it is about as essential for the Jews themselves as for us that we should not intensify the demand already existent in some quarters that we adopt the Princeton system of no Jews at all" (Hopkins Papers, DC).

51. Hopkins, *This Our Purpose,* p. 179; Hopkins to Bill, April 28, 1932, Hopkins Papers, DC; Broun and Britt, *Christians Only,* p. 57; *Yale Daily News* is cited in Synnott, *Half-Opened Door,* p. 159.

52. Hopkins to Allan H. MacDonald, May 5, 1936; Hopkins to Bill, August 19, 1932, both in Hopkins Papers, DC.

53. The view that noneastern schools were unusually receptive to Jewish students is intimated in Steinberg, *Academic Melting Pot,* p. 21. My research, however, indicates otherwise. See Robert M. House Papers for a copy of the out-of-state application form; *Tar Heel Topics,* April 1938, p. 2; Kemp Battle to Frank P. Graham, November 17, 1936, Graham Papers, UNC. See also McWilliams, *Mask for Privilege,* p. 133.

54. For the University of Chicago, see "Report on Student Promotion" (1930), box 79, and C. F. Huth to Emery T. Filbey, October 20, 1927, box 76, both in Presidential Papers, 1925–45, UC; Wechsler, *Qualified Student,* pp. 221–30, 375–77. For a contemporary view of Columbia, see Keppel, *Columbia,* pp. 111, 179–81. For the University of Pennsylvania, see Slosson, *Great American Universities,* pp. 346, 361–63; Samuel Lipshutz, "Four Years of College," *American Mercury,* October 1929, pp. 131–35; Cheyney, *University of Pennsylvania,* p. 475; Broun and Britt, *Christians Only,* pp. 72–76; Baltzell, *Protestant Establishment,* p. 211; Baltzell, *Puritan Boston and Quaker Philadelphia* (New York, 1979), pp. 258–68. For Western Reserve University, see Report of the President and Other Officers, 1922–23, p. 12, and Survey Commission of the Cleveland Foundation, 1925, pp. 42–43, both in CWRU. See also Steinberg, *Academic Melting Pot,* pp. 9–10, 17; Rudy, *College of the City of New York,* pp. 292–94. Finally, Baltzell has shown that the proportion of men listed in the 1940 *Social Register* who had graduated from Harvard, Yale, Princeton, and Stanford after 1920 was about twice as high as among earlier college graduates (*Protestant Establishment,* pp. 209–10).

55. Hopkins' defense of the quota is discussed in "Anti-Semitism at Dartmouth," *New Republic,* August 20, 1945, pp. 208–9; "Sense or Nonsense," *Time,* August 20, 1945, p. 92; McWilliams, *Mask for Privilege,* pp. 130–40; Dan W. Dodson, "College Quotas and American Democracy," *American Scholar* 15 (Summer 1946):267–76 (Dodson was executive director of the Mayor's Committee); Lewis S. Feuer, "The Stages in the Social History of Jewish Professors in

American Colleges and Universities," *American Jewish History* 71 (June 1982):432–65. The imposition of an admissions quota at Sarah Lawrence College was the topic of a controversial article in *Commentary*, May 1983, by Louise Blecher Rose, titled "The Secret Life of Sarah Lawrence," and of many letters from readers published in the August 1983 issue.

56. The finest monograph on black colleges and black students in the 1920s is Raymond Wolters, *The New Negro on Campus* (Princeton, 1975), esp. pp. 17, 314–29. The Oberlin anecdote can be found in ibid., p. 322. The Antioch story is in Kirkpatrick, *American College*, pp. 183–84. Lipset and Riesman, *Education and Politics*, pp. 142–43, 177–78, cover these years at Harvard. See also Wechsler, *Revolt on the Campus*, pp. 362–73, for a contemporary view.

57. Seventeen of the 69 land-grant schools that received federal funds were black colleges. Of these 17, none had more collegiate-grade than secondary-grade students until the 1930s. In 1930, only three met accreditation standards of library size; by 1940, 15 of the 17 did. In the early 1930s, while blacks constituted nearly one-quarter of the total population of the 17 southern states, black colleges received less than 6 percent of the funds appropriated to those states for the support of the land-grant colleges. See Eddy, *Colleges for Our Land*, pp. 257–66, for more on black land-grant schools. See also Wolters, *New Negro*, pp. 18–30, 82–83, 339–48; Eagan, *Class*, pp. 34–36. Frazier is quoted in Wolters, *New Negro*, pp. 82–83.

58. Alexander Meiklejohn, "What Does the College Hope to Be in the Next Hundred Years?" *Amherst Graduates' Quarterly* 10 (August 1921):337–38, 344.

59. Louis I. Newman, *A Jewish University in America?* (New York, 1924), esp. pp. 11–13, 15–22; Ralph P. Boas, "Who Should Go to College?" *Atlantic Monthly*, October 1922, pp. 441–48. See also Broun and Britt, *Christians Only*, p. 86; McWilliams, *Mask for Privilege*, pp. 114–15.

8 / The Junior College and the Differentiation of the Public Sector

1. *Biennial Survey of Education, 1936–38*, chap. 4, p. 10.

2. Duffus, *Democracy Enters College*, p. 177; William O. Thompson, president of Ohio State, is quoted in *DePauw University Bulletin*, 3d ser., 10 (August 1913):35.

3. Rudolph, *American College*, pp. 361–63; *Biennial Survey of Education, 1916–18*, 1:481; Coffman, in Fairchild, *Obligation*, pp. 25–28, 38. For an example of a state university's public relations efforts, see *It Belongs to You*, a pamphlet distributed by the University of Illinois, in *University of Illinois Bulletin* 22 (February 23, 1925), UI. See also Allan Nevins, *The State Universities and Democracy* (Urbana, 1962), esp. p. 43.

4. Donald Donnelly, 1936 Campus Oration, Massachusetts State College, UM; President's Annual Report to the Trustees, May 1923, p. 1, API; *University*

of North Carolina Record, no. 171 (December 1919), p. 17, UNC; President's Report for the Year 1922–23, pp. 6–9, UI.

5. Harry W. Chase, "Address to the Faculty," September 18, 1930, pp. 4–5, in Chase Papers, UI.

6. Foerster, *American State University,* pp. 178–84, 194; George F. Sabine, "Are State Universities Different?" *School and Society,* September 12, 1931, pp. 350–56. See also President's Annual Report to the Trustees, May 1925, p. 14, API.

7. Charles H. Judd, *Education and Social Progress* (New York, 1934), pp. 193–94; *A Survey of Educational Institutions of the State of Washington,* U.S. Bureau of Education Bulletin, 1916, no. 26, pp. 99–102; *State Higher Educational Institutions of Iowa,* U.S. Bureau of Education Bulletin, 1916, no. 19, pp. 7–8, 58–72, 134; *Survey of Public Higher Education in Oregon,* U.S. Office of Education Bulletin 1931, no. 8, pp. 47–53. See also *The Problem of Duplication,* U.S. Office of Education Bulletin, 1934, no. 19, pp. 8–13.

8. William S. Learned, William C. Bagley, et al., *The Professsional Preparation of Teachers for American Public Schools* (New York, 1920), pp. 75–76, 260; *Biennial Survey of Education, 1924–26,* p. 4, includes the reference to the Missouri Board of Curators.

9. The curriculum at Kirksville Normal School is discussed in Learned et al., *Professional Preparation of Teachers,* pp. 71–72. In 1915 there were 100,325 students in teachers' colleges and normal schools; in 1925 there were 270,206.

Information on teacher training and teachers' colleges can be found in a variety of contemporary sources, including Lotus D. Coffman, *The Social Composition of the Teaching Profession* (New York, 1911), esp. pp. 31–36, 54, 65; *Biennial Survey of Education, 1916–19,* 4:21; *State Higher Educational Institutions of Iowa,* p. 26; Learned et al., *Professional Preparation of Teachers,* esp. pp. 22–41, 55–56, 71–73, 364–76; George F. Zook, "The Emergency in Higher Education," in *Addresses and Proceedings of the Fifty-eighth Annual Meeting of the National Education Association* (Washington, D.C., 1920), p. 233; Rollo W. Brown, "Educational Unleavening," *Harper's Magazine,* May 1921, p. 744; Homer R. Seerley, *The American Teacher,* U.S. Bureau of Education Bulletin, 1922, no. 44, esp. p. 13; Annual Report of the President and Other Officers, 1925–26, Stanford University, p. 28; Lynd and Lynd, *Middletown,* p. 183; M'ledge Moffett, *The Social Background and Activities of Teachers College Students* (New York, 1929), esp. p. 14; Arthur J. Klein, *Survey of Land-Grant Colleges and Universities,* U.S. Office of Education Bulletin, 1930, no. 9, 1:300 and 2:122; *National Survey of the Education of Teachers,* U.S. Office of Education Bulletin, 1933, no. 10, esp. 5:66–67; Reeves et al., *Liberal Arts College,* pp. 55–61, 227–37; Judd, *Education and Social Progress,* pp. 46, 187; Wilkins, "Major Trends," pp. 444–45; Foerster, *American State University,* p. 72; Robert S. Lynd and Helen M. Lynd, *Middletown in Transition* (New York, 1937), p. 215; Arthur L. Thomasson, "A Half Century of Teacher Training in State Normal Schools and Teachers Colleges of the United States, 1880–1940," Ph.D. dissertation, University of Illinois, 1943, esp. p. 80; Curti and Carstensen, *Uni-*

versity of Wisconsin, pp. 251–59; McGiffert, *Higher Learning in Colorado,* pp. 10–12, 150–53; Gorelick, *City College,* p. 90.

10. Johnston, *Liberal College,* pp. 77–78, 104–5, 128, 161–66, 229–31, 313–14.

11. C. Robert Pace, *They Went to College* (Minneapolis, 1941), p. 11.

12. Stone and De Nevi, eds., *Portraits,* p. 92.

13. Ernest C. Moore, *I Helped Make a University* (Los Angeles, 1952), esp. pp. 3–86.

14. This and the following three paragraphs are based on Carnegie Foundation for the Advancement of Teaching, *State Higher Education in California* (Sacramento, 1932), esp. pp. 21–26, 41, 50–55, 65.

15. Robert G. Sproul, "Certain Aspects of the Junior College," *Junior College Journal* 1 (February 1931):276–77, 279–81.

16. Learned et al., *Professional Preparation,* pp. 228–46.

17. This and the following paragraph are based on J. Herschel Coffin, *The Role of the State Colleges in Higher Education in California* (Sacramento, 1939), esp. pp. 65–62, 66–81, 104–5.

18. This and the following paragraph are based on F. M. McDowell, *The Junior College,* U.S. Bureau of Education Bulletin, 1919, no. 35, pp. 10–20, and Leonard V. Koos, *The Junior College Movement* (Boston, 1925), esp. pp. 235–39.

19. *Biennial Surveys of Education: 1926–28,* p. 691; *1936–38,* chap. 4, p. 10. Coleman R. Griffith, *The Junior College in Illinois* (Urbana, 1945), estimates that enrollment in the nation's junior colleges climbed from about 50,500 to 196,700 between 1928 and 1938.

20. Kent, ed., *Higher Education,* p. 5; *Junior College Journal* 1, no. 2 (November 1930), p. 81; no. 4 (January 1931), pp. 196–97: and no. 7 (April 1931), p. 461; Greenleaf, *Junior Colleges,* pp. 44–53; *Biennial Surveys of Education: 1926–28,* p. 691; *1936–38,* chap. 4, p. 10.

21. Greenleaf, *Junior Colleges,* pp. 12, 38–39; McDowell, *Junior College,* pp. 26–28; Bruce E. Millikin, "Need of Public Junior Colleges in Utah," *Junior College Journal* 1 (March 1931):351–56; Jencks and Riesman, *Academic Revolution,* p. 481.

22. George F. Zook, ed., *National Conference of Junior Colleges, 1920,* U.S. Bureau of Education Bulletin, 1922, no. 19, p. 2; the dean of Carleton is quoted in Zimmerman, "College Culture," pp. 11–14. See also Reeves et al., *Liberal Arts College,* p. 35.

23. Annual Reports of the President and Other Officers, Stanford University, 1915–16, pp. 35–36; 1919–20, pp. 10–26; 1925–26, pp. 1–2.

24. Zook, ed., *National Conference,* p. v; Stanton C. Crawford, "The Junior College as an Extension of a University," *Junior College Journal* 1 (February 1930):289–98.

25. The junior college president is quoted in Zook, ed., *National Conference,* p. 5; Koos, *Junior College Movement,* pp. 19–28; Walter C. Eells, *The Junior College* (Boston, 1931), pp. 215–16.

26. Davis is quoted in Zook, ed., *National Conference,* p. 51; Lange is discussed in Gregory L. Goodwin, "The Historical Development of the Community-Junior College Ideology," Ph.D. dissertation, University of Illinois, 1971, pp. 78–79 (this work explores the history of the vocational orientation of junior colleges, particularly in Illinois).

27. Zook is quoted in Goodwin, "Historical Development," p. 130; Lowell is quoted in Kelly, ed., *Effective College,* pp. 283–84. See also Koos, *Junior College Movement,* p. 315; Charles Bonham, "The Junior College," *Social Science* 3 (August 1928):86–87; Marion Coats, "The Junior College," *Forum,* July 1928, pp. 86–87; Charles Odell, "Are College Students a Select Group?" *University of Illinois Bulletin* 24, no. 36 (May 10, 1927):9; the comments of George A. Works, in Coleman Griffith, ed., *Conference on the Problems of Higher Education* (Urbana, 1939), p. 94; Rudolph, *American College,* p. 463; and the comments of the president of the University of Baltimore, T. H. Wilson, in Walter C. Eells, *Why Junior College Terminal Education?* (Washington, D.C., 1941), p. 290.

28. Thomas L. Hardin, "A History of the Community Junior College in Illinois: 1901–72," Ph.D. dissertation, University of Illinois, 1975, pp. 49–64; the Massachusetts survey is reported in William G. Carr, "The Junior College in State School Surveys," *Junior College Journal* 1 (March 1931):359; G. Vernon Bennett, *Vocational Education of Junior College Grade* (Baltimore, 1928), pp. 5, 24–94.

29. Carr, "Junior College," p. 357; *Biennial Survey of Education, 1926–28,* pp. 7–8; L. R. Hiatt, "Curricular Changes in Junior Colleges," *Junior College Journal* 1 (October 1930):6; William M. Proctor, "Student Interest in Junior Colleges," *Junior College Journal* 1 (November 1930):84–88.

30. Willey, *Depression,* pp. 265–66; Goetsch, *Parental Income,* p. 118; the editor's comments can be found in Eells, *Why Junior College?* p. 161; *Biennial Survey of Education, 1922–24,* p. 28; Alvin C. Eurich, ed., *The Changing Educational World* (Minneapolis, 1931), p. 39.

31. Eells, *Why Junior College?* esp. pp. 1, 36, 41, 67, 78, 88; Foerster, *American State University,* p. 181; Warner et al., *Who Shall Be Educated?* p. 56; Educational Policies Commission, *Education and Economic Well-Being in American Democracy* (Washington, D.C., 1940), pp. 96–97; W. W. Kemp, "Junior College Development in California," *Junior College Journal* 1 (February 1931):286–87.

32. McDowell, *Junior College,* pp. 24–25, 53, 68; William C. Hill to Craven Laycock, November 27, 1917, Hopkins Papers, DC; Zook, ed., *National Conference,* p. 20; Koos, *Junior College Movement,* pp. 150–52; Walter C. Eells and Robert Brand, "Student Opinion in Junior Colleges in California," *School Review* 38 (March 1930):183.

33. McDowell, *Junior College,* pp. 53, 86; L. C. Marshall, "The Collegiate School of Business at Erewhon," *Journal of Political Economy* 34 (June 1926):292–93; Eells, *Why Junior College?* pp. 60–61; Sproul, "Certain Aspects," pp. 276–81.

34. Eells and Brand, "Student Opinion," p. 178, called this trend "at once a

gratification and a warning" and "a distinct danger signal" to educators' plans. See also Koos, *Junior College Movement*, pp. 95–97; Eells, *Junior College*, pp. 254–74; Kemp, "Junior College Development," p. 283; W. S. Allen, "University Success of Junior College Graduates," *Junior College Journal* 1 (December 1930):147–48; Annual Reports of the President and Other Officers, Stanford University, 1934–35, p. 443; 1935–36, p. 427; and 1936–37, p. 462.

35. Walter E. Morgan, "Junior College Development in California," *Junior College Journal* 1 (October 1930):64–66; Bennett, *Vocational Education*, pp. 201–2; Nicholas Ricciardi, "Vital Junior College Problems in California," *Junior College Journal* 1 (October 1930):25.

36. Sproul, "Certain Aspects," p. 281.

37. Carnegie Foundation, *State Higher Education*, pp. 32–43.

38. Quoted in Eells, *Why Junior College?* p. 90.

9 / *Higher Education during the Depression*

1. Robert E. Rogers, "Is College Worth While?" *Forum*, September 1933, p. 137.

2. Installation address, May 1, 1931, in Chase Papers, UI.

3. *Biennial Survey of Education, 1934–36*, vol. 1, chap. 3, p. 8.

4. *The DePauw*, March 10, 1933, p. 1; *The Plainsman*, March 18, 1933, p. 2, and May 6, 1933, p. 1; Annual Report of the President, 1937, pp. 2, 7–8, 16, API.

5. David D. Henry, *Challenges Past, Challenges Present* (San Francisco, 1975), pp. 23–28; Educational Policies Commission, *Education and Economic Well-Being*, p. 4; Duffus, *Democracy Enters College*, p. 106; Verne A. Stadtman, *The University of California: 1868–1968* (New York, 1970), pp. 259–60; "74th Annual Report of Massachusetts State College," *Massachusetts State College Bulletin*, March 1937, p. 2; "79th Annual Report of Massachusetts State College," *Massachusetts State College Bulletin*, March 1942, p. 2; "A Brief Preliminary Report of Financial Operations for the Year Ended November 30, 1940," p. 4, in Baker Papers, UM; Martin, *Lamp in the Desert*, pp. 160–64, 279.

6. Private institutions received in 1934 only slightly more than half the amount they received in 1930. See *Biennial Survey of Education, 1934–36*, vol. 1, chap. 3, p. 17; Lyon, *History of Pomona*, pp. 283–85, 328; Duffus, *Democracy Enters College*, p. 106.

7. Willey, *Depression*, pp. 164–66; Calvin B. T. Lee, *The Campus Scene: 1900–1970* (New York, 1970), p. 50; Fred J. Kelly and Ella B. Ratcliffe, *College Projects for Aiding Students*, U.S. Office of Education Bulletin, 1938, no. 9, pp. 4–22; *Journal of Higher Education*, May 1937, p. 278.

8. Reeves et al., *Liberal Arts College*, pp. 632–34; *Biennial Survey of Education, 1934–36*, vol. 1, chap. 3, pp. 28–29; Trevor Arnett, *Trends in Tuition Fees* (New York, 1939), pp. 34–36; Annual Report of the President, 1931–32, Case School of Applied Science, p. 2, CWRU; *Tar Heel Topics* (UNC), March 1933, p. 1.

9. Reports of the President and Other Officers, 1933–34, Western Reserve University, p. 36, CWRU; Robert C. Angell, "The Influence of the Economic Depression on Student Life at the University of Michigan," *School and Society*, November 14, 1931, pp. 650–51; Emery T. Filbey to the Deans of the Divisions and the Professional Schools (1932?), in box 75, Presidential Papers, 1925–45, UC; Annual Report of the President and Other Officers, 1933–34, Stanford University, p. 454; *Biennial Survey of Education, 1934–36,* vol. 2, chap. 4, pp. 14–15.

10. The working student is quoted in Goetsch, *Parental Income,* pp. 59–60; Russell T. Sharpe, "College and the Poor Boy: Is the Door Closing?" *Atlantic Monthly,* June 1933, pp. 698–702; Charles A. Maney, "College Graduates Face the Future," *Journal of Higher Education,* October 1935, pp. 372–73.

11. Marcia Edwards, "College Enrollment during Times of Economic Depression," *Journal of Higher Education,* January 1932, pp. 11–15; Willey, *Depression,* pp. 226–38; Fred L. Kerr, "A Ten-Year Study of Enrollments and Degrees," *Journal of the American Association of Collegiate Registrars,* October 1940, p. 6; *Journal of Higher Education,* January 1939, p. 41; *Biennial Survey of Education, 1934–36,* vol. 1, chap. 3, p. 45; Annual Report of the President, 1938–39, Case School of Applied Science, p. 1, CWRU.

12. Between 1934 and 1936, while the number of men in liberal arts programs increased 17 percent, the number of men in undergraduate professional programs jumped 40 percent. See *Biennial Surveys of Education: 1934–36,* vol. 2, chap. 4, pp. 48–49; *1938–42,* vol. 1, chap. 3, p. 8. See also Kerr, "Ten-Year Study," p. 6; *Reserve Tribune* (CWRU), May 25, 1937; Annual Report of the Officers, 1935–36, p. 19, DPU.

13. Annual Reports of the President and Other Officers, Stanford University, 1931–32, pp. 1–3, 405; 1932–33, pp. 10–13; 1936–37, p. 5.

14. *The Plainsman,* May 23, 1941, pp. 1–4.

15. The *Journal of Higher Education,* January 1940, p. 43, reported that between 1930 and 1938, private universities' enrollment increased 6 percent, private colleges' enrollment increased 11 percent, and public universities' enrollment increased 24 percent.

16. Kerr, "Ten-Year Study," p. 6, and *Biennial Surveys of Education: 1932–34,* chap. 4, p. 12; *1938–42,* vol. 2, chap. 4, p. 6.

17. Willey, *Depression,* pp. 288–89, 301. Angell, "Influence of the Depression," p. 649, reported enrollment in Michigan's junior colleges increased 23 percent between 1929 and 1931, in contrast to a 3 percent drop in enrollment at the University of Michigan.

18. Wechsler, *Revolt on the Campus,* pp. 91–94; Studs Terkel, *Hard Times* (New York, 1970), pp. 398–401; Lipset and Riesman, *Education and Politics,* pp. 298–99.

19. James Conant, "The Future of Our Higher Education," in James B. Conant and Francis T. Spaulding, *Education for a Classless Society* (Cambridge, Mass., 1940), p. 38; "Memorandum on Financial Aid, 1929–35," February 22, 1935, in Hopkins Papers, DC; James L. McConaughy (president of Wesleyan University), "Education in a Democracy," *School and Society,* September 25, 1937, p.

386. Numerous examples of the decline in admissions standards can be cited: Yale's admissions are discussed in Pierson, *Yale,* pp. 265–67; *School and Society* reported on May 21, 1932, p. 699, that M.I.T. was accepting all applicants in the top fifth of their high school classes without requiring entrance examinations; and 1,300 of the 1,460 applicants to the University of Chicago in 1933 were accepted, even with an informal Jewish quota, as is indicated in R. W. Bixler to Emery T. Filber, September 12, 1934, in box 76, Presidential Papers, 1925–45, UC. See also Goetsch, *Parental Income,* p. 87; Foerster, *American State University,* p. 151; and Willey, *Depression,* pp. 241–42.

20. The Office of Education reported that between 1931–32 and 1933–34, enrollment in New York state declined 11 percent, Indiana 13, Pennsylvania 15, and Michigan 21; see *Biennial Survey of Education, 1932–34,* chap. 4, pp. 17–18. See also Willey, *Depression,* p. 247; Kerr, "Ten-Year Study," p. 11; *The Campus* (CCNY), October 15, 1930, p. 1; Parke R. Kolbe, "Is the American College in Danger?" *School and Society,* April 9, 1932, pp. 511–12; O. C. Held, "Admissions Trends in a Liberal Arts College of an Urban University during the Depression," *School and Society,* March 1936, p. 375; Report of the President and Other Officers, 1932–33, p. 31, CWRU; McGiffert, *Higher Learning in Colorado,* p. 207.

21. Wechsler, *Revolt on the Campus,* pp. 373–74, 51–59; *The Campus* (CCNY), October 17, 1930, p. 1; *Emory Wheel,* January 18, 1934, p. 4; Terkel, *Hard Times,* pp. 399–400.

22. *Biennial Survey of Education, 1934–36,* vol. 1, chap. 3, p. 7; Eagan, *Class,* pp. 20, 82; *The DePauw,* May 10, 1933, p. 2; George W. Condit, "A.B. Unemployed," *Forum,* May 1932, pp. 265–69; *Massachusetts Collegian,* April 21, 1932, p. 4, and December 1, 1932, p. 2; Henry, *Challenges,* pp. 27–28; Richard E. Lauterbach, "Youth Comes of Age," *Class Book of the Class of 1935,* pp. 51–52, DC; *Tar Heel Topics* (UNC), May 1934, pp. 1, 4; Lee, *Campus Scene,* p. 48; Maney, "College Graduates," p. 373; Lynd and Lynd, *Middletown in Transition,* p. 211.

23. A copy of the subcommittee's resolution can be found in the Frank P. Graham Papers, UNC.

24. Fred J. Kelly and John H. McNeely, *Federal Student Aid Program,* U.S. Office of Education Bulletin, 1935, no. 14, p. 2; *Biennial Survey of Education, 1934–36,* vol. 1, chap. 3, p. 9. Hutchins' visit to the White House is described in a clipping from the *Chicago Daily News,* August 14, 1933, in box 28, Presidential Papers, 1925–45, UC.

25. Frank R. Elliott, "Uncle Sam's Call to College," *Literary Digest,* September 15, 1934, p. 24; Kelly and McNeely, *Federal Student Aid Program,* pp. 1–2.

26. Quoted in Eagan, *Class,* p. 22.

27. *The DePauw,* February 14, 1934; *Reserve Weekly,* February 20, 1934, p. 4; W. H. Cowley, *A Study of National Youth Administration Projects at the Ohio State University* (Washington, D.C., 1938), pp. 21–23; Hutchins to Zook, June 9, 1934, in box 28, Presidential Papers, 1925–45, UC.

28. Graham to Zook, June 4, 1934, in Graham Papers, UNC; George P.

Rawick, "The New Deal and Youth," Ph.D. dissertation, University of Wisconsin, 1957, pp. 181–85, 191–92, 212; Dixon Wecter, *The Age of the Great Depression* (New York, 1948), p. 188.

29. Brubacher and Rudy, *Higher Education in Transition,* p. 210; Rawick, "New Deal and Youth," pp. 20–30, 200–226.

30. Rawick, "New Deal and Youth," pp. 206–7; Goetsch, *Parental Income,* p. 30; Eells, *Why Junior College?* p. 22.

31. *Biennial Survey of Education, 1934–36,* vol. 1, chap. 3, pp. 11–12, and vol. 2, chap. 4, p. 20; W. G. Leutner to Harry Hopkins, March 12, 1934, Leutner Papers, CWRU; Henry, *Challenges,* p. 25; Clark, *Indiana University,* 2:xiv–xv.

32. A Minnesota survey reported that 75 percent of the applicants for the work-study program were rejected; the University of Illinois received 3,000 applications for 1,250 places. An example of how existing funds were distributed can be found at Emory University, where an allocation intended for 133 students was spread among 202 students. The final National Youth Administration report reported the average student wage was $12.50 per month. See Willey, *Depression,* p. 282; Cowley, *NYA Projects,* p. 19; Eells, *Why Junior College?* pp. 35–36; Clark, *Indiana University,* 2:253; Kelly and McNeely, *Federal Student Aid Program,* p. 34; Rawick, "New Deal and Youth," pp. 180–90; Kelly and Ratcliffe, *College Projects,* p. 4; Fred H. Turner, "Students of the Depression," *Saturday Evening Post,* February 2, 1935, p. 14; Annual Report of the President, 1934–35, p. 6, EU; National Youth Administration (NYA), *Final Report of the National Youth Administration, 1936–43* (Washington, D.C., 1944), p. 57.

33. NYA, *Final Report,* pp. 75–77; Kelly and McNeely, *Federal Student Aid Program,* p. 29; Cowley, *NYA Projects,* pp. 16–17; President's Report, 1936–37, p. 24, UI; Griffith, ed., *Conference,* p. 140. The success of work-study students at the University of North Carolina is indicated in the Frank P. Graham Papers, UNC.

34. James T. Patterson, *Congressional Conservatism and the New Deal* (Lexington, Ky., 1967), is the best general treatment of this trend. See also NYA, *Final Report,* p. 51; Fred J. Kelly and Ella B. Ratcliffe, *Financial Aids for College Students,* U.S. Office of Education Bulletin, 1940, no. 11, pp. 1–2; *Biennial Survey of Education, 1938–42,* vol. 1, chap. 3, p. 16.

35. NYA, *Final Report,* pp. 47–50; Blanshard, *Aydelotte of Swarthmore,* pp. 256–58.

36. Francis J. A. Neef to Hopkins, July 16, 1936, DC; *Princeton Alumni Weekly* clipping in box 28, Presidential Papers, 1925–45, UC; Lipset and Riesman, *Education and Politics,* pp. 161–62.

37. *The DePauw,* November 10, 1937, p. 2; Willey, *Depression,* p. 293.

38. These data were made available to me by James A. Davis of Harvard University and the National Opinion Research Center of the University of Chicago.

39. For a personal view of the growing heterogeneity of the Massachusetts State College student body during the 1930s, see an oral interview with Maxwell Goldberg, conducted June 8–10, 1976, by Julia E. Melrose, University of Massachusetts Oral History Project, UM. See also Willey, *Depression,* p. 307.

40. Steinberg, *Academic Melting Pot,* pp. 10–11; John Whitney Evans, *The Newman Movement: Roman Catholics in American Higher Education, 1883–1971* (Notre Dame, Ind., 1980), pp. 32–33, 55, 74–75; Eagan, *Class,* pp. 161–62.

41. Gannon, *Up to the Present,* p. 215.

42. McGiffert, *Higher Learning in Colorado,* pp. 207–8; "Report of the Faculty Committee to Study the Curriculum," December 1933, p. 1, and August 1934, p. 2, UM; NYA, *Final Report,* pp. 67–72.

43. Willey, *Depression,* p. 293; Lee, *Campus Scene,* pp. 71–72 cites *Fortune's* observation; "College Editors Hail End of 'Rah-Rah' Era," *Literary Digest,* March 9, 1935, p. 20; Joseph P. Lash, *The Campus: A Fortress of Democracy* (New York, 1938), p. 6.

44. Willey, *Depression,* pp. 308–21; Joseph R. De Martini, "Student Protest during Two Periods in the History of the University of Illinois," Ph.D. dissertation, University of Illinois, 1974, pp. 319–75. CCNY's archives include an extensive collection on radicalism there in the 1930s and thereafter.

45. Wechsler, *Revolt on the Campus,* esp. pp. 4–9, 455.

46. Eagan, *Class,* esp. pp. 33, 57–71, 111–15, 120–27, 190–93; Wechsler, *Revolt on the Campus,* esp. pp. 123–48, 163–81; Gorelick, *City College,* pp. 179–81.

47. Eagan, *Class,* discusses conservatism on the campuses at great length; her references to the universities of Pennsylvania and Chicago, Temple, UCLA, and Catholic colleges, particularly on student reaction to the peace movement, are found on pp. 84–89, 104–5, 131, 161, 187, 195–203. Wechsler, *Revolt on the Campus,* pp. 4–5, cites Lippmann; p. 446 quotes the Catholic church official; p. 361 cites the DePauw official; and see pp. 189, 280–83, 354–62 for a discussion of student radical efforts. Lipset and Riesman, *Education and Politics,* pp. 157–61, 171–73, also discusses radical student groups.

48. Henry G. Leach, "A Challenge to the Colleges," *Forum,* September 1933, p. 129; Rogers, "Is College Worth While?" p. 138; Lynd and Lynd, *Middletown in Transition,* p. 210; Willey, *Depression,* pp. 276–77. See also Tugwell and Keyserling, eds., *Redirecting Education,* p. 120; Pace, *They Went to College,* p. 5.

49. *Education for Democracy* (New York, 1939), p. 258.

50. Warner et al., *Who Shall Be Educated?* p. 157; Eells, *Why Junior College?* p. vii.

10 / Is Higher Education a Privilege or a Right?

1. President's Report, 1927–28, pp. 15–16, UI.

2. Koos, *Junior College Movement,* pp. 118–21, 256–59.

3. Harry W. Chase, "Address to the Faculty," September 18, 1930, UI.

4. Kolbe, *Urban Influences,* p. 154.

5. Donald Donnelly, "1936 Campus Oration," UM; the president of Ohio University is quoted in Coleman R. Griffith, ed., *Conference on the Problems of Higher Education* (Urbana, 1939), p. 43. Before World War I tuition accounted

for about 40 and 10 percent, respectively, of a private institution's and a public institution's income. By 1930 the figures were 48 and 14 percent, respectively; in 1940, nearly 53 and 19 percent. See P. A. Cowen, "College Tuition Trends," *School and Society*, May 30, 1931, pp. 738–40; Arnett, *Trends in Tuition Fees*, esp. pp. 26, 53–55; Elise Hatt and F. Dean McClusky, *A Study of Enrollment* (Lafayette, Ind., 1926), p. 20; Foerster, *American State University*, p. 189; Willey, *Depression*, pp. 295–300; Educational Policies Commission, *Education and Economic Well-Being*, pp. 137–40; *The Campus* (CCNY), May 20, 1932, and February 8, 1937; *Biennial Surveys of Education: 1932–34*, chap. 8, p. 27, and *1934–36*, vol. 2, chap. 4, p. 20. William Wickenden defended the Case School of Applied Science's decision to raise tuition, but noted that private institutions must be cognizant of price competition from the public sector; see the October 1929 Annual Report, CWRU.

6. Reynolds, *Social and Economic Status*, p. 20; Johnston, *Liberal College*, pp. 54–55; Educational Policies Commission, *Education and Economic Well-Being*, p. 143; Amos et al., *And So to College*, p. 11, includes the statement by the Pittsburgh official.

7. *Case Tech*, December 1, 1933, p. 2; Warner et al., *Who Shall Be Educated?* pp. 51–52; Goetsch, *Parental Income*, pp. 30–31, 91–92; Educational Policies Commission, *Education and Economic Well-Being*, pp. 137–40; *Tar Heel Topics* (UNC), December 1932, p. 2, and December 1938, p. 4; Duffus, *Democracy Enters College*, pp. 2–4; McConaughy, "Education in a Democracy," p. 386.

8. Bell, *Youth Tell Their Story*, esp. pp. 66–67, 96, 122, 79, 52; Warner et al., *Who Shall Be Educated?* pp. 50, 59; Elbridge Sibley, "Some Demographic Clues to Stratification," *American Sociological Review* 7 (June 1942):322–30.

9. Johnston and Goetsch's proposals are in Goetsch, *Parental Income*, pp. 36–37, 117–21; McConaughy, "Education in a Democracy," p. 390; Rawick, "New Deal and Youth," pp. 213–14, 255–56, 265–68.

10. Richard Polenberg, *One Nation Divisible* (New York, 1980), pp. 21–23.

11. President's Commission on Higher Education, *Higher Education for American Democracy*, 6 vols. (Washington, D.C., 1947), 1:1, 6, 47. Educators were surprised at the response of veterans to the educational provisions of the Servicemen's Readjustment Act of 1944, the so-called G.I. Bill of Rights. By the fall of 1947, at the peak of veteran enrollment, attendance was twice as great as in the late 1930s. This critical legislation and its impact are explored in Theodore R. Mosch, *The G.I. Bill* (Hicksville, N.Y., 1975), and Keith W. Olson, *The G.I. Bill, the Veterans, and the Colleges* (Lexington, Ky., 1974).

12. President's Commission, *Higher Education*, 1:25, 27.

13. Ibid., 2:1 and 1:27.

14. Ibid., 1:33–35. Several southern members of the commission dissented from the report's portrayal of and recommendations concerning segregation in the South.

15. Ibid., 1:2.

16. Ibid., 1:36–38, 67–69; 2:22; 5:51–63. Some members of the commission objected to the report's recommendations for increased federal financial involvement in higher education.

17. Ibid., 1:28, 2:5.

18. Curti and Carstensen, *University of Wisconsin,* p. 618, cites Van Hise; Hudson, *College and New America,* p. 128; Horace M. Kallen, *Individualism: An American Way of Life* (New York, 1933), pp. 225–26. See also R. Freeman Butts, *The College Charts Its Course* (New York, 1939), p. 353.

19. Rainey is quoted in Griffith, ed., *Conference,* p. 61; Educational Policies Commission, *Education and Economic Well-Being,* pp. 4–5; Bell, *Youth Tell Their Story,* p. 98.

References

Much of the primary source material included in this book was found at college and university archives across the country; these institutions are listed in an introduction to the notes. Whenever possible, the following records were examined at each school: presidential papers, particularly annual reports; other administrative papers, particularly reports from the deans and the registrar; college promotional publications; and student newspapers and correspondence. In addition, I reviewed the published annual reports of several colleges and universities, which are cited in the notes where appropriate.

Abbott, Lawrence F. "What Is the Matter with Our Colleges?" *Outlook,* September 5, 1923, pp. 12–14.

Allen, C. B. "A Proportionate Decrease." *Journal of Higher Education,* February 1935, pp. 89–93.

Allen, Frederick L. *Only Yesterday.* New York: Harper, 1931, 1964.

——. *Since Yesterday.* New York: Harper, 1939.

"The American College." *New Republic,* October 25, 1922, pt. 2.

Amos, Thyrsa W., et al. *And So to College.* Radio Publication no. 41, University of Pittsburgh, 1928.

Anderson, Dewey, and Percy E. Davidson. *Recent Occupational Trends in American Labor.* Stanford: Stanford University Press, 1945.

Angell, James R. *American Education.* New Haven: Yale University Press, 1937.

——. "The Endowed Institution of Higher Education and Its Relation to Public Education." *School and Society,* April 14, 1928, pp. 431–39.

Angell, Robert C. *The Campus.* New York: D. Appleton, 1928.

——. "The Influence of the Economic Depression on Student Life at the University of Michigan." *School and Society* 14 (November 1931):657–59.

"Anti-Semitism at Dartmouth." *New Republic,* August 20, 1945, pp. 208–9.

"An Aristocracy of Worth." *Independent,* November 10, 1923, p. 211.

Armytage, W. H. G. *The American Influence on English Education.* London: Routledge & Kegan Paul, 1967.

Arnett, Trevor. *Trends in Tuition Fees.* New York: General Education Board, 1939.

"As a College Man Thinks." Claremont, Calif.: Pomona College, 1924.

Ashley, Roscoe. *Our Contemporary Civilization.* New York: Henry Holt, 1935.

Babcock, F. Lawrence. *The U.S. College Graduate.* New York: Macmillan, 1941.

Baker, George M. "Reflections on the American College." *Sewanee Review,* October 1927, pp. 419–30.

Baltzell, E. Digby. *The Protestant Establishment.* New York: Vintage Books, 1964.

———. *Puritan Boston and Quaker Philadelphia.* New York: Free Press, 1978.

Baumann, Mark K. "Warren Akin Candler: Conservative amidst Change." Ph.D. dissertation, Emory University, 1975.

Beard, Charles A., and Mary R. Beard. *The Rise of American Civilization.* 2 vols. New York: Macmillan, 1927.

Bell, Daniel. *The Coming of Post-Industrial Society.* New York: Basic Books, 1973.

———. *The Reforming of General Education.* New York: Anchor Books, 1968.

Bell, Howard M. *Youth Tell Their Story.* Washington, D.C.: American Council on Education, 1938.

Benner, Thomas E. "Teacher Training and the Liberal College." *School and Society,* April 30, 1932, pp. 577–82.

Bennett, G. Vernon. *Vocational Education of Junior College Grade.* Baltimore: Warwick & York, 1928.

Beury, Charles E. "The Mission of the Modern University." *Journal of Higher Education,* December 1936, pp. 469–74.

Bildersee, Adele. *State Scholarship Students.* Contributions to Education, no. 540. New York: Teachers College, Columbia University, 1932.

Bingham, Walter V. *Placement Service in American Colleges and Universities.* New York: Personnel Research Foundation, 1926.

Blanshard, Frances. *Frank Aydelotte of Swarthmore.* Middletown, Conn.: Wesleyan University Press, 1970.

Bledstein, Burton J. *The Culture of Professionalism.* New York: Norton, 1976.

Boardman, Martha T. "The College President Calls It a Year." *Journal of Higher Education,* June 1936, pp. 287–95.

Boas, Ralph P. "Who Should Go to College?" *Atlantic Monthly,* October 1922, pp. 441–48.

Bonham, Charles L. "The Junior College." *Social Science,* August 1928, pp. 367–75.

Bossard, James H., and J. Frederic Dewhurst. *University Education for Business.* Philadelphia: University of Pennsylvania Press, 1931.

Boyd, Paul P. "Entrance Requirements for the Tax-Supported Liberal Arts College." *School and Society,* December 11, 1937, pp. 737–41.

Breitwieser, J. V. "Bargain Baccalaureates." *School and Society,* June 20, 1936, pp. 844–45.

Brossow, Olive. "With Honor." *American Mercury,* October 1929, pp. 136–42.

Broun, Heywood, and George Britt. *Christians Only: A Study in Prejudice*. New York: Vanguard Press, 1931.

Brown, Elmer E. "Too Many College Students?" *North American Review,* June 1921, pp. 743–52.

Brown, E. Richard. *Rockefeller Medicine Men*. Berkeley: University of California Press, 1979.

Brown, Rollo W. "Educational Unleavening." *Harper's Magazine,* May 1921, pp. 728–36.

Brubacher, John S., and J. Willis Rudy. *Higher Education in Transition*. 3d ed. New York: Harper & Row, 1976.

Buck, Paul H. *Social Sciences at Harvard, 1860–1920*. Cambridge: Harvard University Press, 1965.

Bullock, Henry M. *A History of Emory University, 1836–1936*. Nashville: Parthenon Press, 1936.

Butts, R. Freeman. *The College Charts Its Course*. New York: McGraw-Hill, 1939.

Calvert, Monte. *The Mechanical Engineer in America, 1830–1910*. Baltimore: Johns Hopkins Press, 1967.

Capen, Samuel P. "The Effect of the World War 1914–18 on American Colleges and Universities." *Educational Record* 21 (January 1940):40–48.

——. *Recent Movements in College and University Administration*. U.S. Bureau of Education Bulletin 1916, no. 46. Washington, D.C.: Government Printing Office, 1916.

Carnegie Foundation for the Advancement of Teaching. *Papers Relating to the Admission of State Institutions to the System of Retiring Allowances of the Carnegie Foundation*. New York, March 1907.

——. *State Higher Education in California*. Sacramento: California State Printing Office, June 24, 1932.

Carr, William G. "The Junior College in State School Surveys." *Junior College Journal,* March 1931, pp. 357–62.

Carroll, James. "No College for My Son." *Forum,* September 1938, pp. 129–34.

Carter, Paul. *The Twenties in America*. Arlington Heights, Ill.: A.H.M, 1975.

Cary, Harold W. *The University of Massachusetts*. Amherst: University of Massachusetts Press, 1962.

Cavan, Jordan T. "What Kind of College Gets the Bright Students?" *Journal of Higher Education,* May 1937, pp. 265–72.

Cawelti, John G. *Apostles of the Self-Made Man*. Chicago: University of Chicago Press, 1965.

"A Challenge to the Colleges." *Forum,* September 1933, pp. 129–30.

Cheyney, Edward P. *History of the University of Pennsylvania*. Philadelphia: University of Pennsylvania Press, 1940.

Clark, Burton R. *The Distinctive College*. Chicago: Aldine, 1970.

Clark, Thomas D. *Indiana University: Midwestern Pioneer*. 2 vols. Bloomington: Indiana University Press, 1973.

Coats, Marion. "The Junior College." *Forum,* July 1928, pp. 82–84.

Coffin, J. Herschel. *The Role of the State Colleges in Higher Education in California.* Sacramento: California State Department of Education, 1939.

Coffman, Lotus D. "Flexner and the State University." *Journal of Higher Education,* October 1931, pp. 380–83.

———. *The Social Composition of the Teaching Population.* New York: Teachers College Press, 1911.

———. *The State University.* Minneapolis: University of Minnesota Press, 1934.

Cole, Stewart G. *Liberal Education in a Democracy.* New York: Harper, 1940.

"College Editors Hail End of 'Rah-Rah' Era." *Literary Digest,* March 9, 1935, pp. 20–23.

"College Graduates as Business Sees Them." *Literary Digest,* June 16, 1934, pp. 35–37.

Collier, William M. "College Influences before the War and after the War." New York: Hobart College, Geneva, N.Y., June 14, 1920.

Collins, Randall. *The Credential Society.* New York: Academic Press, 1979.

Commission on the Reorganization of Secondary Education appointed by the National Education Association. *Cardinal Principles of Secondary Education.* U.S. Bureau of Education Bulletin 1918, no. 35. Washington, D.C.: Government Printing Office, 1918.

Commonwealth of Massachusetts. *Report of the Commission in the Investigation of Agricultural Education, January 1918.* Boston: Wright & Potter, 1918.

Conant, James B., and Francis T. Spaulding. *Education for a Classless Society.* Cambridge: Harvard University Graduate School of Education, June 1940.

Condit, George W. "A.B. Unemployed." *Forum,* May 1932, pp. 265–69.

Conference on Commercial Education and Business Progress. Urbana: University of Illinois, 1913.

"The Confessions of an Undergraduate." *Outlook,* July 18, 1915, pp. 711–14.

Cooke, Morris L. *Academic and Industrial Efficiency.* New York: Carnegie Foundation for the Advancement of Teaching, 1910.

Cooper, W. J. "Present-Day Trends in Our Colleges." *Current History,* June 1930, pp. 514–18.

Copeland, Melvin T. *And Mark an Era: The Story of the Harvard Business School.* Boston: Little, Brown, 1958.

Counts, George S. *Dare the School Build a New Social Order?* New York: John Day, 1932.

Cowen, Phillip A. *College Entrance Enquiry.* Bulletin no. 1007. Albany: University of the State of New York Press, 1932.

———. "College Tuition Trends." *School and Society,* May 30, 1931, pp. 737–40.

Cowley, William H. *The Large Place of the Small College.* Albany: University of the State of New York Press, October 17, 1941.

———. *A Study of National Youth Administration Projects at the Ohio State University.* Washington, D.C.: National Youth Administration, 1938.

Cramer, Carl H. *Case Western Reserve: A History of the University, 1826–1976.* Boston: Little, Brown, 1976.

Crawford, Nelson A. "The Nobility of the Campus." *American Mercury,* October 1930, pp. 184–92.

Crawford, William H., ed. *The American College.* New York: Henry Holt, 1915.

Cremin, Lawrence. *Traditions of American Education.* New York: Basic Books, 1977.

———. *The Transformation of the Schools.* New York: Vintage Books, 1961.

Cubberly, Ellwood P. *A Brief History of Education.* Boston: Houghton Mifflin, 1920.

Curti, Merle, and Vernon Carstensen. *The University of Wisconsin: A History, 1848–1925.* 2 vols. Madison: University of Wisconsin Press, 1949.

Cutten, George B. "The Future of the Liberal Arts College." *Journal of Higher Education,* February 1939, pp. 59–67.

Dartmouth College. *150 Years of Dartmouth.* Hanover, N.H., 1921.

Dartmouth College Senior Committee. "The Report on Undergraduate Education." Dartmouth College, Hanover, N.H., May 15, 1924.

De Martini, Joseph R. "Student Protest during Two Periods in the History of the University of Illinois: 1867–94 and 1929–42." Ph.D. dissertation, University of Illinois, 1974.

De Vane, William C. *Higher Education in Twentieth-Century America.* Cambridge: Harvard University Press, 1965.

De Voto, Bernard. "College Education for the Intelligent Few." *Current History,* March 1932, pp. 792–99.

Dewey, John. *Democracy and Education.* New York: Macmillan, 1916.

———. *The Way Out of Educational Confusion.* Cambridge: Harvard University Press, 1931.

A Discussion of the Development and Needs of the College of Engineering and the Engineering Experimental Station of the University of Illinois. Bulletin no. 13. Urbana: University of Illinois, November 25, 1918.

Dodson, Dan W. "College Quotas and American Democracy." *American Scholar* 15 (Summer 1946):267–76.

Duffus, R. L. *Democracy Enters College.* New York: Charles Scribner, 1936.

Dugdale, John. "America's Mass Education." *Current History,* April 1930, pp. 71–75.

Duncan, Otis D., David L. Featherman, and Beverly Duncan. *Socioeconomic Background and Achievement.* New York: New Seminar Press, 1972.

Dyer, John P. *Tulane: The Biography of a University.* New York: Harper & Row, 1966.

Eagan, Eileen. *Class, Culture, and the Classroom.* Philadelphia: Temple University Press, 1981.

Eckelberry, R. H. *The History of the Municipal University in the United States.* U.S. Office of Education Bulletin 1932, no. 2. Washington, D.C.: Government Printing Office, 1932.

Eddy, Edward D., Jr. *Colleges for Our Land and Time.* New York: Harper, 1956.

Edman, Irwin. "Richard Kane Goes to College." *Century Magazine,* October 1924, pp. 723–32.

Education for Democracy. Proceedings of the Congress on Education for Democracy, August 15–17, 1939. New York: Teachers College, Columbia University, 1939.

Educational Policies Commission. *Education and Economic Well-Being in American Democracy.* Washington, D.C.: National Education Association, 1940.

———. *Policies for Education in American Democracy.* Washington, D.C.: National Education Association, 1946.

Edwards, Marcia. "College Enrollment during Times of Economic Depression." *Journal of Higher Education,* January 1932, pp. 11–16.

Eells, Walter C. *The Junior College.* Boston: Houghton Mifflin, 1931.

———. *Why Junior College Terminal Education?* Washington, D.C.: American Association of Junior Colleges, 1941.

——— and Richard Brand. "Student Opinion in Junior Colleges in California." *School Review,* March 1930, pp. 176–78.

Elliott, Frank R. "Uncle Sam's Call to College." *Literary Digest,* September 15, 1934, pp. 24–27.

Ellis, A. Caswell. *The Money Value of Education.* U.S. Bureau of Education Bulletin 1917, no. 22. Washington, D.C.: Government Printing Office, 1917.

Emerson, Guy. "Success in Life and Success in Living: What to Expect of a College Education." *Independent,* April 1, 1922, pp. 319–20.

English, Thomas H. *Emory University: 1915–65.* Atlanta: Emory University, 1966.

Eurich, Alvin C., ed. *The Changing Educational World.* Minneapolis: University of Minnesota Press, 1931.

Evans, John Whitney. *The Newman Movement: Roman Catholics in American Higher Education, 1883–1971.* Notre Dame, Ind.: University of Notre Dame Press, 1980.

Fairchild, Henry, ed. *The Obligation of Universities to the Social Order.* New York: New York University Press, 1933.

Fass, Paula S. *The Damned and the Beautiful.* New York: Oxford University Press, 1977.

Feuer, Lewis S. "The Stages in the Social History of Jewish Professors in American Colleges and Universities." *American Jewish History* 71 (June 1982):432–65.

Ferguson, Harold A. "Trends in College Admission Requirements." *School and Society,* September 24, 1938, pp. 407–11.

"Ferment in the Colleges." *New Republic,* May 3, 1922, p. 266.

Flexner, Abraham. *Universities: American, English, German.* New York: Oxford University Press, 1930.

Foerster, Norman. *The American State University.* Chapel Hill: University of North Carolina Press, 1937.

"The Fortune Survey." *Fortune,* February 1939, pp. 68–70.

Foster, C. R., Jr., and Paul S. Dwyer. *A Study of the Geographical Distribution of*

Students in 363 American Colleges and Universities. New Brunswick, N.J.: Rutgers University Press, 1931.

Fraser, Stewart E., ed. *American Education in Foreign Perspectives.* New York: Wiley, 1969.

Frederick, Marvin L. "Personal Qualities Requisite for Success in Business." *Journal of Business of the University of Chicago* 4, no. 3, pt. 2 (July 1931).

Friedman, Lawrence M. *A History of America Law.* New York: Simon & Schuster, 1973.

"From a Graduate's Window." *Harvard Graduates' Magazine,* March 1931, pp. 337–41.

Fuess, Claude M. *Amherst: The Story of a New England College.* Boston: Little, Brown, 1935.

———. *The College Board: Its First Fifty Years.* New York: Columbia University Press, 1950.

Gager, Delaye. *French Comment on American Education.* New York: Columbia University Press, 1925.

Gannon, Robert I., S.J. *Up to the Present: The Story of Fordham.* Garden City, N.Y.: Doubleday, 1967.

Gavit, John P. *College.* New York: Harcourt, Brace, 1925.

Gelfand, Lawrence E. *The Inquiry: American Preparations for Peace, 1917–19.* New Haven: Yale University Press, 1963.

Gerould, Gordon H. "The Course of Empire in Education." *Scribner's,* January 1930, pp. 60–63.

Gerth, Hans, and C. Wright Mills. *Character and Social Structure.* New York: Harcourt, Brace, 1953.

———, eds. *From Max Weber: Essays in Sociology.* New York: Oxford University Press, 1946.

Gideonse, Harry D. *The Higher Learning in a Democracy.* New York: Farrar & Rinehart, 1937.

Gifford, Walter S. *Addresses, Papers, and Interviews.* New York: American Telephone and Telegraph Co., 1928.

Gist, Noel P., C. T. Philbad, and C. L. Gregory. "Scholastic Achievement and Occupation." *American Sociological Review,* December 1942, pp. 752–61.

Goetsch, Helen B. *Parental Income and College Opportunities.* Contributions to Education, no. 795. New York: Teachers College, Columbia University, 1940.

Goodenow, Ronald K., and Arthur O. White, eds. *Education and the Rise of the New South.* Boston: G. K. Hall, 1981.

Goodsell, Willystine. *The Education of Women.* New York: Macmillan, 1923.

Goodwin, Gregory L. "The Historical Development of the Community-Junior College Ideology." Ph.D. dissertation, University of Illinois, 1971.

Gorelick, Sherry. *City College and the Jewish Poor.* New Brunswick, N.J.: Rutgers University Press, 1981.

Graham, Patricia A. "Expansion and Exclusion: A History of Women in American Higher Education." *Signs* 3 (Summer 1978):759–74.

Grant, Albert. "Educational Supply and Demand in Reference to the University of Chicago." Master's thesis, University of Chicago, 1928.

Green, Arthur M., Jr. *Engineering Education after the War.* U.S. Bureau of Education Bulletin 1921, no. 50. Washington, D.C.: Government Printing Office, 1922.

Green, Paul. *The Enchanted Maze: The Story of a Modern Student in Dramatic Form.* New York: Samuel French, 1939.

Green, William S. "A Study of Attitudes toward Jews on the Dartmouth Campus." Undergraduate thesis, Dartmouth College, 1939.

Greenleaf, Walter J. *Economic Status of College Alumni.* U.S. Office of Education Bulletin 1937, no. 10. Washington, D.C.: Government Printing Office, 1939.

——. *Junior Colleges.* U.S. Office of Education Bulletin 1936, no. 3. Washington, D.C.: Government Printing Office, 1936.

——. *Self-Help for College Students.* U.S. Bureau of Education Bulletin 1929, no. 2. Washington, D.C.: Government Printing Office, 1929.

Griffith, Coleman R., ed. *Conference on the Problems of Higher Education.* Urbana: University of Illinois Press, 1939.

——. *The Junior College in Illinois.* Urbana: University of Illinois, 1945.

Gruber, Carol S. *Mars and Minerva: World War I and the Uses of the Higher Learning in America.* Baton Rouge: Louisiana State University Press, 1975.

Haber, Samuel. *Efficiency and Uplift.* Chicago: University of Chicago Press, 1964.

Halle, Rita S. *Which College?* New York: Macmillan, 1928.

Halsey, A. H., and Martin A. Trow. *The British Academics.* Cambridge: Harvard University Press, 1971.

Hanawalt, Leslie L. *A Place of Light: The History of Wayne State University.* Detroit: Wayne State University Press, 1968.

Hardin, Thomas L. "A History of the Community Junior College in Illinois: 1901–72." Ph.D. dissertation, University of Illinois, 1975.

Hart, Albert B. "Why Go to College?" *Current History,* July 1931, pp. 534–36.

Hassenger, Robert, ed. *The Shape of Catholic Higher Education.* Chicago: University of Chicago Press, 1967.

Hatt, Elise, and F. Dean McClusky. *A Study of Enrollment.* Studies in Higher Education, no. 2. Lafayette, Ind.: Purdue University, 1926.

Havemann, Ernest, and Patricia S. West. *They Went to College.* New York: Harcourt, Brace, 1952.

Hawes, James A. *Twenty Years among the Twenty-Year-Olds.* New York: Dutton, 1929.

Hawley, Ellis W. *The Great War and the Search for a Modern Order.* New York: St. Martin's Press, 1979.

Hays, Samuel P. "The Politics of Reform in Municipal Court in the Progressive Era." *Pacific Northwest Quarterly* 55 (1964):157–69.

Held, O. C. "Admissions Trends in a Liberal Arts College of an Urban University during the Depression." *School and Society,* March 1936, pp. 365–77.

Henry, David D. *Challenges Past, Challenges Present*. San Francisco: Jossey-Bass, 1975.

Herrick, Robert. *Chimes*. New York: Macmillan, 1926.

Higher Education and the State. University of Missouri Bulletin no. 34. Columbia: University of Missouri, December 15, 1933.

Hoffman, W. S. "Occupations of Parents of College Students." *School and Society*, January 2, 1932, pp. 25–26.

Hofstadter, Richard. *Anti-Intellectualism in American Life*. New York: Vintage Books, 1962.

—— and C. De Witt Hardy. *The Development and Scope of Higher Education in the United States*. New York: Columbia University Press, 1952.

Holmes, H. W. "The Colleges Undermine Themselves: An Indictment of the Admissions System." *Educational Record*, January 1933, pp. 94–114.

Hook, Sidney. "A Challenge to the Liberal Arts College." *Journal of Higher Education*, January 1939, pp. 14–23.

Hopkins, Ernest M. *This Our Purpose*. Hanover, N.H.: Dartmouth Publications, 1950.

Horowitz, Helen L. *Alma Mater*. New York: Knopf, 1984.

Hotchkiss, Willard E. *Higher Education and Business Standards*. Boston: Houghton Mifflin, 1918.

Howard, D. T. "Who Ought to Go to College?" *Nation*, October 1, 1930, pp. 344–46.

Hubbard, Haven. "The Relation of Social and Economic Factors to the Obtaining of the College Certificate by the Entering Class of 1931." Master's thesis, University of Chicago, 1934.

Hudson, Jay W. *The College and New America*. New York: D. Appleton, 1920.

Hughes, Raymond M. *A Study of Students Entering Iowa State College in the Fall of 1935 and 1936*. Bulletin no. 3. Ames: Iowa State College, June 1942.

Hunt, Rockwell D. *History of The College of the Pacific*. Stockton, Calif.: College of the Pacific, 1951.

Husic, James F. *Reorganization of English in Secondary Schools*. U.S. Bureau of Education Bulletin 1917, no. 2. Washington, D.C.: Government Printing Office, 1917.

Hutchins, Robert M. "Education and the Public Mind." *School and Society*, August 5, 1933, pp. 161–65.

——. *The Higher Learning in America*. New Haven: Yale University Press, 1936, 1961.

The Inauguration of Ernest M. Hopkins. Hanover, N.H.: Dartmouth College, 1916.

Jarvis, C. D. *Agricultural Education*. U.S. Bureau of Education Bulletin 1921, no. 40. Washington, D.C.: Government Printing Office, 1921.

Jencks, Christopher, and David Riesman. *The Academic Revolution*. Garden City, N.Y.: Anchor Books, 1969.

Jennings, Irwin G. "The Young Man and America's Opportunity." *Scribner's*, May 1917, pp. 626–30.

Johnson, Paul. *Modern Times*. New York: Harper & Row, 1983.

Johnston, John B. *The Liberal College in Changing Society*. New York: Century, 1930.

Judd, Charles H. *Education and Social Progress*. New York: Harcourt, Brace, 1934.

——. *Problems of Education in the United States*. New York: McGraw-Hill, 1933.

—— and Samuel C. Parker. *Problems Involved in Standardizing State Normal Schools*. U.S. Bureau of Education Bulletin 1916, no. 12. Washington, D.C.: Government Printing Office, 1916.

Kallen, Horace M. *Culture and Democracy in the United States*. New York: Boni & Liveright, 1924.

——. *Individualism: An American Way of Life*. New York: Liveright, 1933.

Kandel, Isaac L. *The Dilemma of Democracy*. Cambridge: Harvard University Press, 1934.

——. "The Philosophy Underlying the System of Education in the United States." In *Educational Yearbook, 1929*. New York: Teachers College, 1930.

——, ed. *Twenty-Five Years of American Education*. New York: Macmillan, 1924.

Karabel, Jerome, and A. H. Halsey, eds. *Power and Ideology in Education*. New York: Oxford University Press, 1977.

Kaylor, Earl C., Jr. *Truth Sets Free*. New York: A. S. Barnes, 1977.

Kearney, George F. "The Remaking of College Life." *Scribner's*, July 1916, pp. 77–81.

Keller, Morton. *Affairs of State*. Cambridge: Belknap Press of Harvard University Press, 1977.

Keller, Phyllis. *States of Belonging: German-American Intellectuals and the First World War*. Cambridge: Harvard University Press, 1979.

Kelly, Fred J., and John H. McNeely. *Federal Student Aid Program*. U.S. Office of Education Bulletin 1935, no. 14. Washington, D.C.: Government Printing Office, 1935.

—— and ——. *The State and Higher Education*. New York: Carnegie Foundation for the Advancement of Teaching, 1933.

—— and Ella B. Ratcliffe. *College Projects for Aiding Students*. U.S. Office of Education Bulletin 1938, no. 9. Washington, D.C.: Government Printing Office, 1938.

—— and ——. *Financial Aids for College Students*. U.S. Office of Education Bulletin 1940, no. 11. Washington, D.C.: Government Printing Office, 1941.

Kelly, Robert L. *The American Colleges and the Social Order*. New York: Macmillan, 1940.

——, ed. *The Effective College*. New York: Association of American Colleges, 1928.

Kemp, W. W. "Junior College Development in California." *Junior College Journal*, February 1931, pp. 281–85.

Kent, Raymond A., ed. *Higher Education in America*. Boston: Ginn, 1930.

Keppel, Frederick P. *Columbia.* New York: Oxford University Press, 1914.

Kevles, Daniel J. *The Physicists.* New York: Knopf, 1978.

Kiely, Margaret. *Comparisons of Students of Teachers Colleges and Students of Liberal Arts Colleges.* Contributions to Education, no. 440. New York: Teachers College, Columbia University, 1931.

Kirkpatrick, J. E. *The American College and Its Rulers.* New York: New Republic, 1926.

Klein, Arthur J. *Survey of Land-Grant Colleges and Universities.* 2 vols. U.S. Office of Education Bulletin 1930, no. 9. Washington, D.C.: Government Printing Office, 1930.

Kolbe, Parke R. *The Colleges in War Time and After.* New York: D. Appleton, 1919.

———. "Is the American College in Danger?" *School and Society,* April 9, 1932, pp. 508–12.

———. *Urban Influences on Higher Education in England and the United States.* New York: Macmillan, 1928.

Koos, Leonard V. *The Junior College Movement.* Boston: Ginn, 1925.

——— and C. C. Crawford. "College Aims, Past and Present." *School and Society,* December 9, 1921, pp. 499–509.

Krueger, Thomas A., and William Glidden. "The New Deal Intellectual Elite: A Collective Portrait." In Frederic C. Jaher, ed., *The Rich, the Well-Born, and the Powerful.* Urbana: University of Illinois Press, 1973.

Kuder, Merle. *Trends of Professional Opportunities in the Liberal Arts College.* Contributions to Education, no. 717. New York: Teachers College, Columbia University, 1937.

Kuklick, Bruce. *The Rise of American Philosophy, 1860–1930.* New Haven: Yale University Press, 1977.

Kurani, Habib A. *Selecting the College Student in America.* Contributions to Education, no. 503. New York: Teachers College, Columbia University, 1931.

Lagemann, Ellen C. *Private Power for the Public Good: A History of the Carnegie Foundation for the Advancement of Teaching.* Middletown, Conn.: Wesleyan University Press, 1983.

Langhorne, Maurice C. "A University Takes Inventory." *Journal of the American Association of Collegiate Registrars,* October 1939, pp. 41–51.

Larson, Magali Sarfatti. *The Rise of Professionalism.* Berkeley: University of California Press, 1977.

Lash, Joseph P. *The Campus: A Fortress of Democracy.* New York: American Student Union, 1938.

Leach, Henry G. "A Challenge to the Colleges." *Forum,* September 1933, pp. 129–30.

Learned, William S. "Admission to College." *Educational Record,* January 1933, pp. 23–48.

———, William C. Bagley, et al. *The Professional Preparation of Teachers for American Public Schools.* New York: Carnegie Foundation for the Advancement of Teaching, 1920.

Lee, Calvin B. T. *The Campus Scene: 1900–1970*. New York: David McKay, 1970.

Leslie, W. Bruce. "Localism, Denominationalism, and Institutional Strategies in Urbanizing America: Three Pennsylvania Colleges, 1870–1915." *History of Education Quarterly* 17 (Fall 1977):235–56.

Lester, John A. "When College Stares You in the Face." *Outlook,* November 7, 1923, pp. 408–10.

Leutchenberg, William. *The Perils of Prosperity, 1914–32*. Chicago: University of Chicago Press, 1958.

Levinger, Lee J. *The Jewish Student in America*. Cincinnati: B'nai B'rith, 1937.

Lipset, Seymour M., and David Riesman. *Education and Politics at Harvard*. New York: McGraw-Hill, 1975.

Lipshutz, Samuel. "Four Years of College." *American Mercury,* October 1929, pp. 129–36.

Lowell, A. Lawrence. *At War with Academic Traditions in America*. Cambridge: Harvard University Press, 1934.

Lunden, Walter A. *The Dynamics of Higher Education*. Pittsburgh: Pittsburgh Printing Co., 1939.

Lustberg, Lawrence S. "The Founding of Community Colleges in Massachusetts: A Study of Issues in Political Sociology." Honors thesis, Harvard College, 1979.

Lynd, Robert S., and Helen M. Lynd. *Middletown*. New York: Harcourt, Brace, 1929.

—— and ——. *Middletown in Transition*. New York: Harcourt, Brace, 1937.

Lynn, Kenneth S., ed. *The Professions in America*. Boston: Beacon, 1963.

Lyon, E. Wilson. *The History of Pomona College, 1887–1969*. Claremont, Calif.: Pomona College, 1977.

Lyons, John O. *The College Novel in America*. Carbondale: Southern Illinois University Press, 1962.

McConaughy, James L. "Education in a Democracy." *School and Society,* September 25, 1937.

McConn, Max. *College or Kindergarten?* New York: New Republic, 1928.

McDonald, Edward D., and Edward M. Hinton. *Drexel Institute of Technology: 1891–1941*. Philadelphia: Drexel Institute of Technology, 1942.

McGiffert, Michael. *The Higher Learning in Colorado: An Historical Study, 1860–1940*. Denver: Sage, 1964.

McWilliams, Carey. *A Mask for Privilege: Anti-Semitism in America*. Boston: Little, Brown, 1948.

Malott, J. O. *Commercial Education in 1924–26*. U.S. Bureau of Education Bulletin 1928, no. 4. Washington, D.C.: Government Printing Office, 1928.

Maney, Charles A. "College Graduates Face the Future." *Journal of Higher Education,* October 1935, pp. 371–75.

Mangun, Vernon L. *The American Normal School: Its Rise and Development in Massachusetts*. Baltimore: Warwick & York, 1928.

Manhart, George B. *DePauw Through the Years*. 2 vols. Greencastle, Ind.: DePauw University, 1962.

Mann, Charles R. *A Study of Engineering Education.* New York: Carnegie Foundation for the Advancement of Teaching, 1918.

Marks, Percy. *The Plastic Age.* New York: Century, 1924.

——. *Which Way Parnassus?* New York: Harcourt, Brace, 1926.

Marsh, Daniel L. "Higher Education in Massachusetts." *School and Society,* April 27, 1938, pp. 742–52.

Marshall, L. C. "The Collegiate School of Business at Erewhon." *Journal of Political Economy,* June 1926, pp. 289–326.

——, ed. *The Collegiate School of Business.* Chicago: University of Chicago Press, 1928.

Martin, Douglas D. *The Lamp in the Desert: The Story of the University of Arizona.* Tucson: University of Arizona Press, 1960.

Matherly, Walter J. *Business Education in the Changing South.* Chapel Hill: University of North Carolina Press, 1939.

May, Henry F. *The End of American Innocence.* Chicago: Quadrangle, 1964.

Meiklejohn, Alexander. *The Experimental College.* New York: Harper, 1932.

Melvin, A. Gordon. *Education for a New Era.* New York: John Day, 1933.

Moore, Ernest C. *I Helped Make a University.* Los Angeles: Dawson's Book Shop, 1952.

Morison, Samuel E. *Three Centuries of Harvard.* Cambridge: Harvard University Press, 1936.

Mosch, Theodore R. *The G.I. Bill.* Hicksville, N.Y.: Exposition Press, 1975.

Muir, Ramsay. *America the Golden.* London: Williams & Norgate, 1927.

Mulligan, Raymond A. "Socioeconomic Background and College Enrollment." *American Sociological Review,* April 1951, pp. 188–95.

Nash, Phillip C. "A Municipal University in the Modern Educational Program." *School and Society,* May 27, 1939, pp. 653–59.

National Survey of the Education of Teachers. 6 vols. U.S. Office of Education Bulletin 1933, no. 10. Washington, D.C.: Government Printing Office, 1935.

National Youth Administration. *Final Report of the National Youth Administration, 1936–43.* Washington, D.C.: Government Printing Office, 1944.

Nevins, Allan. *Illinois.* New York: Oxford University Press, 1917.

——. *The State Universities and Democracy.* Urbana: University of Illinois Press, 1962.

Newcomer, Mabel. *A Century of Higher Education for American Women.* New York: Harper, 1959.

Newman, George C. "The Morgan Years: Politics of Innovative Change at Antioch College in the 1920s." Ph.D. dissertation, University of Michigan, 1978.

Newman, Louis I. *A Jewish University in America?* New York: Bloch, 1924.

Nichols, William I. "The Convention of Going to College." *Atlantic Monthly,* September 1924, pp. 355–60.

'90. "Ferguson—Rex: This College Generation." *Atlantic Monthly,* October 1929, pp. 447–56.

Noble, David F. *America by Design.* New York: Oxford University Press, 1977.

Odell, Charles W. *Are College Students a Select Group?* Bulletin no. 34. Urbana: Bureau of Educational Research, University of Illinois, May 10, 1927.

Oleson, Alexandra, and John Voss, eds. *The Organization of Knowledge in Modern America, 1860–1920.* Baltimore: Johns Hopkins University Press, 1979.

Olson, Keith W. *The G.I. Bill, the Veterans, and the Colleges.* Lexington: University of Kentucky Press, 1974.

Otto, M. C. "On the College Frontier: Wisconsin's Experiment." *Nation,* October 29, 1930, pp. 467–69.

Pace, C. Robert. *They Went to College.* Minneapolis: University of Minnesota Press, 1941.

Palmer, George H. "The Junior College." *Atlantic Monthly,* April 1927, pp. 497–502.

———. "The Junior College Again." *Atlantic Monthly,* December 1927, pp. 828–30.

Park, Julian. "A Philosophy of Curriculum Making." *Journal of Higher Education,* May 1932, pp. 233–40.

Parker, Garland G. *The Enrollment Explosion.* New York: School and Society Books, 1971.

Patton, Cornelius H., and Walter T. Field. *Eight O'Clock Chapel.* Boston: Houghton Mifflin, 1927.

Patton, Leslie K. "Undergraduate Student Reports." *Journal of Higher Education,* June 1932, pp. 285–93.

Person, Peter Per. "A History of Higher Education among the Swedish Immigrants in America." Ph.D. dissertation, Harvard University Graduate School of Education, 1941.

Pierson, George W. *Yale: The University College, 1921–37.* New Haven: Yale University Press, 1955.

Potthoff, Edward F. *Enrollments in the Secondary Schools and Higher Institutions of Illinois.* Urbana: Bureau of Institutional Research, University of Illinois, March 1951.

———. "A Statistical and Analytical Study of the Selective Admission of College Students." Ph.D. dissertation, University of Chicago, 1928.

———. "Who Goes to College?" *Journal of Higher Education,* June 1931, pp. 294–96.

Pound, Roscoe. "The Place of Higher Education in American Life." *School and Society,* August 8, 1936, pp. 161–68.

Power, Edward J. *A History of Catholic Higher Education in the United States.* Milwaukee: Bruce, 1958.

President's Commission on Higher Education. *Higher Education for American Democracy.* 6 vols. Washington, D.C.: Government Printing Office, 1947.

President's Committee on Civil Rights. *To Secure These Rights.* Washington, D.C.: Government Printing Office, 1947.

President's Research Committee on Social Trends. *Recent Social Trends in the United States.* New York: McGraw-Hill, 1933.

Proface, Dom. *College Men.* New York: P. J. Kennedy, 1935.

Rainey, Homer P. "The Future of the Arts College." *Journal of Higher Education,* October 1930, pp. 381–86.

Rand, Frank P. *The Village of Amherst.* Amherst, Mass.: Amherst Historical Society, 1958.

———. *Yesterdays at Massachusetts State College.* Brattleboro, Vt.: E. L. Hildreth, 1933.

Rawick, George P. "The New Deal and Youth." Ph.D. dissertation, University of Wisconsin, 1957.

Reeves, Ellis M. "Which College?" *Journal of Higher Education,* February 1932, pp. 67–74.

Reeves, Floyd W. "The Liberal Arts College." *Journal of Higher Education,* October 1930, pp. 373–80.

——— and John D. Russell. *Admission and Retention of University Students.* Chicago: University of Chicago Press, 1933.

——— and ———. *Some University Student Problems.* Chicago: University of Chicago Press, 1933.

———, ———, H. C. Gregg, A. J. Brumbaugh, and L. E. Blauch. *The Liberal Arts College.* Chicago: University of Chicago Press, 1932.

The Relation of the Federal Government to Education. Urbana: University of Illinois Press, 1922.

Remmers, H. H. *Distinguished Students.* Studies in Higher Education, no. 15. Lafayette, Ind.: Purdue University, October 1930.

Report of a Survey of the State Institutions of Higher Learning in Kansas. U.S. Bureau of Education Bulletin 1923, no. 40. Washington, D.C.: Government Printing Office, 1923.

Reynolds, O. E. *The Social and Economic Status of College Students.* Contributions to Education, no. 272. New York: Teachers College, Columbia University, 1927.

Richardson, Leon B. *History of Dartmouth College.* 2 vols. Hanover, N.H.: Dartmouth College Publications, 1932.

———. *A Study of the Liberal College.* Hanover, N.H.: Dartmouth College, 1924.

Riesman, David. *Constraint and Variety in American Education.* New York: Doubleday, 1958.

Ringer, Fritz K. *Education and Society in Modern Europe.* Bloomington: Indiana University Press, 1979.

Rodnitzky, Jerome L. "David Kinley: A Paternal President in the Roaring Twenties." *Journal of the Illinois State Historical Society,* Spring 1973.

Rogers, Robert E. "Is College Worth While?" *Forum,* September 1933, pp. 137–40.

Rosenberg, Rosalind. *Beyond Separate Spheres.* New Haven: Yale University Press, 1982.

Ross, David R. B. *Preparing for Ulysses: Politics and Veterans during World War II.* New York: Columbia University Press, 1969.

Rossiter, Margaret. *Women Scientists in America: Struggles and Strategies to 1940.* Baltimore: Johns Hopkins University Press, 1982.

Rudolph, Frederick. *The American College and University.* New York: Vintage Books, 1962.

———. *Curriculum.* San Francisco: Jossey-Bass, 1978.

Rudy, S. Willis. *The College of the City of New York.* New York: City College Press, 1949.

Rugg, Harold. *An Introduction to the Problems of American Culture.* Boston: Ginn, 1931.

Ryan, W. Carson, Jr. *Recent Developments in Educational Journalism.* U.S. Bureau of Education Bulletin 1923, no. 25. Washington, D.C.: Government Printing Office, 1923.

Sabine, George F. "Are State Universities Different?" *School and Society,* September 12, 1931, pp. 349–57.

Schiesl, Martin J. *The Politics of Efficiency.* Berkeley: University of California Press, 1977.

Schilpp, Paul A., ed. *Higher Education Faces the Future.* New York: Liveright, 1930.

Schmidt, George P. *The Liberal Arts College.* New Brunswick, N.J.: Rutgers University Press, 1957.

Seashore, Carl E. "Is There Overproduction in Higher Education?" *School and Society,* April 15, 1933, pp. 478–82.

Seerley, Homer H. *The American Teacher.* U.S. Bureau of Education Bulletin 1922, no. 44. Washington, D.C.: Government Printing Office, 1923.

Segal, David, and Maris M. Profitt. *Some Factors in the Adjustment of College Students.* U.S. Office of Education Bulletin 1937, no. 12. Washington, D.C.: Government Printing Office, 1938.

"Sense or Nonsense." *Time,* August 20, 1945, p. 92.

Servin, Manuel P., and Iris H. Wilson. *Southern California and Its University.* Los Angeles: Ward Ritchie, 1969.

Seyler, Earl C. "The Selection of Students at the University of Illinois." Master's thesis, University of Illinois, 1931.

Sharp, Dallas L. "Education Goes Ahead." In Kirby Page, ed., *Recent Gains in American Civilization.* Chautauqua, N.Y.: Chautauqua Press, 1928.

Sharpe, Russell T. "College and the Poor Boy: Is the Door Closing?" *Atlantic Monthly,* June 1933, pp. 696–705.

Shipley, Arthur E. *The Voyage of a Vice Chancellor.* New York: Putnam, 1919.

Sibley, Elbridge. "Some Demographic Clues to Stratification." *American Sociological Review,* June 1942, pp. 322–30.

Silvers, Earl R. *A College Man.* Boston: Walter H. Baker, 1917.

Sinclair, Upton. *The Goose-Step: A Study of American Education.* New York: Cornwall Press, 1922.

Skowronek, Stephen. *Building a New American State.* New York: Cambridge University Press, 1982.

Slosson, Edwin E. "Cultivating the Mob Mind in College." *Independent,* April 10, 1920, pp. 52–53.

———. *Great American Universities.* New York: Macmillan, 1910.

Smith, Mapheus. "University Student Intelligence and Occupation of Father." *American Sociological Review,* December 1942, pp. 764–71.

Smith, Rufus D. "The Tide of Youth." *Educational Record* 21 (January 1940):49–63.

Smith, T. V. *The American Philosophy of Equality*. Chicago: University of Chicago Press, 1927.

———. *The Democratic Tradition in America*. New York: Farrar & Rinehart, 1941.

Smith, Timothy L. "Immigrant Social Aspirations and American Education, 1880–1930." *American Quarterly*, Fall 1969, pp. 523–43.

Snedden, David. "Colleges: For What Purposes?" *Journal of Higher Education*, October 1930, pp. 365–72.

Society for the Promotion of Engineering Education. *Report of the Investigation of Engineering Education, 1923–29*. Pittsburgh, 1930.

Solomon, Barbara M. *In the Company of Educated Women*. New Haven: Yale University Press, 1985.

Some Addresses from the Book of the Opening of the Rice Institute. Rice Institute Pamphlet 3 (October 1916):231–310.

Sproul, Robert G. "Certain Aspects of the Junior College." *Junior College Journal*, February 1931, pp. 274–80.

Stadtman, Verne A. *The University of California: 1868–1968*. New York: McGraw-Hill, 1970.

Stagg, Amos A., Jr. "Factors Leading to Choosing the University of Chicago." Master's thesis, University of Chicago, 1935.

Starr, Paul. *The Social Transformation of American Medicine*. New York: Basic Books, 1982.

Starrett, Agnes L. *Through One Hundred and Fifty Years: The University of Pittsburgh*. Pittsburgh: University of Pittsburgh Press, 1937.

State Higher Educational Institutions of Iowa. U.S. Bureau of Education Bulletin, 1916, no. 19. Washington, D.C.: Government Printing Office, 1916.

State Higher Educational Institutions of North Dakota. U.S. Bureau of Education Bulletin 1916, no. 27. Washington, D.C.: Government Printing Office, 1916.

Stearns, Harold E., ed. *America Now*. New York: Scribner's, 1938.

———. *Civilization in the United States*. New York: Harcourt, Brace, 1922.

Steinberg, Stephen. *The Academic Melting Pot*. New York: McGraw-Hill, 1974.

Stevens, Rosemary. *American Medicine and the Public Interest*. New Haven: Yale University Press, 1971.

Stone, James C., and Donald P. De Nevi, eds. *Portraits of the American University, 1890–1910*. San Francisco: Jossey-Bass, 1971.

Stovall, J. Willis. "The Dark Ages of Today." *Social Science*, August 1926, pp. 345–48.

Strang, Ruth. *The Behavior and Background of Students in College and Secondary School*. New York: Harper, 1937.

Strayer, George D., et al. *Report of a Survey of the Colleges under the Control of the Board of Higher Education of the City of New York*. Albany: New York State Printing Office, 1944.

The Students Speak Out! New York: New Republic, 1929.

Survey of Education in Utah. U.S. Bureau of Education Bulletin 1926, no. 8.

"A Survey of Educational Institutions of the State of Washington." *U.S. Bureau of Education Bulletin*, 1916, no. 26.

"Survey of Public Education in Oregon." *U.S. Office of Education Bulletin*, 1931, no. 8. Washington, D.C.: Government Printing Office, 1931.

Susser, Malcolm. "Portrait of a Rolling-Mill." *American Mercury*, April 1927, pp. 486–95.

Swarthmore College Faculty. *An Adventure in Education*. New York: Macmillan, 1941.

Sweet, William W. *Indiana Asbury–DePauw University: 1837–1937*. New York: Abington, 1937.

Swiggert, Glen L. *Objectives in Commercial Education*. U.S. Bureau of Education Bulletin 1924, no. 16. Washington, D.C.: Government Printing Office, 1924.

Synnott, Marcia G. *The Half-Opened Door: Discrimination and Admissions at Harvard, Yale, and Princeton*. Westport, Conn.: Greenwood, 1979.

Taggart, Leona. "The Price Society Pays for Specialization." *Social Science*, November 1927, pp. 32–40.

Talbot, Marion. *The Education of Women*. Chicago: University of Chicago Press, 1910.

Tead, Ordway. *Two Constructive Years in Public Higher Education in the City of New York*. New York: Board of Higher Education, May 1940.

Terkel, Studs. *Hard Times*. New York: Pocket Books, 1970.

Thomasson, Arnold L. "A Half-Century of Teacher Training in State Normal Schools and Teachers Colleges of the United States, 1890–1940." Ph.D. dissertation, University of Illinois, 1943.

Thrasher, Frederic M. "Social Backgrounds and Education." *Journal of Educational Sociology*, October 1927, pp. 69–76.

Thurstone, L. L., and Thelma G. Thurstone. "The 1931 Psychological Examination." *Educational Record*, April 1932.

Thwing, Charles F. *The College Gateway*. Boston: Pilgrim Press, 1918.

Todd, J. Edward. *Social Norms and the Behavior of College Students*. Contributions to Education, no. 833. New York: Teachers College, Columbia University, 1941.

"The Trouble with the Colleges." *Forum*, December 1933.

Trow, Martin A. "The Democratization of Higher Education in America." *European Journal of Sociology*, Spring 1962.

———. "Reflections on the Transition from Mass to Universal Higher Education." *Daedalus*, Winter 1970.

Tugwell, Rexford G., and Leon Keyserling, eds. *Redirecting Education*. New York: Columbia University Press, 1934.

Turner, Fred H. "Students of the Depression." *Saturday Evening Post*, February 2, 1935, pp. 12–13.

U.S. Department of the Interior, Bureau of Education. *Biennial Survey of Education, 1916–18*. 4 vols. Washington, D.C.: Government Printing Office, 1921.

———, ———. *Biennial Survey of Education, 1918–20*. 2 vols. Washington, D.C.: Government Printing Office, 1923.

——, ——. *Biennial Survey of Education, 1920–22.* 2 vols. Washington, D.C.: Government Printing Office, 1924.

——, ——. *Biennial Survey of Education, 1922–24.* 2 vols. Washington, D.C.: Government Printing Office, 1927.

——, ——. *Biennial Survey of Education, 1924–26.* 2 vols. Washington, D.C.: Government Printing Office, 1928.

——, ——. *Biennial Survey of Education, 1926–28.* 2 vols. Washington, D.C.: Government Printing Office, 1930.

——, ——. *Biennial Survey of Education, 1928–30.* 2 vols. Washington, D.C.: Government Printing Office, 1932.

——, ——. *Biennial Survey of Education, 1930–32.* Washington, D.C.: Government Printing Office, 1935.

——, ——. *Biennial Survey of Education, 1932–34.* Washington, D.C.: Government Printing Office, 1937.

——, ——. *Biennial Survey of Education, 1934–36.* 2 vols. Washington, D.C.: Government Printing Office, 1938.

——, ——. *Biennial Survey of Education, 1936–38.* Washington, D.C.: Government Printing Office, 1942.

——, ——. *Biennial Survey of Education, 1938–42.* 2 vols. Washington, D.C.: Government Printing Office, 1947.

——, ——, and Federal Security Agency. *Higher Education.* Vols. 1–3. Washington, D.C.: Government Printing Office, 1945–47.

The University and the Municipality. U.S. Bureau of Education Bulletin 1915, no. 8. Washington, D.C.: Government Printing Office, 1915.

University Training for Public Service. U.S. Bureau of Education Bulletin 1916, no. 30. Washington, D.C.: Government Printing Office, 1916.

Vandebunt, Margaret J. "Characteristics of Students Entering the Various Divisions and Professional Schools from the College in the University of Chicago." Master's thesis, University of Chicago, 1937.

Vanderlip, Frank A. *Business and Education.* New York: Duffield, 1907.

Van Doren, Mark. "The College of the Few." *New Republic,* April 16, 1924, pp. 203–5.

Veblen, Thorstein. *The Higher Learning in America.* New York: B. W. Huebsch, 1918.

Veysey, Laurence R. *The Emergence of the American University.* Chicago: University of Chicago Press, 1965.

——. "Stability and Experiment in the American Undergraduate Curriculum." In Carl Kaysen, ed., *Content and Context.* New York: McGraw-Hill, 1973.

Vinson, Robert E. "The Emerging American University." Columbus: Ohio State University Press, 1931.

Warner, W. Lloyd. *Democracy in Jonesville.* New York: Harper, 1949.

——, Robert J. Havighurst, and Martin B. Loeb. *Who Shall Be Educated?* New York: Harper, 1944.

Wechsler, Harold S. "The Rationale for Restriction: Ethnicity and College Admissions in America." *American Quarterly* (Winter 1984):643–67.

———. *The Qualified Student.* New York: Wiley, 1977.

Wechsler, James. *Revolt on the Campus.* New York: Covici, Friede, 1935.

Wecter, Dixon. *The Age of the Great Depression.* New York: Macmillan, 1948.

Weeks, Helen F. *Factors Influencing the Choice of Courses by Students in Certain Liberal Arts Colleges.* Contributions to Education, no. 465. New York: Teachers College, Columbia University, 1931.

Weigle, Edith D. "Hide Your B.A." *Outlook,* April 6, 1921, pp. 543–44.

Wellemeyer, J. Fletcher. "The Junior College as Viewed by its Students," *School Review,* December 1926, pp. 760–67.

Weller, George A. *Not to Eat, Not for Love.* New York: Harrison Smith & Robert Haas, 1933.

West, James. *Plainsville, U.S.A.* New York: Columbia University Press, 1945.

West, Rodney M., and Leonard V. Koos. "The Freshman Class in 1940." In *Addresses and Proceedings of the Fifty-eighth Annual Meeting of the National Education Association.* Washington, D.C.: National Education Association, 1920.

"What Profit Education?" *Survey,* May 15, 1929, pp. 246–47.

"What the Undergraduate Wants." *New Republic,* July 30, 1924, pp. 258–60.

White, William C., and Louis J. Heath. *A New Basis for Social Progress.* Boston: Houghton Mifflin, 1917.

Whitehead, Alfred N. "Harvard: The Future." *Atlantic Monthly,* May 1928, pp. 260–70.

———. "Universities and Their Function." *Atlantic Monthly,* May 1928, pp. 638–45.

Whitener, Thomas A. *College Education and Professional Opportunity.* University of North Carolina Extension Bulletin. Chapel Hill: University of North Carolina Press, 1925.

———. "Guidance of College Freshmen." Master's thesis, University of North Carolina, 1924.

Whitney, Frederick L. *The Junior College in America.* Greeley: Colorado State Teachers College, 1928.

"Why Boys Go to College." *Literary Digest,* September 16, 1922, p. 33.

Widmayer, Charles E. *Hopkins of Dartmouth.* Hanover, N.H.: University Press of New England, 1977.

Wilkins, Ernest H. *The Changing College.* Chicago: University of Chicago Press, 1927.

———. "Higher Education and Social Change." *School and Society,* January 13, 1934, pp. 41–45.

———. "Major Trends in Collegiate Enrollment." *School and Society,* September 28, 1935, pp. 442–45.

Willey, Malcolm M. *Depression, Recovery, and Higher Education.* New York: McGraw-Hill, 1937.

Williams, Robin M., Jr. *American Society.* 2d ed. New York: Knopf, 1961.

Willis, Elbert V. *The Growth of American Higher Education.* Philadelphia: Dorrance, 1936.

Wilson, Louis R. *The University of North Carolina, 1900–1930.* Chapel Hill: University of North Carolina Press, 1957.

Winston, Sanford. "Social Background of College Freshmen." *Southern Association Quarterly,* November 1938.

Wolters, Raymond. *The New Negro on Campus.* Princeton: Princeton University Press, 1975.

Woolley, Edward M. "How Our Colleges Teach Business." *Collier's,* March 11, 1922, pp. 5–6.

Works, George A. "Some Factors Influencing the Development of Higher Education." *University of Chicago Record,* October 1932.

Wyllie, E. G. "The Businessman Looks at the Higher Learning." *Journal of Higher Education,* June 1952, pp. 295–300.

Zimmer, Brother Agatho. *Changing Concepts of Higher Education in America since 1700.* Washington, D.C.: Catholic University of America Press, 1938.

Zimmerman, Joan G. "College Culture in the Midwest, 1890–1930." Ph.D. dissertation, University of Virginia, 1978.

Zook, George F. "The Emergency in Higher Education." In *Addresses and Proceedings of the Fifty-eighth Annual Meeting of the National Education Association.* Washington, D.C.: National Education Association, 1920.

——. "Is the Junior College a Menace or a Boon?" *School Review,* June 1929, pp. 415–21.

——. *Residence and Migration of University and College Students.* U.S. Bureau of Education Bulletin 1926, no. 11. Washington, D.C.: Government Printing Office, 1926.

——. *The Residence of Students in Universities and Colleges.* U.S. Bureau of Education Bulletin 1922, no. 18. Washington, D.C.: Government Printing Office, 1922.

——, ed. *National Conference of Junior Colleges, 1920.* U.S. Bureau of Education Bulletin 1922, no. 19. Washington, D.C.: Government Printing Office, 1922.

Index

277

Library of Congress Cataloging-in-Publication Data

Levine, David O., 1955-
  The American college and the culture of aspiration, 1915–1940.

  Includes index.
  1. Universities and colleges—United States—History—20th century.
2. Student aspiration—United States. 3. Achievement motivation. I. Title.
LA227.1.L48   1986   378.73   86-4169
ISBN 0-8014-1884-4